AF505817

Negotiating European Union

Negotiating European Union

Edited by

Paul W. Meerts and Franz Cede
International Institute for Applied Systems Analysis, Austria

First published 2004 by
PALGRAVE MACMILLAN
Houndmills, Basingstoke, Hampshire RG21 6XS and
175 Fifth Avenue, New York, N. Y. 10010
Companies and representatives throughout the world

PALGRAVE MACMILLAN is the global academic imprint of the Palgrave
Macmillan division of St. Martin's Press, LLC and of Palgrave Macmillan Ltd.
Macmillan® is a registered trademark in the United States, United Kingdom
and other countries. Palgrave is a registered trademark in the European
Union and other countries.

ISBN 1–4039–4161–0 hardback

This book is printed on paper suitable for recycling and made from fully
managed and sustained forest sources.

A catalogue record for this book is available from the British Library.

Library of Congress Cataloging-in-Publication Data

Negotiating European Union / edited by Paul Meerts and Franz Cede.
    p. cm.
  Includes bibliographical references and index.
  ISBN 0–4039–4161–0 (hardback)
    1. European Union–Decision making. 2. Negotiation. I. Meerts, Paul. II. Cede, Franz.

JN30.N43 2005
341.242′2–dc22   2004057665

10   9   8   7   6   5   4   3   2   1
13   12   11   10   09   08   07   06   05   04

Printed and bound in Great Britain by
Antony Rowe Ltd, Chippenham and Eastbourne

Contents

Foreword

Paul W. Meerts and Franz Cede, Editors

One way of perceiving the European Union (EU) is as an enormous bilateral and multilateral process of internal and external negotiation. This is indeed one way of looking at the EU, but the EU has never really been looked at in this respect—at least, not in depth. It is for this reason that the Processes of International Negotiation (PIN) Network has taken the initiative of asking twelve authors from different corners of Europe to contribute to the present book, *Negotiating European Union.*

In *Negotiating European Union* authors have looked at negotiations within member states, among member states, within and among the institutions of the Union, and between the EU and other countries. They have analyzed processes, actors, and interests. They have evaluated power, effectiveness, and trust. They have detected strategies, skills, and styles. And, most importantly, they have discovered that the EU negotiation process, though an enigma, has a great deal to impart to those who are involved in other processes of supranational and intergovernmental negotiation. There are lessons to be learned here for other forums, other regions, other people, and future eras. This book is a first try, a first probe into the relatively unknown arena of negotiation processes in the European Union. More may follow, but this "pilot" is already a very valuable attempt to obtain a better understanding of the character and the characteristics of negotiations processes as an opportunity—or as an obstacle—to European Union.

Preface

By Dr. Bernard Rudolf Bot
Minister of Foreign Affairs of the Kingdom of the Netherlands
Former Permanent Representative of the Netherlands to the
European Union

Ten Commandments for Negotiators in the Post-Enlargement EU

In the twenty-first century it is no longer possible for diplomacy merely to be the art of the possible. In a world in which national borders are increasingly losing their power to protect, this traditional adage is no longer adequate. It reflects the realpolitik of the past which saw nation states scoring points off each other to maneuver themselves into better positions. But a world in which cross-border challenges can be met only through cross-border cooperation will oblige us to elevate diplomacy to the art of working together to *make* things possible. This is especially true in the case of member states of the European Union (EU). After all, member states may defend their own interests and principles *within* the European Union but they want the Union to have a single internal market and to speak with one voice in its *external* economic and political policies. Thus, while it is true that negotiations within the European Union still display some features of traditional international diplomacy between nation states, they also increasingly resemble the decision-making processes that occur *within* national governments. Or, as Paul W. Meerts puts it in the concluding chapter of this book, "The classical Westphalian situation with sovereign actors negotiating on a voluntary basis has largely disappeared in a European Union where a substantial part of sovereignty is vested in the EU institutions." Accordingly, the process of negotiation within the European Union can justifiably be described as a hybrid affair.

Negotiations within the European Union are also unique in that they involve not only nation states, private-sector enterprises, not-for-profit representative organizations, and professional lobbyists, but also supranational players held to represent the general interests of the entire Union. In the latter category the European Commission is of course the first body that springs to mind. Commissioners and Commission officials do not shed their national plumage on taking office, but they do take an oath of allegiance to the general interests of the Union. The Commission usually acts as the impartial referee between divergent national interests, but sometimes it engages actively in negotiations, adopting a position of its own that appears primarily to serve the bureaucratic or political interests of the Commission itself.

In practice, the European Council of heads of state or government is emerging as the real power base within Europe. A growing number of initiatives and orientations for future policy derive from the European Council's decisions. This trend is in line with the "new bilateralism," in which the outcome of negotiations is more and more frequently determined by advance negotiations among all the players before member states have even arrived at the official negotiating table.

This trend will be reinforced by the enlargement of the European Union. After all, the law of large numbers teaches us that a Union of twenty-five member states will be more volatile. Their increasing number will also have the effect of reducing the individual clout of each of them, irrespective of size. To achieve what they want member states will have to work harder and be quicker to respond to new opportunities and circumstances in the knowledge that others will seek to do the same. This will foster greater rivalry. Moreover, the larger number of players and the reduced predictability of the negotiation procedure will mean more room to maneuver. This could increase the temptation to indulge in greater opportunism and "freeloading."

Two factors may be expected to compensate, however, for this potenual unpredictability: a) the need to agree on solutions at the end of the day; and b) the increase in majority voting. Taken together, these two factors will probably encourage like-minded countries to get together at an early stage to work out common positions. In my experience, decision making in Brussels did not become any slower in the wake of earlier enlargements. There is an obvious explanation: the more member states attend a meeting, the less time each of them has to make its own points. Member states are therefore forced to confine themselves to the essentials of their arguments. All other issues have to have been settled in advance. This is not only true of Council meetings but of COREPER as well, and it will be even more applicable in the future when decisions are taken by majority vote.

In the Union of the future I should like to see all member states still having an opportunity to achieve progress together. I fear that concepts such as pioneering groups or a multispeed Europe could sow division. In cases where pioneering groups are truly inevitable, we should ensure that they remain within the limits that the treaty defines for them under the heading of "enhanced cooperation." This will have the advantage of providing guarantees concerning matters such as transparency, access for new members, the role of the Commission, and the continuing integrity of the EU *acquis*. The Schengen area and the Eurozone are good examples of enhanced cooperation *avant la lettre*.

Will the recent enlargement significantly change the process of negotiation as such? And if so, how would this affect the negotiators? Some time ago I devised the following "ten commandments for the successful negotiator," drawing on my own experience as a Brussels negotiator. They provide a useful framework for predicting the effects of enlargement on the negotiator's role. Most of them seem just as valid now as when I devised them; indeed, I think that some have actually gained in importance.

Ten commandments for the successful negotiator:

1. *Retain the trust of those you represent*: in an enlarged Union this will be even more important. Voters in member states will increasingly doubt whether their own country is in a position to exert sufficient influence. Given that such doubts can easily harden into euroskepticism, representatives must be aware of the mood on the "home front"; they must be able to count on their government's support; and they must constantly demonstrate that they are successfully defending national interests.

2. *Make it clear that you appreciate the position of other negotiating parties*: in an enlarged Union the entire process of negotiation will be more fluid. As already suggested, like-minded countries will try to form coalitions in advance. Those seeking to do so would be wise to demonstrate their appreciation of considerations that matter to other members of the group envisaged; this will help make it possible to act in concert. Thus, there will be more attempts to form coalitions, and it will be important for the individual member state to make major concessions within its chosen coalition so as to be able to defend the key tenets of its own position at a later stage of the game.

3. *Know your dossier well*: this will continue to be important, as a negotiator who really knows what he/she is talking about will always be more persuasive than one who clearly does not; on the other hand, there will be a tendency toward specialization of knowledge within groups of like-minded member states; certain countries will take the lead on particular issues or be designated as the main spokespersons on them. This will require confidence in each other's knowledge and expertise.

4. *Maintain good networks*: this will be an increasingly decisive factor. Good networks of experts or friends can help negotiators sound out possible coalition

partners on an informal basis or indeed to gain a better understanding of opponents' positions without having to seek direct clarification. The network is a forum in which information is bartered.

5. *Cultivate a feel for the balance of political power and the ability to spot a political bluff*: these strengths will be equally important in an enlarged Union. On the other hand, no negotiator will be able to know all twenty-five member states equally well; he/she will need to focus on key figures—the representatives of the largest member states or of those that adopt an especially firm stance on particular issues and may therefore tip the balance one way or the other. Moreover, Brussels negotiators will be even more reliant than in the past on the knowledge and expertise of their colleagues at the bilateral embassies. After all, the embassies are well versed in the affairs of the other individual member states and are in a better position to identify the internal and often unexpressed reasons for the adoption of particular stances in Brussels. Three-way consultation between central government, the bilateral embassy, and the Brussels negotiator will help the negotiator estimate the likely fallback position of another member state and decide the possible terms of a compromise.

6. *Guard against your opponents' losing face*: this, in my view, is a crucial commandment, valid in every epoch and culture. Any opponent who loses face will be more intransigent and less inclined to reach a compromise as a result. Within the European Union the effect is exacerbated by loss of face occurring not just between two parties but, at worst, at the actual negotiating table in the presence of all the parties involved. For that reason, the tone in which a point of view is expressed needs to be pitched carefully: the harsher the message, the milder the tone. Many negotiators find the combination difficult to achieve, but this "commandment" will be even more vital in the enlarged Union with its increasing number of different national cultures around the negotiating table.

7. *Learn to act a part*: by playacting, negotiators can disguise their true intentions and so create extra room for negotiation. This is probably the most difficult talent to acquire. Negotiators from eastern and southern Europe tend to be better at it than their northern colleagues.

8. *Build up your stamina*: negotiators who want to control the endgame have to be ready and able to continue negotiating into the small hours and beyond, if necessary. After hours of continuous negotiation a hard-fought compromise can often be won on issues over which negotiators may have crossed swords for months, simply because everyone is exhausted and the self-imposed deadline for agreement is fast approaching. Negotiators who still have their wits about them at this late stage can in any case prevent nasty surprises and may even be able to milk the situation for agreement on something that had previously appeared nonnegotiable.

9. *Make concessions in time to obtain a quid pro quo*: many negotiators get things wrong in this respect. Because it has been impressed upon them that they must negotiate hard on their country's behalf, it seems almost a sign of weakness to make a timely concession. But one must not forget that a good concession is always part of a deal. And there is nothing wrong with a sensible deal once the negotiations are well under way. Wait too long and you run the risk of giving ground when the concession is no longer needed because trade-offs between the other negotiators will already have produced a compromise on the main issues. Good timing in this respect will be even more important in an enlarged Union than it has been in the past.

10. *Be yourself, and always hold fast to your own style of negotiating*: this commandment may seem rather at odds with the requirement for playacting but in the end "being yourself" is a basic point of departure without which it is impossible to meet the other requirements. A negotiator who tries to adopt a negotiating style that does not come naturally will inevitably be unmasked. After all, at the end of the day it is important that negotiators know what they can expect from each other. For negotiations to be successful in a club like the European Union they must be based on a relationship of trust that, once established, can pay off over time. Negotiators who remain true to themselves will have genuine and lasting credibility in the eyes of their colleagues.

Given the continuing need for consensus, it is unlikely that the enlargement of the European Union will bring any fundamental change in the process of negotiation. Majority decision making will provide a degree of compulsion in this respect, but the member states will probably continue to strive for the widest possible consensus on really important points before votes are counted. In the enlarged Union the "new bilateralism" will gain in importance; it will be increasingly common to prepare the ground for compromises even before member states enter the negotiating room. There will be more room to maneuver but less predictability. This will increase the pressure on Brussels negotiators. Of the ten commandments cited above, four in particular will become even more important: retaining the trust of those of the home front; cultivating a feel for the balance of political power; preventing loss of face; and the shrewd timing of concessions.

Glossary

AC	advisory committee
acquis communautaire	the body of EU law, rules, and decisions that each member state agrees to when it joins the EU
BATNA	best alternative to a negotiated agreement
CAP	common agricultural policy
CEEC	Central and Eastern European countries
CEEP	*Centre européen des entreprises à participation publique*; in English, the European Center of Enterprises with Public Participation
CFSP	common foreign and security policy
CGS	Council General Secretariat
Committee of PRs	Committee of Permanent Representatives
CORDIS	Community Research and Development Information Service
COREG	Committee of the Regions
COREPER	Committee of Permanent Representatives
COREPER I	Committee of Permanent Representatives: meetings of deputies of the ambassadors
COREPER II	Committee of Permanent Representatives: meetings of the ambassadors
COREU	*CORespondance EUropéenne.* COREU is an EU communication network between member states and the Commission for cooperation in the fields of foreign policy to make it easier for decisions to be taken swiftly in emergencies.
COSAC	Conference of Community and European Affairs Committees of Parliaments of the European Union; in

	French, *Conférence des organes specialisés dans les affaires communautaires et européennes des parlements de l'Union européenne*
CREST	Scientific and Technical Research Committee
CRP	Council rules of procedure
DG	Directorate-General
DG I	DG External Relations
DG III	DG Industry
DG IV	DG Competition
DG VI	DG Agriculture
DG ELARG	Directorate-General for Enlargement
DG EMPL	Directorate-General Employment and Social Affairs
DG ENTR	Directorate-General Enterprise
DG I-E	Directorate-General for Eastern Europe
DG Markt	Directorate-General Internal Market
DG SANCO	Directorate-General for Health and Consumer Protection
EC	European Communities
EC treaty	Treaty of Rome, signed 25 March 1957, establishing the European Economic Community (EEC)
ECB	European Central Bank
ECJ	European Court of Justice
ECOFIN	Economic and Financial Council of Ministers
ECSC	European Coal and Steel Community
EEA	European Economic Area
EEC	European Economic Community
EESC	European Economic and Social Committee
EFSA	European Food Safety Authority
EFTA	European Free Trade Association
EMU	economic and monetary union
EP	European Parliament
ERA	European Research Area
ETUC	European Trade Union Confederation
EU	European Union
EU treaty	Treaty on European Union signed at Maastricht on 7 February 1992

EUCP	European Union common position
EURAB	European Research Advisory Board
Euratom	European Atomic Energy Community
Eurojust	EU body that supports investigations and prosecutions by member states of serious cross-border and organized crime
GAC	General Affairs Council
GAERC	General Affairs and External Relations Council
GATT	General Agreement on Tariffs and Trade
GDP	gross domestic product
GMO	genetically modified organisms
ICT	information and communication technologies
IGC	Intergovernmental Conference
IR	international relations
ITRE	Industry, External Trade, Research, and Energy Committee
JHA	justice and home affairs
"Med" countries	Mediterranean (partner) countries
MEP	Member of the European Parliament
Mercosur	Mercado Commun del Sur (Southern Common Market)
MFA	ministry of foreign affairs
MP	Member of Parliament
NAFTA	North American Free Trade Agreement
NGO	nongovernmental organization
PAM	public-affairs management
PD	prisoner's dilemma
PHARE	a program of Community aid for Central and Eastern European countries
Pillar – first pillar – second pillar – third pillar	The architecture of the EU is usually illustrated by three pillars. The first pillar represents the European Communities, the second, the common foreign and security policy (CFSP), and the third, cooperation in the area of justice and home affairs (JHA)
PIP	people, interests, and power
PR	permanent representation
Presidency	Presidency of the Council of Ministers
QMV	qualified-majority voting

RTD	research and technological development
SCF	Scientific Committee on Food
SEA	Single European Act
SHH	safety, hygiene, and health protection at work
SNT	single negotiating text
SVC	Standing Veterinary Committee
TEC	Treaty Establishing the European Community (Treaty of Rome)
TEU	Treaty on European Union (Treaty of Maastricht)
Triple P	procedures, positions, and people
UNICE	*Union des industries de la Communauté Européenne*
WTO	World Trade Organization

List of Contributors

Leendert J. Bal (b. 1966) graduated with distinction from the University of Utrecht. He joined the Netherlands Institute of International Relations, Clingendael, in 1991 and set up its training program on European integration. From 1996 he worked at the European coordination unit of the Dutch ministry of transport focusing mainly on EU Transport Council meetings. Since 2000 he has been transport attaché at the Netherlands Permanent Representation to the European Union in Brussels. He has published some twenty-five articles and book reviews on, for example, European decision making and negotiations, and institutional reforms. From mid-April 2004 he has worked as policy adviser at the bureau of the executive director of the European Maritime Safety Agency.

Derek Beach (b. 1970), received his PhD from the University of Southern Denmark and his MSc from the London School of Economics and the University of Aarhus, Denmark. His research activities currently deal with the role and influence of the EU institutions in history-making negotiations in the EU and explaining compliance with EU law. He has written several books, the latest of which (2004) deals with importance of the EU institutions in the dynamics of European integration. His most recent article, covering the role and impact of the Council Secretariat in treaty-reform negotiations, appeared in the *Journal of European Public Policy* in 2004.

Franz Cede was legal adviser to the Austrian Foreign Ministry and has participated in numerous international conferences and bilateral negotiations. He was also a regular delegate to the General Assembly of the United Nations. In 1999 Franz Cede became Austrian Ambassador to the Russian Federation, and since 2003 he has been Austrian Ambassador to Belgium, also representing his country at NATO.

Ole Elgström (b. 1950) is professor of political science at Lund University, Sweden. He has published articles on EU negotiation and mediation in many eminent journals, including the *Journal of European Public Policy*, the *Journal of Common Market Studies*, *International Negotiation*, *Scandinavian Political Studies*, and the *European Foreign Affairs Review*. A board member of the standing group on the

European Union of the European Consortium for Political Research, Professor Elgström was editor of the book, *European Union Council Presidencies* (2003).

Peter C. J. van Grinsven (b. 1976) studied political science in the Netherlands at Leiden University. Since 2000 he has worked as researcher and program coordinator at the department of training and education of the Netherlands Institute of International Relations, Clingendael. (Inter)nationally he publishes and lectures on the institutional structure and decision-making processes of the EU and the development of the European Council. For his academic work on this last topic he was awarded the Peccei Scholarship by the International Institute for Applied Systems Analysis, Austria in 2004.

Alain Guggenbühl graduated in political science, European administration, and negotiations. He has worked at the European Commission's delegation to the United Nations in New York and directed an EC law office in Brussels. He is currently directing the program on European negotiations at the European Institute of Public Administration which trains national and European officials. He also teaches European politics at the Catholic University of Mons in Belgium. He has published books and articles, notably dealing with relations between the EU and Eastern Europe, EC social legislation, the simplification of European law, the Treaty of Amsterdam, and openness and transparency.

Dorothee Heisenberg is an assistant professor of European studies at the Johns Hopkins School of Advanced International Studies in Washington, D.C. She received her PhD from Yale University and is the author of *The Mark of the Bundesbank: Germany's Role in European Monetary Cooperation*, as well as a forthcoming book on the U.S.–EU conflict over data protection. She has published in a number of journals, including the *Journal of Common Market Studies* and the *Journal of European Public Policy*.

Mendeltje van Keulen (b. 1975) holds masters degrees in European studies from the University of Twente in the Netherlands and the College of Europe in Bruges, Belgium. She has worked at the European Parliament as a political assistant and since 2000 has worked in the European integration section at the Netherlands Institute for International Relations, Clingendael. She coordinates training courses in EU affairs and lobbying for national government officials in The Hague and abroad. Since 2001 she has been a PhD student at the Centre for European Studies, University of Twente, preparing a dissertation on national governments in the European Union. She has published on the Netherlands in the EU, national EU policy coordination, and EU enlargement.

Alice Landau is professor of international relations at the University of Geneva.

She has taught in many places, including Montreal and Calgary, and has published extensively on the European Union, negotiations, and international economic relations. Her latest publications are *Redrawing the Global Economy*, and *Demystifying the Multilateral Trading System*.

Pieter J. Langenberg (b. 1953) studied contemporary history at Utrecht University in the Netherlands. A professional diplomat since 1979, he has served at the Netherlands foreign ministry and in several posts abroad. He is currently a counselor at the Netherlands Permanent Mission to the European Union where he is spokesman for research issues and nuclear matters.

Paul W. Meerts studied political science and international relations at the universities of Amsterdam and Leiden. He has been research fellow in Dutch political history at the universities of Leiden and Groningen as well as coordinator of diplomatic training at the Netherlands Society of International Affairs and the Netherlands Institute of International Relations, Clingendael, of which he has been deputy director since 1990. As a consultant in diplomatic negotiation he has trained diplomats and civil servants in more than seventy countries. He has written on interstate bargaining, focusing on its political dimensions. Paul W. Meerts holds an honorary doctorate from the National University of Mongolia.

Rinus van Schendelen (b. 1944) graduated from the University of Amsterdam, and has been a full professor of political science at Erasmus University, Rotterdam, since 1980. He is also a visiting professor in North America, China, the Middle East and throughout Europe. His research activities mainly cover European Union issues, politics-business relationships, business lobbying, public affairs, parliamentology, Dutch politics, and the mass-elite relationship. Professor van Schendelen is an editorial board member of the German *Zeitschrift für Parlamentsfragen*, the *International Review on Comparative Public Policy*, the *Journal of Legislative Studies* and the *Journal of Public Affairs*, and has published thirty books and over two hundred articles. He is also founding chairman of the research committee of the European Centre for Public Affairs, Oxford, and a member of many research networks.

Chapter 1

Introduction

Franz Cede

The EU as the Epitome of a Negotiating Process

The history and growth of the European Union (EU) have often been recognized as the product of an extraordinarily successful negotiating process. A wealth of literature is currently available that allows the study of nearly every aspect of European integration, a subject that looks set to become a scientific research discipline in its own right. Surprising as it may seem, however, the great majority of publications devoted to European studies focus on the outcomes of negotiations rather than on the processes themselves. This relative scarcity of contributions to the study of the EU from the angle of negotiation theory and practice is all the more astonishing as the European integration phenomenon can be described as the epitome of a negotiating process.

In that regard one may cite Walter Hallstein, the first President of the Commission of the then European Economic Community (EEC), who once compared the process of European integration to a bicycle that falls over at the very moment the person riding it stops pedaling. In this book the coeditors and authors of the various contributions try to examine precisely how the bicycle of European integration is kept in motion. Their endeavor is to present the distinctive features of the negotiation process within the EU framework. Their hope is that the book will fill what is often perceived as a lacuna in the academic research and study of this particular subject matter.

It is hoped that a better understanding of the EU as a "negotiating system in action" will provide insights that will be of interest to all the players involved in EU negotiations. Whereas today "learning by doing" seems to be the prevailing training method for acquiring and mastering the necessary negotiating techniques, it may well be that a more systematic approach to gaining expertise in "negotiating the EU" will become the rule in the future. With that in mind the authors were faced with the challenge of presenting findings that will be useful precisely because they transcend the empirical experience gained by those who gyrate professionally around the EU.

The authors come from various backgrounds, either from universities and academic institutions with a strong emphasis on European studies or from the foreign-policy establishment of their respective countries; as such, they are directly involved in the day-to-day business of EU negotiations.

Short Description of the Central Issues of Each Chapter

A glance at the table of contents will show that, as well as this introduction and a closing chapter, each of which has been written by a coeditor and does not require a special introduction, the present book consists of ten substantive chapters that address a broad spectrum of issues:

Rinus van Schendelen (Chapter 2) offers an interesting analysis of the pluralist environment of EU negotiations. He sheds new light on the fragmentation of the power structure inside member states and the impact this has on the EU negotiating system. This aspect is often neglected in the usual efforts to present the EU as a clear-cut system. Van Schendelen presents a different picture, using the metaphor of an arena to describe the pluralist environment of EU negotiations—a good description of the complex "playing field" of EU negotiations with the various players interacting. "Pluralism," "fragmentation," and "interdependency" are the catchwords van Schendelen uses to capture the real world of EU negotiations. He cites many examples to support his propositions and provides an excellent demonstration of the changing character of the negotiating pattern in the EU context in which "public-affairs managers" (PAMs) are gradually replacing the traditional actors (diplomats, lobbyists, experts).

Mendeltje van Keulen (Chapter 3) turns the spotlight on the domestic aspects of EU policy by illustrating the impact of EU negotiations on the political and administrative systems of EU member states. Like van Schendelen, the author dispels the notion that member states behave in Brussels as unitary actors. She examines the interface between the "home front" of EU negotiations and the decision-making process in Brussels. From the point of view of negotiation theory, comparative research in this area is still hard to find. The author explains this neglect by the sheer intricacy and specificity of EU policy processes which seriously complicate attempts to get to grips with them. Given the ever-growing importance of the European integration process and its enormous impact on the domestic political scene within member states, van Keulen's efforts to conceptualize the interaction between national EU coordination and negotiations at the institutional EU level certainly merit close attention. Van Keulen illustrates her findings with well-informed insights into the complexities of EU coordination in the Netherlands. Her observations on the tension between the "administrative" and the "political" actors, the latter being less prone to taking integrationist European positions than the former, are of particular interest. The author provides a clear explanation of the similarities and the differences between EU negotiations in Brussels and the coordination schemes within member states. Her contribution will, without any doubt, lead to a more systematic discussion and study of this important subject. The old saying that diplomacy begins at home appears particularly appropriate for describing the often-difficult negotiations at the domestic level that aim to coordinate national positions before these are taken to the EU level.

Pieter Langenberg's contribution (Chapter 4) discusses the role of member states in the EU negotiating process. With the insight of a diplomat having wide experience in EU negotiations, the author has chosen EU research and technological development (RTD) policy to demonstrate the peculiarities of the EU negotiating process. His chapter comes to the conclusion that the potential for influencing the decision-making processes in the EU is rather limited as the leverage of individual member states is gradually decreasing and the influence and number of other powerful players are increasing. He concludes, therefore, that member states, in order to make their voices heard in Brussels, must engage as early as possible in the various consultative processes. They should plan more strategically and operate tactically. In this regard, Langenberg sees value in the forging of ad hoc coalitions on relevant issues with as many like-minded countries as possible. The give-and-take in a negotiating exercise that is so typical of the EU framework certainly deserves close scrutiny from the viewpoint of negotiation theory and practice to test whether Langenberg's findings are not limited just to the case of RTD policy but, in fact, point to a more general pattern.

The fifth chapter by **Derek Beach** concentrates on negotiations within the framework of EU intergovernmental conferences (IGCs), with particular emphasis on the role of the EU institutions. Using a solid body of empirical evidence, he demonstrates the mighty influence of these institutions in the preparation and the course of IGCs. This is not to belittle the decisive role of the member governments in shaping the final outcome of the IGCs, but Beach does ably show the "discreet power" of the institutions throughout the entire negotiating process. Again, it is surprising that negotiations research has so far ignored the subject of IGCs, and it is to Beach's credit that he has chosen this topic. In one section of his analysis Beach shows how the Presidency, the Council Secretariat, the Commission, and the European Parliament played their cards at a recent IGC (1996–1997). He finds that the Council Secretariat often outwitted the Commission, thus gaining considerable influence over the course of the negotiations. In dealing with these issues Derek Beach combines a high level of conceptual abstraction with empirical findings that make this chapter recommended reading for both social scientists and students of the practice of European politics. In his concluding remarks Beach tries to explain to what extent EU negotiations differ from other negotiations in a multilateral framework (e.g., the World Trade Organization [WTO] and the North American Free Trade Agreement [NAFTA]). Although this question is addressed only briefly in his contribution on the IGCs, Beach does describe many of the features that set EU negotiations apart from other international negotiation processes.

Dorothee Heisenberg (Chapter 6) examines the procedure of taking decisions by consensus as the prime decision-making mechanism in the Council of Ministers and the governing council of the European Central Bank (ECB). Having outlined the structural factors in EU negotiations and the ways in which they compare with those of other international negotiations, Heisenberg surveys the voting pattern in the Council of Ministers only to make the discovery that smaller member states hardly ever cast a negative vote or abstain. In her assessment, the consensus mechanism in the EU often turns out to be a double-edged sword. Even though, as Heisenberg points out, the Presidency is always proud of being able to convince all the partners to go along with a compromise it has proposed, she does not see great value in decisions being reached by way of consensus. Quite the opposite, Heisenberg believes that the application of the consensus principle fails all too often to further the cause of integration as it holds the EU back from attaining a new and higher level of international governance. Heisenberg's chapter appears to be the first serious analysis to date of the consensus principle as applied within the EU framework; it thus makes a significant contribution to negotiation theory.

In Chapter 7 **Ole Elgström** provides a close look at the interplay of the Commission and the Council of Ministers in the EU decision-making process. He devotes a good deal of his analysis to the capacity of both institutions to advance progress in negotiations through mediation. In this context Elgström sees the Commission in the role of a preventive mediator, while the Presidency and the Council of Ministers often seem to intervene as mediators, the former acting as a "facilitative compromise broker" in the later stages of negotiations. With the benefit of Heisenberg's clarifications on the consensus rule it is useful to learn Elgström's views on EU voting and what he calls "the shadow of the vote." In particular, Elgström considers the bargaining dynamics under the shadow of the vote, a constantly shifting situation in which the sheer possibility of a majority vote makes constructive negotiations imperative. Elgström concludes his chapter with an observation relating to the impending EU enlargement, forecasting that there will be a more frequent use of majority voting which will lead to less concern for the views of minorities and, given the diversity of member countries, a more difficult decision-making process. Elgström's allusion to enlargement opens the window on a completely new EU negotiating scenario which has only just begun to attract the interest of negotiation researchers.

Leendert Jan Bal (Chapter 8) shares his inside impressions of how member states operate in the Council of Ministers. A practitioner himself, the author gives a quite candid assessment of the negotiating behavior of the various member states, too candid perhaps in the eyes of readers from some countries but all the more interesting for it. He expands on the mechanics of the negotiation process between member states and discusses the time element involved in the deliberations of the Council, thereby drawing attention to another often-neglected factor in negotiation research. Unlike the European Parliament, the Council is not obliged to follow a fixed time frame, giving it the choice of working "fast" or "slow" as the case may be. Bal also describes in some detail the various stages of the negotiation process in which the role of the individual member states may vary. For instance, when an issue is dealt with by the European Parliament, member states have less influence in determining the course and outcome of the negotiations.

Peter van Grinsven (Chapter 9) offers a general overview of the working methods of the European Council and discusses the shortcomings of the current procedures. He criticizes the decreasing ability of the General Affairs and External Relations Council (GAERC) both to adequately prepare the European Council meetings and to coordinate EU policies. He calls for a refocusing of the European Council on strategic and political decision making. The author addresses the current proposals for a reform of the European Council as they were formulated by the Convention on the Future of Europe. After the recent intergovernmental conference on the EU constitution, this chapter merits particular consideration.

Alain Guggenbühl (Chapter 10) deals with the scope of influence that the Presidency may exert. Comparing the program of the Presidency with a cookbook, Guggenbühl offers his own recipe for successful negotiations: the Presidency has the best chance of being successful if it does should not push forward its own national agenda but seeks rather to act as an honest broker and as an agent for the promotion of European integration. This, according to Guggenbühl, is the indispensable ingredient that will make the dish palatable for every guest.

Alice Landau (Chapter 11) concentrates on the negotiations surrounding EU enlargement, giving an in-depth account of the role of the Commission in them and presenting the negotiating strategies of member states in the recent rounds of talks. Landau gives an excellent account of the multilayered bargaining process with its cluster of actors, all of which are all involved in some way in power struggles. Landau is convinced that the Commission has shown a tendency to expand its own power base during the recent enlargement negotiations.

Conceptual Propositions

This section will briefly describe the workings of the EU institutions. Particular emphasis will be placed on the interaction between the EU institutions and the member states. The principal challenge of this book, however, will be to ascertain whether the negotiating process within the framework of the EU follows a distinctive pattern and thus allows the particular features that set EU negotiations apart from other negotiating processes to be discerned.

The following conceptual propositions can be made without taking too many risks:

1. One of the essential differences between the EU negotiation process and other international negotiation processes is the question of *assured outcomes*, in other words, whatever happens the result of the process cannot be too vague or ambiguous. Assured outcomes are much less self-evident at the international level than in national negotiations. In national negotiations there is always a third party able to take a decision should the negotiating parties fail to reach a satisfactory solution. If national negotiations are the first step in an international process, then there must be an assured outcome at this level or the member state will be unable to mandate its representatives. In standard international practices, diplomatic conferences are not obliged to come to substantive conclusions and often result in unclear outcomes, if any at all. Especially on issues where opposing views dominate (e.g., Kyoto Protocol, Comprehensive Test-Ban Treaty) implementation is a major problem, to say the least.

In the European Union, however, there is no alternative to an assured outcome—no other choice—in those domains where substantive sovereignty has been delegated to the European institutions. If no decisions are taken, then EU mechanisms will come to a grinding halt and will start to slip, and even slide back; this would affect the member states so adversely that no standstill can be countenanced on issues in the supranational area. Assured outcomes are needed there just as they are needed on the national level. Of course, it does make a difference if the negotiations are taking place under the consensus rule or under the qualified-majority rule; and we postulate that assured outcomes are more probable under the latter regime than the former. Moreover, as the different territories and levels of the EU are interconnected, we also postulate that the drive for assured outcomes is a distinctive feature of the European negotiation process as a whole compared with non-EU processes. Our thesis is that assured outcomes are most likely to be seen at the intrastate level, least likely at the international level, and in between at the EU level. In the EU, there are more assured outcomes than in regular international negotiations but fewer than in intrastate processes. Inside the EU arena a distinction can be made between decision making under the consensus rule, which comes closer to international negotiation processes, and decision making under the qualified-majority-voting rule, which is closer to the national processes. In the coming chapters we will test this hypothesis.

It should be noted that this book, *Negotiating European Union*, is but a first attempt to define the ingenious character of EU negotiation processes. The "subarenas" with which we will be dealing represent only a part of the full spectrum of EU negotiations. Many other such "subarenas" will be analyzed in other compilations of practical and academic wisdom. This, at least, is a start, and, the authors and editors hope, a fruitful one: the start of a process of analyzing negotiation processes in and around a European Union that is in constant flux, chiefly because of the enlargement process and the deepening of the processes that are already in place.

2. Another proposition is that EU negotiations are largely different from other international negotiating processes in that their outcome, by virtue of the EU treaty, has a direct effect on the member states and their citizens. The *supranational character* of EU negotiations merits in-depth analysis to elicit the lessons for negotiation theory and practice.

3. A third element which makes the conceptual framework of EU negotiation quite unique concerns the *democratic dimension* of the EU. In fact, there is no other international organization in the world in which a parliamentary body (European Parliament) and democratically elected representatives (Council of Ministers, European Council) have comparable influence on the decision-making process in virtually all important matters. The democratic quality of EU negotiations has not only been embodied in the respective EU institutions (i.e., in the European Parliament) from the start but is also mirrored at the level of the member states where national parliaments are eager to make their voice heard in all matters of European integration. The democratic dimension of the EU and its parameters, as defined by the EU treaties, are certainly among the key factors that must be included in any serious research on the EU as a negotiating process.

4. A fourth proposition that helps to elucidate the specific nature of EU negotiations relates to the particular type of interaction between EU institutions and member states. Interaction is not a phenomenon that makes EU negotiations different from others. In any negotiation a close interface can be observed between, on the one hand, the negotiators, and on the other hand, the various actors entitled and competent to direct the course of the negotiations. The conceptual difference between the necessary interaction of the key players in any negotiation and the nec-

essary interaction of the key players in the EU negotiating framework resides in the specifics of the EU system of integration.

In less-integrated systems the interaction of the various actors is rather limited. The EU system, characterized by a high level of integration covering a broad area of common competences, necessitates a particularly dense, permanent, and multi-layered network of contacts between the actors both in Brussels and the member states. The conceptual proposition can be made that EU negotiations are usually conducted in a framework of *enhanced interaction*, in the sense of a qualitatively new and intensified cooperation.

5. As the process of European integration deepens, it becomes evident that competence over more and more matters is being shifted from the sphere of member states' domestic legislation to becoming the common responsibility of the EU. For instance, only a few years ago, the areas of justice and home affairs were typically considered as falling within the competence of member states; they have now become matters of joint competence. The monetary union and the introduction of the euro are other examples of how far the integrative force of the EU has advanced the process of European integration. In terms of negotiation doctrine one may observe a *shift of sovereignty* from member states toward joint EU competences. This transfer of power and its effects on negotiations need further study and investigation.

The Complex Nature of the EU

The problem of definition

From the point of view of negotiation theory, the EU is not easy to encapsulate. This would not be too much of a problem if the negotiating framework of the EU were comparable in practice with that of any other international organization, but that is definitely not the case. A brief exposition of the complex nature of the EU would thus appear to be appropriate. In terms of the classic definition of an international organization, the EU poses a serious challenge. It is often described as an entity *sui generis* as it does not meet many of the criteria usually associated with inter-governmental organizations. In many respects the EU cannot be categorized as an international organization in the formal sense. Because of its partly supranational character and its far-reaching competences the EU exerts an enormous impact on the daily life of the member states and their people, all the more because the EU is gradually eroding the sovereignty of its member states, leaving less and less scope for purely domestic affairs. Within the EU framework the dividing line between foreign and domestic affairs has become blurred.

It is not always easy therefore to determine the competences of the EU on the one hand and those of the member states on the other. A distinction is generally made between the competences that are reserved to member states, others that are shared between the EU and member states, and those that have completely shifted from the member states to the EU. Within that last domain the EU has the final word. Furthermore, the EU treaty introduced the principle of "subsidiarity" which holds that the European Union can act in areas where it does not have exclusive power only if the member states cannot sufficiently achieve the stated objectives (i.e., "only if and in so far as the objectives of the proposed action cannot be sufficiently achieved by the Member States and can, therefore, by reason of the scale of effects of the proposed action, be better achieved by the Community" [Article 5 of the Treaty Establishing the European Community]). In accordance with these rules of competence government ministers and public officials from EU capitals meet regularly in Brussels to discuss and negotiate matters that are to be decided fully or partly in Brussels. Given the advanced state of European integration, the body of law governing the EU has become something special that is quite different from international law proper and from domestic law. The EU legislative process, where it is no longer possible to distinguish between domestic and foreign affairs, is a case in point. The need for coordination and interaction between the various government departments within member states has become such that, in some countries, the competence for European affairs has shifted from the ministries of foreign affairs to the prime minister's office or to a ministry of European affairs. The transfer of competences is just one aspect of the complex nature of the EU. Another factor that has immediate bearing on the way negotiations are conducted has to do with the special legal character of the various EU components. Parts of it present a supranational character; parts are still shaped in accordance with the intergovernmental model. In reality, it makes a great difference whether negotiations are set in the supranational or in the intergovernmental framework. Bearing in mind the peculiarities of the relevant negotiation situation it seems useful to recall the institutional setup of the EU which has turned out to be an amalgam of very different organizational schemes. In each of them a variety of distinct negotiating styles has developed.

By the Treaty of Maastricht, signed on 7 February 1992 (effective as of 1 November 1993), the member states established among themselves a European Union. The European Union is based on the European Communities (EC) (i.e., the European Economic Community, the European Coal and Steel Community, and the European Atomic Energy Community). The architecture of the EU is commonly compared to the roof of a Greek temple supported by three pillars, one consisting of the European Communities, the second encompassing the European common foreign and security policy (CFSP), and the third comprising provisions on cooperation in the fields of justice and home affairs (JHA).

Although the European Communities have had a common set of institutions since 1967 the negotiating framework of the EU is still remarkably complex. This state of affairs can be explained by the distinct composition of and the complicated procedures provided for each institution (the main ones being the European Commission, the Council of Ministers, the European Parliament, and the European Court of Justice) as well as by the dissimilar legal effects of the decisions taken by the various organs. The intricate system of interaction between the institutions and the member states adds to the difficulties of understanding the workings of the EU. Another salient feature of the process of European integration, as embodied in the EU, is its unclear finality. Defining European integration as a "work in progress" does not particularly help one to grasp the essence of a negotiation process whose final destination is still unknown. At present, nobody can tell for sure whether the EU is moving toward a system in which the member states remain the principal actors (intergovernmental model) or whether the EU is going in the direction of some kind of "United States of Europe" in accordance with the federal model (integration concept). This uncertainty about the finality of the EU also contributes to the conceptual vagueness and to the ambivalent nature of the EU negotiating process. EU affairs are neither domestic nor foreign in the classic sense. They are somewhere in between. The officials involved in the multifaceted EU negotiations should no longer be considered as typical diplomats but, in most cases, as specialists in their fields, often moving on the edge between community competences and national prerogatives. The strong involvement of the EU bureaucracy in decision making further complicates matters.

The phenomenon of supranationality

As indicated above, one of the key elements of European integration within the EU consists in the supranational quality of major parts of its legal system. Under the first pillar comprising the European Communities most matters are governed by the principle of supranationality which provides that legal acts adopted in conformity with EU rules immediately become the law of the land of member states, effectively replacing the respective national legislation. As the EU norms falling within the purview of the first pillar take precedence over national legislation, the legal systems of the member states are strongly influenced by EU law, and the domain of domestic legislation is gradually shrinking.

In a general context the "integration impact" of supranationality—the irreversible binding together of the destinies of EU member states in the economic and monetary field—has been described as the most advanced form of cooperation ever developed in the modern world between independent states. It is true that, step-by-step, EU member states are losing a large amount of their sovereignty and independence as more and more competences are being shifted to the EU. The continuous transfer of sovereignty from member states to the EU makes the EU a formidable power center. Currently, over half of all legislative acts in force within member states are community law. Moreover, these EU regulations, directives, and decisions claim absolute legal authority and take precedence over the national legislation of member states. From the point of view of negotiation research, the question as to how European law is made and what forces are at play in the tough bargaining triangle between member states, EU institutions, and various lobbies is an intriguing one. A closer look at the law-making process pertaining to EU norms under the first pillar (i.e., bearing the characteristics of "supranationality") reveals that negotiations in this core area of European integration are different from those conducted in an intergovernmental context. EU negotiations within the supranational framework compare rather with the activities of a legislator as the outcome of the process is a legal norm applicable without exception within all member states. Given the rigid and complicated procedures typical for the creation of EU laws, all negotiations regarding legal texts are bound to be formalistic and meticulous. One of the criticisms raised with regard to the EU from a citizen's standpoint concerns the overly legalistic language of the EU treaty in general and of EU legislation in particular. The legal texts negotiated and adopted in the EU have become so complicated that only a few experts are able to understand them. On the other hand, it is hard to see how legal documents regulating very complex matters for all member states can be drafted in such a manner as to be understood by the average EU citizen. In short, in dealing with community matters a high measure of expertise is required in both the substance of the issue under consideration and the legal mechanism at play. Negotiators need a good knowledge of the interplay between the different EU institutions, the national actors in the member states, and the lobbies involved.

The intergovernmental framework

In all matters not governed by the principle of supranationality, the coordination of member states' positions is still based on the traditional intergovernmental framework. The second pillar of the EU treaty, CFSP, is decided and executed under this premise; CFSP and most matters related to the third pillar, JHA, have not yet reached the high degree of integration typical of the supranational framework. The same holds true for defense matters where the EU is just beginning to develop its own security and defense identity. Foreign affairs, justice and home affairs, not to mention defense, form the inner core of what is commonly perceived as a state's sovereignty. Once the national competences over these areas have shifted to Brussels, little to nothing will be left of the national states as we know them today. The reluctance of member states to give up these strongholds of national sovereignty is not surprising. In the foreseeable future, progress in shaping a cohesive and effective common foreign and security policy for the EU seems hard to achieve. In spite of all the serious efforts undertaken, a realistic assessment must be that member states will revert frequently to the classic instruments of bilateral diplomacy rather than put all their energies into pursuing a common EU policy. The coordination of a common EU foreign and security policy, as prescribed by the EU treaty, sometimes resembles a façade behind which certain key member states engage in "parallel actions" completely outside the EU framework. Negotiations under the second pillar therefore show only part of the picture, which further complicates the analysis. On the one hand, specific EU particularities and, on the other hand, the ways and means of traditional diplomacy, all have to be taken into account. Negotiations in the context of the second and third pillar, although conducted within the EU institutional system, can be compared to a certain extent to the multilateral process used in other international organizations. Whereas under the first pillar the negotiating process is typically geared to the creation of EU law (legislative procedures), under the second and third pillar it aims to elaborate a common position or to take political decisions that engage member states to state a common position or to take common actions. In matters of foreign and security policy, and to some extent also in justice and home affairs, the intergovernmental character of negotiations provides a limited role only for the Commission and the Parliament, while the key players remain the member states as represented in the European Council or in the Council of Ministers.

The various actors

In any negotiating system the actors involved are the principal masters of the game. Within the EU these actors are the EU institutions, the member states, and the powerful lobbies. As outlined above, the complex nature of the EU means that key actors have to play different roles; and various actors are subject to different rules depending on where they are in the three-pillar structure. In an intergovernmental negotiating situation, the weight of the member states is definitely heavier than in a situation characterized by the principle of supranationality where the Commission and the Parliament hold a very strong position. To correctly assess the leverage exerted by the various actors, the relevant mechanisms at work must first be taken into consideration. It is not enough to understand the system in theory. The EU schemes must be studied in practice taking cognizance of the fact that the key players are operating within a concrete context of international and domestic policy. The actors form part of the political leadership of the respective member states or are part of the influential EU bureaucracy. As the bearers of political responsibility at home or in Brussels, the various players clearly have to defend interests and positions that may run counter to the underlying principle of an ever-closer European Union.

The EU negotiating situation can be influenced considerably by the parameters of domestic politics within member states (e.g., electoral considerations) and by the particular role played by the rotating Presidency. It is no secret that some member states use the term of their Presidency to promote a national agenda rather than to advance the cause of European integration. Furthermore, in assessing the diverse factors that determine the actual negotiating scenario, due consideration must be given to what can be called "European public opinion." Mainstream public opinion on widely discussed key issues should by no means be underestimated.

Interaction and coordination

Two key words capture the essence of the multilayered EU negotiating system: "interaction" and "coordination." Both at the horizontal and vertical level the institutions and actors involved in EU affairs are constantly engaged in an intricate and intensive process of consulting, negotiating, and decision taking. This continuous activity of interaction and coordination in matters of vital importance to the member states makes the EU a unique negotiating system. The project of European integration in action can best be understood by examining how the nuts and bolts of the interface between the different layers of the system fit together. Vertically, the highest political level is incarnated by the European Council which regularly brings together the heads of state or governments to provide political guidance to the work of the EU institutions. Together with the Council of Ministers, the European Council represents the intergovernmental face of the EU. The Commission embodies the supranational function and the European Parliament ensures democratic control. The European Court of Justice sees to it that the law of the EU is interpreted and implemented in the same way in all member states. The EU Presidency which rotates each semester among member states, animates EU business as it presides over the European Council and the Council of Ministers, and it may also set the overall EU agenda.

Below ministerial level the negotiating framework for day-to-day business comprises the Committee of Permanent Representatives (COREPER), consisting of the heads of diplomatic missions of the member states to the EU. The bulk of the substantive work of the EU is carried out at the level of COREPER in close cooperation with the Commission and its bureaucracy and/or the Council Secretariat. The European Parliament also comes into play here in conformity with its prerogatives in the decision-making process. The vertical and horizontal EU coordination procedures are mirrored in the capitals of member states where the harmonization of national positions can be as tough as the negotiations in Brussels. In the EU context "diplomacy begins at home" means that the governments of member states have to formulate and defend to the political players on the home front the positions that they intend to present in Brussels. This may turn out to be a cumbersome task as, in certain matters, what may or may not be in the national interest is often disputed among the government, the opposition parties, and other powerful pressure groups.

Enlarging the EU

The historical perspective shows that EU negotiations have often been conducted on a shifting terrain characterized by a perpetual changing of the rules of the game through the dynamics of reform and by continuous enlargement through which, over time, membership has expanded from the original six founding states to the current twenty-five-strong Union, ten new members having acceded on 1 May 2004.

Without doubt, the biggest wave of member states ever to be admitted will profoundly alter the EU and bring about qualitative changes that have little in common with the substantive problems encountered with previous admissions of member states. The Treaty of Nice attempted to set the ground rules for the upcoming EU expansion. After Nice, however, it became clear that much more radical reforms were needed to bring the system into line with the requirements of an EU with ten new member states. It is obvious that this, the biggest enlargement ever, will cruelly test the capacity of the EU to reform its institutions and the procedures by which the negotiating processes are presently carried out in Brussels. It has become public knowledge that the present mechanisms are ill adapted to meet the gigantic challenges posed by the fundamental changes looming on the horizon.

Enlargement and the need for institutional reform call for totally new approaches to the ways and means by which future negotiations should be conducted on matters of European integration. The conviction has sunk in at the highest political level that, in view of the growing disenchantment of EU citizens and their frustration with the bureaucratic features of the EU and of what they perceive as the Union's "democratic deficit," a completely new negotiating basis is needed for the future. For this reason, at the meeting of the European Council in Nice in December 2000, the heads of state or government called for a broad and detailed discussion of the future prospects of the EU. They invited the citizens of Europe to participate in this debate on the future of Europe so that the people's aspirations could be better taken into account beyond the Nice treaty. It was in this context that a declaration on the future of Europe was annexed to the treaty. Within the framework of a large debate involving the European Parliament, national parliaments, politicians, the business world, academics, and representatives of the European civil society, a number of subjects were chosen for consideration. In the declaration, the simplification of the legal framework of the EU, the demarcation of the responsibilities to be attributed to member states and to the EU, as well as the EU Charter of Fundamental Rights, were singled out as priority subjects for the reform debate.

Following, in certain respects, the innovative mechanisms established for the elaboration of the Charter of Fundamental Rights, a consensus emerged on the need for a new negotiating framework designed to prepare for the next intergovernmental conference of the EU. The Convention on the Future of Europe was thus established, consisting of representatives of the member states, the European Parliament, national parliaments, and the Commission. The convention was given the mandate to work out options for draft amendments to the EU treaty. Provision was also made for involving the applicant countries in its work. In parallel, a forum of civil society was established to serve as a "structural network" and to provide a consultative mechanism for the convention. As a process of international negotiations, the convention on the reform of the EU became a laboratory of new ideas. The convention and its interaction with the civil-society forum departed from the well-trodden procedural paths that had governed previous intergovernmental conferences. In the past, procedures had lacked that precise "preconference" element that the convention provided. As it turned out, however, the introduction of a broader negotiating platform to prepare the ground for the formal intergovernmental conference did not, per se, ensure the success of the latter. When on 20 June 2003 the chairman of the convention, the former French president, Valéry Giscard d'Estaing, presented the result of the deliberations of that body in the form of a proposal for a EU constitution, expectations ran high that the intergovernmental conference would be able to successfully conclude its work on the basis of this draft document. In spite of the intensive efforts of the Italian Presidency, the European Council in December 2003 finally failed to settle the few outstanding issues that would have enabled it to wrap up the whole package deal. Superficially and with hindsight, it is easy to identify the stumbling blocks that stood in the way of a successful conclusion of the conference. The uncompromising position of some member states regarding the weight of voting rights in the Council of Ministers are usually given as the main reason for the conference's ultimate failure.

From the standpoint of negotiation theory and practice the outcome of that European Council meeting raises the deeper question of "failed negotiations" in general. Why do negotiations break down? In answering this question with regard to the European Council held in December 2003, it would be simplistic to engage in the sort of "blame game" that has pointed the finger at the Italian Presidency and at "stubborn Poles and Spaniards" who did not want to go along with the solutions proposed by the convention. A more profound understanding of the workings of EU negotiations is needed to address the issues more seriously. May we express the hope that this book will make a contribution to that understanding.

Chapter 2

The EU as a Negotiations Arena: Diplomats, Experts, and PAM Professionals[1]

Rinus van Schendelen

Negotiating in a Pluralist Environment

The European Union (EU) is a formal grouping of member states whose governments are, in a sense, its shareholders and as such responsible for its institutional skeleton as outlined in the relevant treaties. Being shareholders, however, does not necessarily make them stakeholders, let alone important stakeholders. Every member state is, in fact, a *member country* made up of a characteristic combination of government and private entities, both of which are extremely fragmented. "Government" is organized not only horizontally—ranging from national, through regional, to local government—but also vertically, with specific public authority in the financial-services, public-transport, food-safety, or other domain. The private domain, which is also fragmented, is composed of organizations that differ according to whether or not they are profit-orientated, to manpower and capital size, to type of product or service, and more. Between all these distinctions there is, in fact, a fair amount of gray area. For example, between governments and companies there are the nongovernmental organizations (NGOs), not-for-profit bodies that fall under private law although many of them are, in essence, offshoots of a government or company. In short, every member country of the EU is a pluralist system.

All the member countries are part of the framework of the EU to which treaties have given the authority to make hard law (directives, regulations, and decrees) that overrules domestic decisions. The EU also produces soft law, such as guidelines and benchmarks, and makes use of mild instruments, such as subsidies, all of which can be just as influential as hard law. It is not surprising that in pluralist member countries, many sectors consider the EU as highly relevant. Here, they can win or lose on legislation, on subsidies, and on anything that can bring them closer to those prizes, such as benign procedures, positions, and people (Triple P). This EU framework, however, is not a political system standing high above the member countries but essentially an open playing field. Given the *relevance and openness* of the EU framework, many public and private interest groups wish to participate in the processes of decision making, be it through formal structures, semiformal arrangements, and/or informal lobbying. Many also put most trust in self-reliance and participate directly or indirectly through networks in those processes, thereby experiencing the aggregate pluralism of Europe. A decision is usually the outcome of negotiations; but the actual question here is: who are the negotiators?

The EU Playing Field

The formal EU *skeleton* of decision making as it existed under the Treaty of Nice until May 2004 (the fifth enlargement date), comprises the following parts (see *Figure 2.1*):

- The European Commission is the administrative body of twenty Commissioners (the College) managing about twenty small ministries (called Directorates-General or DGs), and about twenty thousand civil servants (including linguistic, secretarial, and technical staff). Within the limits of the treaties (primary law), the Commission has the exclusive right to initiate proposals for secondary legislation for adoption by the Council and by the European Parliament (EP) where the codecision procedure applies. Such legislation amounted to 15 percent of total EU law in 2001 (General Report 2002). The Commission also produces—practically without the involvement of the Council and European Parliament—the 85 percent of legislation delegated to it by secondary legislation passed previously.
- The Council is composed of national ministers acting mainly through specialized councils, for example, the Environment Council or the Transport Council.
- The three main representative bodies: the European Parliament for political parties; the European Economic and Social Committee (EESC) for socioeconomic

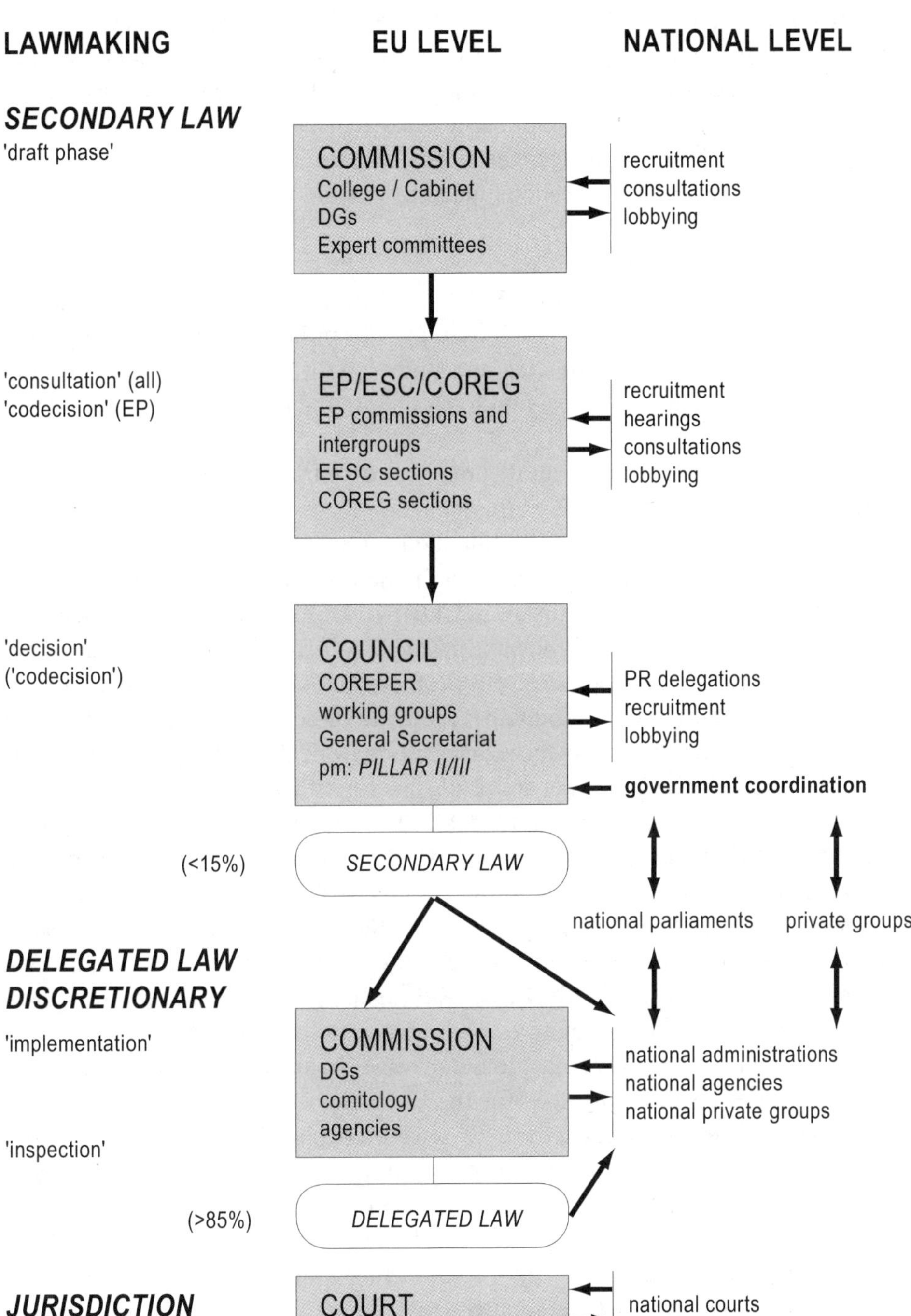

Figure 2.1. Main decision-making flows: EU and member states.

interest groups; and the Committee of the Regions (COREG) for regional and local governments. As prescribed by the treaties these bodies must be consulted on proposals for secondary legislation. Under codecision the European Parliament can also amend or veto secondary legislation.

- The European Court of Justice (the Court) which, upon request and based on the treaties, can overrule decisions made by the aforementioned bodies or can urge them to make decisions.

This skeleton applies to pillar I of the EU, the old European Economic Community which is by far the main domain of EU activity. For pillar II (common foreign and security policy) and pillar III (justice and home affairs), the Council is formally both the start and finish of EU decision making but, to date, it has started little and finished even less.

All the major sectors of the pluralist member countries have some formal position inside the EU framework. For example, national governments sit in the Council and nominate their commissioner(s) while their ministries usually have specialized Councils. Major national political parties sit in the European Parliament, just as regional and some local governments sit in COREG. Umbrellas of private socioeconomic interest groups have positions within EESC. There also exists a semiformal and an informal reality that, together, put flesh on the bones of the EU skeleton. In the ambit of the Commission particularly, there are more than one thousand expert committees where more than fifty thousand experts from all kinds of domestic interest groups sit semiformally to prepare proposals for either secondary or delegated legislation (van Schendelen 1998 and 2003). Through its hearings and intergroups the European Parliament has a similar setup. The Council takes decisions mainly through the three hundred or so working groups of its Committee of Permanent Representatives (COREPER or Committee of PRs). To work on legislation delegated to it, the Commission has some four hundred fifty special expert committees, known as its "comitology." Finally, Brussels is an open city, where everybody, even those from outside a member country, can lobby an official informally.

The fragmentation of power inside the member countries, caused by domestic pluralism, has had its consequences for the EU framework. In pillar I, on which we focus here, there is *no single center of power*. The governments of the member states now possess the power of veto only over new treaty formation, a few cases of secondary legislation, and special issues such as the nomination of the chair of the Commission. For all secondary legislation the Council is dependent on a proposal from the Commission, must take into account the opinions of the representative bodies, and has increasingly been required to accommodate its codecision maker, the European Parliament. The Commission is dependent on the Council and, under codecision, on the European Parliament for both secondary legislation and the granting of delegated powers. Because of its small size the Commission is also highly dependent for the gathering of information and support on its "assistant bureaucracy" of expert committees and on all sorts of lobbyists acting on an informal basis. The three representative bodies are most dependent on support from the Commission and from elsewhere. For its jurisprudence the Court is dependent on formal requests and complaints, and for its effectiveness, on respect for EU law, particularly on the part of national governments.

There are many intrainstitutional as well as interinstitutional dependencies. For example, there is a partial overlap in the division of labor between the Commissioners and the DGs, which requires them to accommodate their differences especially if the decision they need requires majority approval by the College. On most policy dossiers, however, the key person in the Commission is a mid-level ("lower A") civil servant (*chef de dossier*), who manages the policy process via expert committees and through consultation of colleagues. There are comparable *interdependencies* inside the three representative bodies, where the division of labor is centered on the rapporteur who has to muster sufficient support from all the parliamentary parties involved and commissions, as far as these are involved, and ultimately the plenary.

In the Council the staff of the Presidency, which rotates every six months, run all the working-group meetings, as well as the COREPER and Council sessions, with the help of staff from the preceding and succeeding Presidency ("troika") and the Council Secretariat. The division of labor here frequently causes friction with the national capitals where there may be a division of labor along quite different lines. At any level inside the Council a decision usually requires the (at least silent) test of qualified-majority voting (QMV) or roughly two thirds of all voting points, and on some proposals even unanimity, thus making the internal interdependencies even more intense. Moreover, inside all the institutions there are many informal interdependencies based, for example, on interests, nationality, language, age, career, and friendship.

Order and Examples of Variety

"Pluralism," "fragmentation," and "interdependency" are the catchwords that summarize the essentials of the EU playing field. Decision making in the EU usually results in an arena full of different stakeholders and issues representing the different interests of the fragmented institutions and the pluralist countries. Every game is usually wide open because of the absence of a power holder, competitive because of the presence of many stakeholders and issues, complex because of the many formal procedures and informal realities, and dynamic because the tide can always turn in a different direction. The arena, in short, is usually "multi-n" by the number of institutions, semiformal and informal layers, stakeholders and issues, levels and laterals, and more. It is outstandingly suitable for negotiations, as its openness usually provides an entry, its competition a fair chance, its complexity another way out, and its dynamics a new momentum.

The EU system is not, however, "anarchical," as may sometimes be the case in global politics, although even on that kind of playing field there is usually some order behind the clashes (Bull 1977). The EU *order* comes from two general sources. One is the collection of treaties, the other the accepted behavior in practice; together they form the EU constitution, written and unwritten (Friedrich 1974). The written part contains mainly the formal agreements regarding the division of labor and the rules on decision making: which institution decides on what, and how. The unwritten part refers mainly to the practices of decision making considered as legitimate, such as the aforementioned characteristics of openness and competition in a complex and dynamic setting, which result in negotiations as the way to peaceful compromises. Together, the two parts impose a basic order on any EU arena. Variations are caused by specific factors, such as legislative procedures, domain characteristics, or the "multi-n" mentioned before. As an intermezzo we shall now provide brief examples of the two main types of EU legislative process.

Secondary Legislation: The European Food Safety Regulation

On 8 November 2000 the Commission published its proposal for better food-safety regulations, to be adopted by the Council and the Parliament under codecision (COM 2000/716), thus making this a case of secondary legislation. The objective of the Commission was to make the practices of decision making in this field less fragmented and less incomplete through a directly binding regulation. For a long time, various DGs, such as Agriculture, Research, Health and Consumer Protection, and Environment, had covered aspects of food safety. On specific issues eight expert committees, for example, the Scientific Committee on Food (SCF), played a policy-shaping role. Nine comitology committees, for example, the Standing Veterinary Committee (SVC), were in charge of delegated legislation. On issues not delegated to it, the Commission had to propose, each time anew, legislative measures to the Council and the European Parliament.

In the second half of the 1990s such practices became more and more openly criticized. Citing various animal diseases, such as bovine spongiform encephalopathy (BSE) and swine fever, the media and consumer groups started to blame the EU for its failures in food-safety policy. The food industry and food retailers, led respectively by French company, Carrefour, and Anglo–Dutch company, Unilever, also asked for an improved EU policy approach; so, too, did members of both the European Parliament and the Council. More criticism was unleashed. The failures had wasted money in the form of compensation handouts to farmers. New products developed by industry took too long to be approved. Other food products remained outside the controls. There was no balanced approach that took into account the interests of agriculture, health, environment, and consumers. Certain special issues intensified the criticism, such as biotechnology, genetically modified organisms (GMOs), novel foods (not used for human consumption in the past), imports from the United States (different food-safety regimes), and exports to less-developed countries (inferior products).

All in all, the Commission felt the need to propose a more integrated food-safety policy approach ("from farm to fork"), the main contents of which are:

1. The establishment of the European Food Safety Authority (EFSA) as the expert body for advice and research, replacing the old expert committees and composed of one scientific committee with various panels, plus an advisory forum representing national authorities;
2. One standing committee instead of the many comitology bodies for delegated regulation; and
3. The DG Health and Consumer Protection (DG SANCO) being placed in the driver's seat.

In addition to this division of labor, the Commission proposed decision-making rules both for general principles (for example, safeguards, traceability, and liability) and for specific principles (for example, regarding definitions, recruitment of experts, and internal rules).

This arena is formally composed of the Commission, Parliament, and Council, acting under codecision. At the proposal of its main body responsible for this matter (the commission for Environment, Public Health, and Consumer Protection: rapporteur Phillip Whitehead), the European Parliament adopted 189 amendments at its first reading. The Council accepted many of these and the European Parliament dropped a number of others, leaving the remainder for a second reading of which the European Parliament considered nineteen as central. Key issues in COREPER and its working group which was preparing the Council's decision became: the scope of the regulation (including plants, animals, and GMOs or not); the number of EFSA board members to be nominated by the Council; and the location of EFSA (in Helsinki, Finland, or Parma, Italy, with Brussels being chosen for the time being). On 28 January 2002 the Agricultural Council (*sic*) in its second reading approved without debate (as a rubber-stamped A-point) the remainder of the European Parliament's amendments, thus avoiding conciliation procedures and making the regulation final (EC 178/2002; OJ L 31/1).

The real arena has been much more complex. Experts of the old expert committees and comitology bodies representing their private- or public-interest group frequently participated in the process under the Commission, both semiformally on committees and informally as individuals. Inside the Commission, various DGs responsible for aspects of food safety had their own arena with regard to the proposed new powers of DG SANCO and EFSA which, of course, implied a loss of their own power. Public and private lobby groups, which had apparently failed to influence the draft text of the Commission, were effectively behind the bulk of amendments presented by the European Parliament. They had also been most active through their national capitals, as well as through their permanent representatives and their delegates in the COREPER working group. Some multinational groups (companies and NGOs) orchestrated their activities through various capitals. It was not a coincidence that Unilever and Carrefour each gained one of the fourteen seats on the EFSA board; one put forward a Dutchman and the other a Belgian, thus leaving open other positions for France and the United Kingdom (UK).

According to some scholars (Nugent 1999, 257; Greenwood 1997, 13) a case of secondary legislation such as this belongs to the world of "high politics" (accounting for 15 percent of EU law in 2001), which is considered much more relevant than the "low politics" of delegated legislation (the other 85 percent). There is not, however, one decision in the whole regulation about the substantive area of food safety. Much of the text is also diffuse and unspecific in order perhaps to cover disagreements, for example, with regard to definitions of food, internal rules, and the planned review of the issue by the year 2005. The regulation is little more than a political agreement about division of labor, decision-making rules, and legitimate practices. By defining formal procedures, positions, and people (Triple P), it provides the skeleton of a new playing field. The substantive negotiations arena on food safety started in 2003, as soon as EFSA and the standing committee began their operations under delegated legislation, with the European Parliament and Council at a distance.

Delegated Legislation: Safety, Hygiene, and Health Protection at Work

The policy field of safety, hygiene, and health protection at work is one of the oldest in the EU, as it began with the treaty establishing the European Coal and Steel Community (ECSC) in 1952 with its special concern for the mining industry. The Commission soon acquired delegated powers for regulating this field almost directly, needing to consult only with an advisory committee representing those industries (comitology). In 1974 the Council approved by secondary law the Commission proposal to establish a similar Advisory Committee (AC) for Safety, Hygiene, and Health Protection at Work (SHH) for all other industrial sectors (Daemen and van Schendelen 1998). Its composition became tripartite: governments, trade unions, and employers' organizations. The two latter groups are the so-called social partners and represent their umbrellas: the European Trade Union Confederation (ETUC) representing trade unions; *l'Union des Confédérations de l'Industrie et des Employeurs d'Europe* (UNICE) representing private employers; and the *Centre Européen des Entreprises à Participation Publique* (CEEP) representing public employers. There are two members for every member country plus alternates for each of the three groups, making a total of ninety members and ninety alternates (2002), all nominated via national governments and formally approved by the Council. The AC, chaired and staffed by a few officials from the Commission (DG Employment and Social Affairs, DG EMPL), functions mainly through its ten or so working groups, each comprising fewer than twenty people, which prepare the plenary opinions.

The AC acts as the central adviser to the Commission in as much as it holds delegated powers to legislate the SSH field. The Commission has to give "the utmost attention" to an AC's plenary opinion which, if necessary, can be taken by a simple-majority vote. In contrast with the management and the regulatory committees under comitology, however, it remains formally free to deviate from simple majority decision making. In reality, the process of consultation works much more subtly and informally. DG EMPL likes to use the AC as a platform for legitimizing its SHH measures and thus prefers consensus rather than conflict. The *consensus culture* is based on expertise which is also depoliticizing. Senior experts of the AC behave as grandfathers who try to keep good order and good spirits inside the family. Usually a working group discusses a request or proposal from DG EMPL until sufficient consensus has been created both internally and with DG officials. This subtle shuttling is spread over a number of meetings and takes time; and it is frequently effective. Sometimes, however, the ACSHH comes to an internal agreement to disagree, resulting in different positions on the part of the various groups or national delegations with apparently different interests in SHH legislation; DG EMPL is then completely free to decide what it wants. There is, incidentally, a common agreement to disagree with DG EMPL, as happened with regard to the drafting of the Fourth Action Programme (1994–2000). This case also makes clear that DG EMPL can use the ACSHH as an ordinary expert committee for the preparation of proposals for either secondary or delegated legislation, a double use that is fairly customary in comitology.

The ACSHH obtained its *breakthrough* with the 1987 Single European Act (SEA), which explicitly framed the SHH agenda and weakened the Council (both in codecision and QMV terms). In 1989 the European Parliament and the Council approved the SHH Framework Directive giving delegated powers to the Commission—comparable, as such, with the Food Safety Regulations. Soon almost forty specific directives passed the ACSHH. The 1993 Maastricht treaty emphasized the importance of the SHH policy domain and, through its Social Protocol (UK abstaining until 1997), it strengthened the position of the "social partners" in that they became entitled to jointly initiate secondary legislation, independently of the Commission and outside the ACSHH. In fact they obtained a second route both for agenda building and legislation by successfully adopting numerous common opinions and by initiating directives on parental leave (1996), part-time work (1997), and fixed-term contracts (1999). In 2002 the Commission published its new SHH policy programme for the years 2002–2006 and reemphasized the importance of SHH legislation, the role of the AC (from then on [the end of the ECSC treaty] also acting for the mining industries), and the Social Protocol.

The SHH arena is *open and competitive*. DG EMPL and the ACSHH are only two of the major players. The "social partners" inside the AC have an alternative route via the Social Protocol, while the representatives from the national administrations can exert hindrance value through the Council with regard to other relevant dossiers falling under secondary legislation. Inside the AC the groups represented or some of their members can even try to directly push or to block legislative proposals in this field. ETUC and UNICE, in particular, frequently do so both formally and informally. Outside interest groups, such as consumer groups and different national ministries, as stakeholders, use their own ways of intervening at both the domestic and the European level. Other DGs than DG EMPL can also behave as stakeholders as they may consider SHH policies to be intervening in their domain of, for example, internal market (DG Markt), enterprise (DG ENTR), public health (DG SANCO) and enlargement (DG ELARG). They also try to intervene, both inside the Commission via the interservice procedure (i.e., inter–DGs) and College, and outside, via friends in the European Parliament, the Council, or (even applicant) member countries.

Arena Variability

These two cases exemplify both the basic "structuring" of an EU arena and the variety of legislative procedure. Of course, the two cases cannot be taken as representative of the standard pattern of secondary and delegated legislation because such a pattern simply does not exist for the specific reasons mentioned before. *Variability* is the catchword here. For example, the story of EFSA is different from that of GMOs (van Schendelen 2002, 159 ff), although both belong to the same larger arena of secondary legislation on food safety. In every game there are specific factors caused by the "multi-n" of every EU arena, thus even more gray areas. For two reasons, however, these two cases are exceptionally useful here. First, they clarify the considerable difference between secondary and delegated legislation. Secondary legislation is mainly about placing crucial markers (division of labor, decision rules, and legitimate practices) on a playing field; delegated legislation deals with the playing of the ball itself. As mentioned above, some people mistakenly view this as the difference between "high" and "low" politics. Second, the two cases help to show that the aforementioned general characteristics of any EU arena are in reality variable. Nothing is static; everything is variable.

First, *openness* has many faces. At first sight the EFSA case looks much more open than the SHH one. In the EFSA case three institutions are involved; in the SHH case only one. This, however, is only the formal face. If the semiformal and informal realities are taken into account, the EFSA case is much more open than it actually looks, as many interest groups sit in adjacent committees and carry out informal lobbying. Similarly, the SHH case also shows a greater openness than it formally has. For the "social partners" and the interest groups behind them especially, the ACSHH is only one of the major routes for pushing or blocking legislation in this field, while stakeholders left outside the AC can also intervene here. Openness, in short, is a continuum as two other cases may show to the extreme: on the one side, the new arena on "EU governance" in which the EU website ostentatiously invites stakeholders to participate and, on the other side, the Economic and Financial Council of Ministers (ECOFIN), a committee of high officials of the national ministries of finance, which is sensitive almost only to domestic politics.

Second, *competition* is another variable. It is, of course, different from openness because those entering an arena may arrange a cartel. In the EFSA case a great deal of competition can be seen among many different stakeholders, each with its own interests that are normally at issue in the EU. Thus, during the decision-making process coalitions and compromises were made, except for one stalemate issue on the new EFSA location; this wheeler-dealing did not take place before the negotiations, however, but after them, and thus indicates a great deal of competition. ACSHH is less competitive to the extent that the "social partners" sometimes create their own cartel and can more easily do so under the flag of the Social Protocol. For example delegations from the North wanting to get rid of lesser SHH practices in the South ("unfair market competition") sometimes form a cartel too, as does the South on the rebound, so to speak. The SHH arena is usually full of competition, however, because of internal divisions and external challengers. Competition is not necessarily greater under secondary legislation and lower under delegated legislation. The ECOFIN route from Commission to Council is frequently closed off to challengers from outside, while in the field of waste management there are now (unlike in the past) many competitive comitology committees (van Kippersluis 1998).

· Third, *complexity* seems to be everywhere; but the contents are usually different. In the EFSA case, the officials and stakeholders had to fall back on general guidelines, such as treaty texts, Commission papers and Council declarations, which gave a great deal of room for interpretation and thus for infighting. Their product—the regulation—intended to simplify previous decision practices, will probably be complex in its future application. ACSHH looks simple; it is asked formally for its opinion but this binds the Commission only morally (the Commission having only to pay "utmost attention" to its opinions). Its groups and delegations do, however, have hindrance value both inside and outside the AC, as they can delay the shuttling process, take an external route, open another arena, or lobby informally. Complexity in this case does not so much concern the goalposts as the ball that is being played. There can, of course, be more or less variability. At the one extreme there is the trade agreement procedure that formally links the Commission, European Parliament, and Council to the national governments and parliaments (Woolcock 2000). At the other extreme there is the standard format for a regional fund subsidy, although many applicants still find this very complex.

Dynamics, finally, also seems to be everywhere. After a time every EU arena shows continual changes in policy paradigms, regime values, procedures, officials, stakeholders, interests, issues, and much more. The EFSA case is an example of organized change itself. The story of its regulation shows a rapidly changing policy paradigm with new coalitions and compromises, and new winners and losers. The SHH arena also shows more dynamics, especially since 1987; but here it is not that the policy paradigm is shifting, more that the domain is expanding. There are, of course, more dramatic cases of EU dynamics. At one extreme there is, for example, the common agricultural policy (CAP) with its change of paradigm from "production and income" toward "sustainable rural development," bringing into its arena many new stakeholders and issues. At the other extreme one could place the coal and steel policy, once the engine of EU integration, now an almost rudimentary appendix of EU activity.

From Diplomats to Experts as Negotiators

Arenas that are so open, competitive, complex, and dynamic, as just outlined, and also so commonplace in the current EU, clearly require very special skills on the part of the participating negotiators. In the early decades of what is now called the EU, it was mainly national *diplomats* who negotiated on behalf of their government, both with each other and with EU officials. They must have felt at ease then. Pluralism, fragmentation, and interdependency were low-scoring variables in those days. The community of the six was largely a community of member states, not of pluralist member countries. Decentralized governments, private companies, and NGOs were almost absent from the playing field, with the exception of the "social partners" in the coal and steel sector and, at a later stage, the agricultural organizations; but these groups then behaved as subordinates of their national governments. Power was less fragmented than it is today, concentrated as it was in the Council. "Codecision" and "QMV" were unknown terms. The bulk of legislation was secondary, not delegated. The machinery of ordinary decision making showed less interdependency, thanks in particular to the Community's then smaller size and the esprit de corps of the pioneers. The people inside the Commission, European Parliament, and Council could "orchestrate Europe" by negotiating informally, quietly and, avoiding opposition, indirectly; in short, they could negotiate diplomatically (Middlemas 1995).

The arenas of negotiation were *different* from those of today. Run by the diplomats themselves in precisely the way they wanted their openness was limited. Of course there was competition but it was mainly limited to six governmental positions and moderated by the German postwar ambition of complying with French interests, the indifference of Italy due to its domestic instability, and the compliant behavior of the three small countries which were incapable of acting as one. Complexity had a different meaning then. It did not refer to an intricate division of labor or set of decision-making rules as these had yet to be constructed. The complexity lay mainly in the conundrum of how to bring the six into stable and peaceful integration and thus in the creative engineering of the construction itself. Dynamics, too, had a different meaning. Dynamics did not refer to shifting policy paradigms, rapidly changing stakeholders and issues, and other surprising turns in the tide. The dynamics lay in the steady buildup of the decision-making machinery and in the expansion of policy fields, all of which was so normal that their stagnation ("Eurosclerosis") was the big surprise of the early 1980s. The diplomats also liked the challenge of secondary legislation: they liked slaloming along and between the posts of procedures, positions, and people (reactive) or placing the posts according to where their national interest lay (proactive). So-called implementation they considered as "low politics," to be delegated to the Commission and more or less left to experts. Diplomats believed they possessed political expertise rather than technical expertise. They had a better idea of how to play than what to play.

Nowadays, many decades later, the bulk of EU legislation (85 percent) comes from the delegated pipeline of the Commission and comitology; and the preparation of both secondary and delegated legislation is now in the hands of the Commission's *chef de dossier* and expert committees. *Technical experts*, having expertise in a specific matter and representing their organization, have largely replaced diplomats; nowadays the latter are in charge of only the last phase (Council) of the small amount (15 percent) of secondary legislation. The expertise of the experts is usually thorough but, of course, limited to only one part or aspect of a policy domain. Therefore more than fifty thousand experts are needed. They act not for their national government but for their organization, for example, their ministry, trade union, or company, and frequently only for smaller units within these. It is by this means especially that the pluralism of the member countries has found its way to Brussels, thus contributing to the integration of Europe below the level of national governments. The experts also contribute to the fragmentation of power. They want to be among other experts, like the people inside ACSHH, and they dislike intervention by nonexperts. In committee they want to be the king of their island but in reality they are this only to a certain degree, for every committee remains dependent on support and information from the Commission, other committees, and external stakeholders. Willy-nilly, the expert committees keep the parts of the EU machinery interdependent.

The shift *from diplomats to experts* has also contributed to the current characteristics of a EU arena. Paradoxically, openness has greatly increased because the more an expert committee wants to become a "closed shop" the more it attracts curious intruders. The *chef de dossier* of the Commission has a personal interest here: the more intruders, the less a single committee (let alone one member inside it) has a chance of becoming a monopolist in its field and the more the *chef* can shop for information and support, and so, in fact, take the driver's seat. The strong competition in an arena is stimulated not only by the more pluralist backgrounds of experts, now coming from twenty-five instead of six member countries, but also by the Machiavellian tactics of the *chef* and the attentive outsiders such as the unrepresented stakeholders and the media. The experts have also become a cause of the complexity. Committees tend to develop their own rules, definitions, procedures, practices, and more. For comitology, a complex set of procedures has been institutionalized. In such a system high dynamics can take anyone by surprise. Authoritative experts can plead successfully for a new policy paradigm or method, and so can challenging outsiders. Experts also feel most at ease in the area "low politics." Here, they can discuss what the substance of the game is all about and go and play the ball itself.

The Rise of PAM Professionals

In the meantime many organizations have discovered that the protection or promotion of their interests at stake in the EU cannot be left just to their experts. The *weaknesses* of technical experts are more or less threefold.

- As "being an expert" is part of their self-image, experts tend to play solo, reluctant to accept instructions from and report to the superiors at home. In large-sized government organizations, companies, and NGOs, the management seldom has a list of the names of their people acting as experts in Brussels; in small ones, it usually knows thanks to social control mechanisms.
- Experts have a strong belief in being right (in German, *expertenkultur*), thus are also frequently reluctant to compromise on their cherished facts and values. This lowers their legitimizing value in the eyes of the Commission, which then looks elsewhere for advice.
- As mentioned, experts enjoy discussing the substance of the game and playing the ball itself. This is naïve as, in reality, playing the ball correctly frequently depends on respecting the position of certain "markers." Only those who have won the benign procedures, positions, and people (Triple P), can play on an advantageous playing field with better chances of actually putting the ball in the net.

Many interest groups are now trying to repair the weaknesses of their experts. Their search for *improvements* in their arena performance is usually a learning process. It starts with better training for their experts. Frequently, this is followed by the nomination of a EU lobbyist, traveling to and from Brussels or even having a Brussels office. Such a lobbyist is a sort of pathfinder and has two functions: first of all to monitor (to be the "eyes and ears" of) developments potentially relevant for the group and, in addition, to build up a position of interest (by acting as "the mouth") with stakeholders and officials. The lobbyist reports to a high official inside the organization. Frequently a clash will then occur between the lobbyist in Brussels and the experts back home. More recently there has been a tendency to try to optimize the home situation of the group by fostering a more integrated approach on the EU playing field. As it is multinational groups (both companies and NGOs) that are particularly setting this trend, it is also known as the "multinational model" (van Schendelen 2002, chapter V). Its basic elements are now described.

Under the direct responsibility of a member of the central board of the organization a special unit is placed in charge of the design of both the preparatory homework and the optimal fieldwork. In modern speak, this is called the *Public-Affairs Management* (PAM) unit for EU affairs. Its organized emphasis on preparation and planning makes it particularly different from old-style lobbying and thus eligible for the new label. The specific tasks of the unit are threefold. First, it has to study general and specific EU developments that are potentially relevant to the group. The main activities here are identifying threats and opportunities, compiling the long list of relevant dossiers, scanning the arenas, drafting a short list of key dossiers (fewer than ten), developing plans of action, and assessing causes of success and failure. A few times a year the central board member has to approve strategic proposals, such as defining what is on the shortlist. The second task of the unit is the internal implementation of the shortlist. For the selected dossiers "ad hoc teams" (real or virtual) are formed, which also include other staff members (for example, those working with EU law) at headquarters and line experts (familiar with "ball play") belonging to the relevant divisions in the countries. Every team thus brings on board varied expertise as well as links to divisions and countries. In fact, the PAM unit represents the internal arena in terms of obtaining the desired outcomes from the EU. Finally, the unit has to organize the fieldwork with regard to EU officials and stakeholders relevant to those outcomes. One tool is that the team, just like the aforementioned experts, may hold a position in an EU expert committee or working group and thus be composed of different national colors. The other tool is the aforementioned Brussels lobbyist or lobby office which is now the coping stone of the integrated approach.

In this newest practice *PAM professionals* coming under the central board now supervise the technical experts who replaced the diplomats. In fact they bring together the old roles of the diplomats (the people who place the "markers"), the experts (the people who play the ball), and the lobbyists (the pathfinders) in a much more systematic approach, based on a large amount of preparatory homework and run by an "ad hoc team," all managed by them but supervised by the "top dog" at their company, NGO, or ministry. If it works well, then the central board may become the real negotiator with the EU. Many more private and public groups now take this multinational model as an example to follow, and establish a central PAM unit or, when country units are missing, a European network as a sort of multinational family. Inside the EU this new development may strengthen the pluralism of the member countries and increase the fragmentation of power and the many interdependencies; as a consequence, it may also further weaken the already mainly symbolic "national coordination" at central government level. In addition, it may enhance the current characteristics of the playing field because usually openness is greater for well-organized interest groups than for "amateurish" ones, competition grows with professionalism, and complexity and dynamics increase as a result of both. The PAM professionals may also bridge the different worlds of secondary and delegated legislation, as they have a better understanding of the game of playing the ball by (re)positioning the markers.

EU Arenas of Professionals: Good or Bad?

Poorly trained, weakly organized or, in short, largely amateurish interest groups from government or the private sector may feel afraid of EU arenas that are characterized by even more openness, competition, complexity, and dynamics. They may feel bewildered by the many players, be insecure amid the fighting stakeholders, lost in the labyrinth of Triple P, and uncertain on the trampoline of ever-changing developments. In essence, they lack sufficient *knowledge and skills.* In contrast, professional groups and people usually have few problems with such arenas. Psychologically, they take it as a fact of life. As professionals they have better knowledge and skills regarding taking a good entry, coping with other fighters, finding a way out of the labyrinth, and keeping their feet firmly on the trampoline. They may even feel happy with the characteristics of EU arenas just mentioned, as they can manage better than the many amateurish groups can, and they can even use them as an opportunity to create better chances to get a desired outcome. If needed, the professional may know, for example, how to bring new friends on board, how to divide more in order to rule, how to create more complexity and thus confuse others, and how to destabilize an opponent coalition. Of all the factors of success (or failure), knowledge (or the lack of it) is frequently the single most important one. The "multinational model" is a fine example of critical learning.

The professionalization of interest groups may also be beneficial to the *quality of arena negotiations.* The professionals, more so than amateur groups and individuals, are conscious of the basic requirements of the playing field. They make their preparatory homework proactive rather than reactive, for example, by studying in advance the stakeholders and issues involved and the procedures, positions, and people in charge. They give respect to officials and stakeholders, not because of their charm but because of their weapons. They develop their own supply side of specific support and information that is so necessary for matching the demand side of others and thus for satisfying their own demands. They build broader coalitions that cut across national, sectoral, and cultural borders and, more and more they become supporters of what would appear to be the general interest. Knowing that every dossier is different at every moment even, they base their fieldwork not on rules of thumb but on careful homework. Usually they prefer the quiet, informal, and indirect styles of negotiation, but they also know under what circumstances the opposite styles should be applied. Their negotiations are, in short, more tailored, well timed, and fine-tuned. Realizing that they live in the pluralist EU and that they cannot end up as the "winner takes all," they are prepared to make compromises. All this contributes to the quality of negotiations, just as it diminishes the chance of misperceptions, misunderstandings, and mistakes and, in the final analysis, mismatches. For their part, EU officials and politicians appear to have a high appreciation of this growing professionalism (Kohler-Koch 1998).

The PAM-driven style of negotiating can also be considered as positive for the *integration of Europe.* Even amateurish groups from the world of governments, companies, and NGOs already contribute to the better integration of Europe below the level of state governments. At the very least, they articulate their pluralist interests, thus making possible the formation of new EU agendas and policies closer to the citizens. If they learn from their mistakes, they may sooner or later contribute to the accommodation of EU issues in the professional way already mentioned. Under the current circumstances they will probably enhance the arena characteristics of openness, competition, complexity, and dynamics. As a consequence, an even more sophisticated professionalism will be required. The time of EU negotiations by mainly diplomats or experts in the field seems to be coming to an end as PAM professionals take over more and more by replacing them or integrating them. Representing their "leader" at home, they connect the EU to the well-organized interest groups of the pluralist member countries, and they do so in a more prepared way.

Notes

1. The main observations and conclusions of this article are rooted in van Schendelen (2002), which contains more detailed references.

Chapter 3

What Happens at Home—Negotiating EU Policy at the Domestic Level

Mendeltje van Keulen

Introduction

This chapter is concerned with what happens at the domestic level of Europen Union (EU) negotiations. Public and media attention directed at the EU generally focuses on *history-making* decisions (Peterson and Bomberg 1999) and European Council summitry. What happens in Brussels, however, accounts for only a fraction of the resources and efforts national governments devote to the different stages of the EU bargaining game. As "shapers" and "takers" of EU legislation, they are key players in the preparatory as well as implementing phase of EU policy making (Börzel 2003). As the distinct stages of the EU bargaining game are closely interrelated—the effective implementation of binding European legislation is considerably facilitated by the successful negotiation of national preferences in the earlier stages—all governments have designed complex procedures and mechanisms "at home" to manage the interactive relationship, both upward and downward, between their domestic constituency and the European level of governance. Any understanding of the way EU negotiating works in practice must take into account what happens "down the line," in other words, the organizational and management efforts by national governments. This chapter is devoted to an analysis of the principles, peculiarities, working practices, and recent trends and developments with regard to EU negotiations at the domestic level.

The Context: Complicating Features of EU Bargaining

The EU is a particularly dense form of international organization. Its leveled system of integrative bargaining, based on the principles of consensus, cooperation, compromise, and compensation (Rood and van Keulen 2001) constitutes more than the classic *two-level games* in international negotiations (Putnam 1988). A key difference from this theoretical analogy is that EU domestic interplay lacks the figure of the *chief negotiator*. Although representatives of national governments continue to play a key role in the different (European) Council formations, the widening of the scope of policies to be decided at the EU level has led to the circumventing by various government departments, interest groups, and private lobbies of the traditional coordinating authority of foreign and economic affairs ministries. This practice demands different and more complex ways of effectively constructing and negotiating national preferences than is the case in "ordinary" interstate bargaining. A number of system characteristics directly impact upon the way domestic negotiations over EU policy making proceed. Three of these will be dealt with in the next section.

The EU bargaining game is characterized by procedural complexity

The EU decision-making system is far from being a clear separation of powers. The *trias politica* as an organizational principle is nonexistent in Brussels. To give two examples: there is no single authoritative legislator, as the power to legislate is shared between the member states and the European Parliament, and the executive embodied by the European Commission is highly dependent on national governments. To complicate things further, the concept of a neat *policy chain* or the distinction between *prenegotiating* and the actual negotiating stages are misleading in the working practice of EU negotiating. Often, dossiers pass back and forth between different levels—proposals may skip certain phases, accelerate because of political pressures, or be stored away for years until the advent of a new national Council Presidency with a fresh interest in that particular matter. A small number of highly sensitive dossiers are never treated in working groups or in the Committee of Permanent Representatives (COREPER) but only at a high political level in ministerial Council meetings or summits. Nonetheless, the negotiating mandate representing national preferences regarding the matter at hand—in Eurospeak, the *national position*—should ideally be voiced coherently and consistently throughout the different negotiation stages. The *quality* of national positions is even more important as Brussels produces binding decisions on a daily basis, and the proliferation of *qualified-majority voting* has accelerated the policy process and necessitated *coalition formation* at an early stage. Moreover, the *drive for supranationalism* (Stone Sweet and Sandholz 1998; see also Meerts in this volume) causes member states' lobbying efforts to be directed not only toward their national counterparts on a bilateral and multilateral basis but also at the Commission, Council and, increasingly, European Parliament.

Most EU policy-making textbooks proscribe national input into the EU negotiating process during the Council phase. However, an oft-cited estimate is that some 80 percent of the original Commission proposals still stand after negotiations at Council level (Hull 1993). This underlines the need for national governments not to focus exclusively on the Council but to have adequate human resources deployed and to be actively present in these writing and fine-tuning stages, in other words, to *anticipate* new legislation and to operate *proactively* (Peters and Wright 2001). The extent to which national governments make active use of the expert committees and lobby the Commission directly is very variable. Traditionally, influencing the Commission, the embodiment of the European interest, was seen as "not done." Some member states such as the Netherlands have held this "ideal view" of the traditional EU institutional setup longer than others such as France and the United Kingdom. Representations from member states in the meetings is thus ad hoc and rather spontaneous. In other capitals Commission-instigated expert committees are seen as potential lobbies and there is central listing and coordination of who is going to represent what view on matters tabled and which experts will be participating where. It seems that the proposal-drafting phase is more and more regarded as an opportune time for member states to make a sustained lobbying effort to inject national preferences into the EU policy process, often via contacts between ministers and Commissioners (Dinan 2000a, 225).

Combined with another estimate, namely, that 85 percent of all dossiers are settled before they reach the ministerial Council level (i.e., 70 percent in Council working groups and another 15 percent in the next stage of negotiations between permanent national representatives [Hayes-Renshaw and Wallace 1997, 78]), these insights increase the importance of coordination "at home" between possibly opposing views on the matter at hand. Those involved in these early phases of drafting and sharpening new policy proposals will, in most cases, be expert officials from different government departments. There is thus a serious risk that representatives of an individual member state will have to negotiate not only with other players in the EU bargaining game but also with each other. Some governments have translated these insights into deliberate coordination attempts by selecting and briefing the expert officials that are to be delegated to these committees and working groups. But apart from coordination of positions "European process management" at the domestic level (Schreurs 2002) requires close cooperation between specialized experts, who provide in-depth knowledge on the dossier, and trained diplomats who have, simultaneously, a knowledge of the negotiating positions of the other players and a *horizontal* overview of the different issues being discussed. Both categories of negotiators should be equipped with the relevant skills, such as training in negotiation and networking, improving language skills, and updating knowledge of procedures in Brussels.

An increasingly heterogeneous playing field

Although most press and media accounts of EU decision making portray it as purely *intergovernmental*, representatives of national governments face severe competition. First, local and regional levels of government have been prevailed upon to be present at the EU level rather than being represented by their national governments. The German *länder*, Spanish *communidades autonomas* and the Dutch provinces all have EU representatives and offices in Brussels. Second, nongovernmental groups as well as private lobbies and their EU consultants have long since found their way to Brussels. It seems that these groups have acknowledged the new working methods in Brussels more rapidly than national governments. Apart from the need to be present in the drafting stages of proposals, they are very active in lobbying the European Parliament. Members of the European Parliament (MEPs), who have seen their competencies increase with two subsequent treaty changes in the 1990s, are more than happy with these inputs, which are often directly translated into amendments to legislative texts.

As the EU bargaining game grows more *multilevel* (Hooghe and Marks 2001), the national position risks being circumvented by newly engaged actors representing competing interests. National governments therefore try to reinforce their grip on these new actors. Some national governments make clever use of nongovernmental interests in an innovative public-private partnership (van Schendelen 2002). To get private and organized interests "on board" at an early stage, they invite their representatives to be actively present in the aforementioned Commission expert groups. The Commission is generally more than happy with the input from this side as the EU institution suffers from a lack of staffing and expertise. Information is actively sought not only from consultants, academics, and professional experts but also from representatives of national government bureaucracies. This is done not only to design and optimally fine-tune technical and legal details but just as much to investigate the probable reactions of national governments to certain proposals. A proposal that has been soundly checked out with the key players obviously has a better chance of making it through the Council negotiating phases (Nugent 2001). This also holds true for lobbying MEPs who, moreover, are electorally dependent on the successful representation of their respective constituencies. As for national government input into this phase, actively informing MEPs and sharing preferences and positions with them, constitutes a change in working culture as, in most member states, government officials are not supposed to contact parliamentarians. In EU working practice, however, much depends on the way individual MEPs perceive their role, be it as national representatives or as true Europarliamentarians. Some national MEPs, for example, are often known to vote in the plenary on the basis of national instructions.

EU policy suffers from an increased politicization

Before the 1987 Single European Act European integration was essentially a technocratic process. Relations with the EU could be managed in a specialized foreign ministry department and, in most member states, the constituency could not be bothered with what was going on among Brussels bureaucrats. In the post-Maastricht era the impact of the EU has become more direct. Less or more integration is now a salient political issue for governments and their constituencies. Most national governments have realized this, and both the process and the outcomes of EU bargaining are now being rapidly *politicized*. Politicians make instrumental use of the EU level which is often used as a scapegoat to blame for unwanted new policies ("Brussels forced us to act").

The only EU-level actor not divided into sectoral parts is the European Council, which facilitates issue linkage and package deals at the level of the national heads of state or government (see van Grinsven in this volume). Although this politicization may be positive from a democratic point of view, however, it adds another layer to an already complicated negotiating system and thus an extra complication for national governments to deal with at the domestic level of EU negotiations.

What Happens at Home? Domestic EU Policy Making

That there is a relationship between securing successful outcomes in EU negotiations and the capacities "at home" to coordinate potentially conflicting political, administrative, and nongovernmental views is often suggested.

> Governments that are well co-ordinated are assumed to be more efficient, to have fewer conflicting an redundant programmes and to utilize scarce public resources more rationally in achieving their policy goals (Kassim and *et al.* 2000, 1).

"Well co-ordinated" generally refers to the degree of *centralization* in national EU-related decision making. Powerful coordination by a single authority responsible for national EU policy making would enable national governments to control the design and adaptation of mandates and instructions for individual negotiators at all levels and stages. In this perspective, national involvement with a dossier would mirror the latter's routing through the different negotiating *feedback loops* from the domestic to the European level and back again, a process in which the national position is carefully fine-tuned and has been (re)designed to take account of (Peters and Wright 2001, see *Table 3.1*). In reality, however, managing the EU at the domestic level is not all that easy.

Although the different stages in *Table 3.1* can easily be discerned in all national models for handling EU policy making, there are many differences in the design of national arrangements. The different models, their pros and cons, and the challenges they constantly face, have been extensively analyzed in a great number of country studies and comparative volumes (Rometsch and Wessels 1996; Hanf and Soetendorp 1996; Mény *et al.* 1996; Zeff and Pirro 2001; and Kassim and *et al.* 2000). This section will be limited to discussing the similarities between the different models as well as a number of recent trends and developments in the art of national EU negotiating: the erosion of the traditional coordinating authority, the growing involvement of national parliaments, and a steady Europeanization of organized interests and subnational governments, as well as more coordination in and from Brussels as the EU center of gravity. In the last section some remarks will be made concerning possible explanations for the enduring heterogeneity among different national arrangements.

Erosion of the coordinating authority

When analyzing national arrangements for dealing with EU negotiations, it is surprising to what extent national coordination structures continue to rely on procedures set up in the early years of membership, sometimes dating back to the1950s, and how little these have been adapted to the developments discussed in the second section of this chapter. In other words, there is no systematically directed domestic organizational or procedural adjustment to changes in the EU environment (Hanf and Soetendorp 1996). Rather, consistency with *neoinstitutionalist* predictions, a tendency to preserve, path-dependency, and slow and incremental adaptation are the norm, with "an emphasis on the immediate" (March and Olson 1998; Schneider and Aspinwall 2001).

In general, national EU coordination continues to be organized *hierarchically* and according to a *functional division of responsibilities*. There are six broad similarities between the different national models, which will be treated in a random order (Kassim and *et al.* 2000, 237). First, the formal link between the domestic level

Table 3.1. National input in EU decision-making stages.

Stage in EU policy cycle	Lead EU institution	Stage	Member state input through:	Lead national actor	Activities at the national level	Coordination
Problem recognition and agenda setting	Commission	Conception	EU Presidency; EP; (European) Council	All ministries	Delivering ideas	None
		Expert Meeting	Expert coordination	Lead Ministry	Review implications, inform organized interests, approach Commission	None
Policy formulation	Commission	Cabinet of Commissioners	Political lobby	All ministries	Interest representation	
Legitimation	Council and EP	Presentation	Interministerial coordination		National line developed	Division of responsibilities
		Working group	Coordinated position		Interest representation	Instruction
		COREPER	Interministerial instruction	Coordinating authority, lead ministry, PR	Consultation	Instruction
Adoption	Council and EP	(European) Council	Government position	Coordinating authority, lead ministry, PR	Review priorities, margins, and fallback positions; agree elements of package deal	Instruction
		Council–EP Conciliation	Government position	Coordinating authority, lead ministry, PR	Review priorities, margins, and fallback positions; agree elements of package deal	Instruction
Implementation	Commission with member states	Comitology	Expert coordination	Line ministry	National line developed	Instruction
Transposition			Interministerial coordination	Coordinating authority, lead ministry		
Compliance			Legal expert coordination	Line ministry		

and Brussels continues to lie with the *ministry of foreign affairs* ([MFA] in Belgium, Denmark, the Netherlands, and Sweden) which for historical reasons often cooperates closely with the ministries of economic affairs and/or finance (Germany, Greece). In the MFA there are special administrative units for EU matters that are responsible for the reception of new Commission proposals and for disseminating this information within the national administrative structure, for which special bodies may be created (the Netherlands). The receipt of new proposals is generally the starting point for domestic-level negotiations to construct a position although, as indicated in the above, some member states attempt to keep a close eye on their national experts in the Commission expert phase (France, United Kingdom).

Second, in almost all member states, the formal authority for EU affairs is embodied by a special *official for European affairs*, normally of the rank of junior minister or state secretary. This position is usually created under the auspices of the minister of foreign affairs. The nature of the position varies: in some member states it is more a politico-administrative post while in others it is a ministerial political appointment. The modest size of the staff of the official, however, and the fact that national ministers or state secretaries for European affairs have no formal functions or meeting place at the EU level, mean that personality and expertise play an important part in establishing the stature of this position at home. An important argument overheard against creating a special ministry for European affairs is that its organization would necessarily mirror the national administration in scope and depth of issues to be dealt with (Rood and van Keulen 2001).

Although the MFA generally continues to be responsible for second-pillar cooperation and large package deals such as budgetary issues and IGCs, all coordinating authorities have been confronted with a gradual *erosion of competencies* concerning day-to-day EU business, both from above and from the bottom up. The latter occurs because the articulation of a coherent national position, as indicated above, almost always starts at the downstream level of expert officials. Knowledge and expertise regarding legislation on specialized issue areas is the domain of line ministries or, in the case of European regional policy, of regional and local authorities. In many member states, EU policy coordination has thus become characterized by the interplay between centralized coordination by the foreign ministry and simultaneous sectoral specialization in favor of the specialized ministries.

The third feature common to national arrangements for dealing with EU policy is that almost all government departments have in the past few years adjusted their internal organizations to the requirements of EU policy making by setting up special intraministerial *EU units* and coordination mechanisms as well as their own *bureau* within the permanent representation (Schout 1997). These direct contacts between line ministries and officials from the EU institutions as well as the transnational links between the experts on different issues have undermined the traditional position of the MFA as *gatekeeper* and *chief negotiator* between the domestic and the international *game board* (Evans *et al.* 1993).

In most member states individual government departments take the lead in preparing the instructions for EU negotiations concerning specialized dossiers. These are constructed either through negotiations with officials within their own organization or through intensive deliberations between the ministries involved. This makes sense because ultimately the individual departments will be responsible for the implementation of the policy to be decided upon in Brussels. Coordination capacities and MFA competencies differ from capital to capital. In an attempt to devise a standard of reference to facilitate comparisons between the member states, Metcalfe (1987) has devised a scale for measuring *policy coordination capacities*. It ranges from the lowest level (*communication and consultation* between government departments), through *avoiding divergence* and *arbitration*, to *prioritizing* and *strategy formation*. The model chosen should "fit" the particular domestic political and administrative constellation: in member states such as the Netherlands *coalition politics* weaken the capacity to centralize policy processes, while in Germany subnational levels impact upon central-level policy processes (see below).

Most national arrangements are built upon supervision through specific *interdepartmental coordination bodies*, labeled *special committees* (Denmark) or *European correspondents* (Luxembourg), which bring together on a regular basis senior civil servants from the various government departments—the *fourth* characteristic common to practically all member states. The MFA, in most cases, chairs this body and/or provides its secretariat. The complexity of these consultation procedures largely depends on the size of the administration and the domestic salience of European integration in general. In practice most detailed legislation is hammered out at an expert level, leaving the politicized cases or the political strategy and guidelines for the upper levels (van den Bos 1991).

The broader or horizontal issues are increasingly and more regularly dealt with by the heads of state or government of the member states. The respective presidents, chancellors, and prime ministers of successive British, French, and German administrations have dictated the European policy ambitions of their own member state. Some member states have therefore chosen to create a coordinating EU unit, either within or adjoining the prime minister's office. The central position of such units facilitates an overall view of the various activities of government relating to EU matters. In other member states this solution has been suggested, but not yet implemented, as a result of strong resistance by the MFAs. This clinging to traditional roles does not prevent the role of the highest political levels in EU negotiating being increasingly routinized—a fifth feature common to all member states. The much-admired, highly centralized systems of domestic coordination, such as the British and the French systems of EU coordination, and the decentralized systems

(Belgium, Germany, the Netherlands) are being confronted with both increasing fragmentation and sectoral segmentation.

Attempts to increase limited parliamentary involvement

The sixth and final feature common to national EU negotiating is the minor role *national parliaments* still play in EU policy making (Maurer *et al.* 2001). The infamous European democratic deficit is caused by just this lack of EU awareness, knowledge, and involvement on the part of the national parliaments as, a number of important treaty changes notwithstanding, this deficit has (still) not been remedied by the close involvement of the European Parliament in most policy areas. This lack of parliamentary involvement is all the more striking as, in EU working practice, national officials play a legislative role at the downstream working-group level and committee level.

In practice there is considerable variation in the scope of national parliamentary participation in the EU, depending on the constitutional structure and political tradition and practice of each member state. Most parliaments established *subcommittees for European affairs* in the 1990s, and Members of Parliament are regularly informed about new EU initiatives. The volume, technicalities, and urgency of EU policy making, however, continue to hamper effective parliamentary involvement at an early enough stage of the process. Discussion is therefore all too often limited to issues with serious constitutional or budgetary implications such as treaty changes or enlargement. These serious obstacles hold just as good for the Danish system of parliamentary mandates which is often admired by national parliamentarians from other member states. As for cooperation in the fields of foreign and defense policy, and justice and home affairs, the situation is slightly different. Because of the requirement for unanimity, the national parliaments hold a mandate here; however, they also lack background and expertise knowledge to provide for a sound evaluation of the proposed legislation.

There have been several initiatives on the part of national parliaments to increase their engagement in what happens at the EU level, such as the founding of the Conference of European Affairs Committees (COSAC) of EU parliaments, a consultation group uniting MEPs and national parliamentarians. From the EU side the role of national parliaments was tabled as a separate issue in the Convention on the Future of Europe. Effective European involvement, however, starts not with competencies or structural change but with increased awareness that what happens in Europe may also impact on national political business.

Europeanization of interest groups and subnational governments

At the domestic level, participation of organized interests and nongovernmental lobby organizations in the domestic coordination of EU affairs is often rather ad hoc and spontaneous. Social partners are informed about EU initiatives and their opinion is asked on new economic and social legislation. The possibility of a dialogue depends on the degree of consultation the responsible government department allows and the lobbying activities of the NGO in question itself.

Many interest organizations are today organized at the European level or associated with transnationally organized lobby groups, thus circumventing the process of preference formation by national governments. The same holds true for subnational governments which have seen their relations with the central government level altered, partly because of policy innovations introduced at the European level such as the regional policy principles of *partnership and additionality.*

Increased coordination in and from Brussels

The national permanent representation (PR) to the EU generally serves as the "eyes and ears" for member states in Brussels. Comparative analysis of the different PRs show that their "upstream" functions are performed rather similarly, while there are differences in the involvement of the national PRs at the domestic level of negotiations. In some cases the PR participates formally in the process, while in others it has no predetermined role. Concerning the staffing policy of the PRs, it is a sign of increasing Europeanization that today nearly all government departments are represented in the national embassies to the EU, assisting experts in EU-level negotiations and providing the necessary information link back to the capital. Increasingly, the PR is used for recruitment policy, that is, for getting nationals into the EU institutions.

But the level of "proactiveness" of the PR differs. The British Permanent Representation, UKREP, is known for its structured and rapid information flow to London of the minutes of all relevant meetings between member states and European institutions.

Explaining Enduring Heterogeneity

A close look at the degree and modes of adaptation of administrative, executive, legislative, and judicial institutions in the fifteen member states shows a rather diverse and diverging pattern of *heterogeneity* among ambitions, roles, responsibilities, and administrative structures. There seems little or no indication to support the thesis of gradual convergence between national models for dealing with EU policy (Kassim *et al.* 2000) which continue to be characterized by "a frenzy of institutional experimentation and innovation" (Peters and Wright 2001, 163). Every member state gets the coordination it deserves; but how can differences between member states be explained?

An important indicator are the differing national *ambitions* toward European integration in general and specific issue areas of cooperation. Does the member state aim to push for more and deeper integration ("shapers")—or should closer cooperation in particular policy fields instead be hindered ("foot draggers") (Börzel 2002)? Are limited resources strategically deployed for certain issues or dossiers (agriculture, economic integration) or is simply everything important? Much also depends on the nature of the issue at stake: is it of high constitutional importance, urgent, and requiring an active stance, or is it merely routine and bureaucratic? Does the member state want to be ranked among either the leading or the laggard states in a certain policy field?

Second, the way national coordination procedures for EU affairs are designed is strongly dependent on the national *politico-administrative culture and traditions* (such as the vision on coordination as an organizational principle) (Knill 1998) and shaped by contextual factors and institutional constraints. In the latter category is the so-called domestic *policy style*, a notion introduced by Bulmer (1983), referring to political and administrative opportunity structures: Is the state strong or weak? Is consensus the leading principle? How about embedding corporatist institutions? An explanation lies in the assumed "logic of divergence" of national politico-administrative systems. In line with (neo)institutional reasoning, "institutions are stickier than politics," in other words, national arrangements and traditions will probably survive, despite the common logic and pressures of Europeanization. Two more suggestions for explaining the continuing divergence between modes of EU coordination point first to the principle of *mutual recognition* of national regulation as established in the famous *Cassis de Dijon* court case (1979) and rely second on an *intergovernmentalist* logic, according to which interstate bargains would result in gains by the large member states thereby freeing those countries from the need to adapt to common European pressures. This last claim, however, has not been supported by empirical analysis (Cowles *et al.* 2001).

Negotiating Effectiveness

From the above one could easily conclude that any national position to be negotiated in Brussels should be formulated at an early stage so that it can be presented proactively, coherent in its definition, and consistent with other national policy positions. This calls for a centralized coordination of negotiating mandates. On the other hand, national instructions need to be sufficiently flexible to be adapted to the changing circumstances or positions of the other negotiators. The aforementioned characteristics of EU bargaining mean that negotiations create their own dynamics. Carefully coordinated instructions produced at home may be outdated when the negotiator finally arrives in Brussels. Because of the negotiating nature of EU decision making, amendments are proposed throughout the process and all outcomes involve intricate compromise. For individual negotiators this implies that room for maneuver and interpretation are needed whereas tight domestic compromises may bind hands. Another argument against centralized EU coordination in the hands of a single authority is that the active participation of all interested parties at the early stages of the decision-making process could serve to improve implementation at a later stage of the policy process.

That the stages of national and European-level interest formation cannot be separated in working practice may be most visible at the COREPER level of pre-Council negotiations. When trying to reach agreement before legislation is tabled at an upcoming Council meeting, a permanent representative is *Janus-faced* in the sense of his/her dual loyalty of being both national representative and ambassador of the EU to his/her member state (Bostock 2002). Although all permanent diplomats receive negotiating instructions, during isolated COREPER meetings there is a considerable margin for maneuver. In working practice, known as *engrenage*, representatives will often depart from instructions and make recommendations back to the capital for changes. If instructions prove impossible, plotting is used to redefine national positions or to reshape national constraints, for instance by purposely exaggerating the fierceness of opposition. When there is no agreement, the representative is left to decide and find solutions. National mandates, however meticulously constructed at the domestic level, can thus be *reconstructed* to ensure a better fit in the general EU consensus, thereby contesting the image of national-preference formation taking place in "splendid (. . .) isolation" (Kassim and Peters 2001, 298).

The aforementioned focus on coordination at the domestic level would imply that *efficiency* is the most important factor in explaining the outcomes of negotiating games at the EU level. Especially in the eyes of intergovernmentalists (Hoffmann 1966; Moravcsik 1998), the performance of unitary member states in Brussels is held to be dependent on rationally organized systems of national coordination. However, if one takes the pattern of heterogeneity that characterizes national EU arrangements together with the fact that evidence of domestic performance in Brussels has until now been mostly anecdotal (Metcalfe 1994), one can conclude that there is no single "good" model to ensure member-state performance. Academically, the complex question of how to define effectiveness in shaping EU policy has thus far been ignored. This lack of academic interest is not surprising given the sheer complexity of the EU bargaining game and its distinctive features which considerably complicate attempts to address it. But the question remains as to whether there is a recipe for success, a particular negotiating strategy that is more successful than the others. Apart from the recurring focus on coordination, academic studies have listed a number of other factors that may influence performance in EU bargaining (Soetendorp and Hosli 2000). First and foremost, the size and weight of a member state, translated into "political clout" undoubtedly plays a role in determining bargaining leverage. The question here is whether large member states are indeed as advantaged in their Brussels operations as their size would predict. Again, large and centralized administrations can be hampered by their lack of flexibility and the difficulty they have in prioritizing among European dossiers, something that smaller administrations may be forced to rely on. Second, the relative size of individual governments can be modified by the membership of winning or blocking coalitions. Moreover, not only would the existing policy climate play a role but so too would the "fit" with the national policy-making style and the prevailing political culture in Brussels. Last, but certainly not least, national ambitions and the "fit" of national preferences may be decisive in whether a national government gets it way in Brussels. Here we come back to the "feedback" character of the EU game, for notwithstanding the size or political clout of member states, the open and multilevel character of the EU as a political system supplies national governments with many opportunities to shape the EU agenda in order to *make* their ambitions and proposals fit with those at the EU level. In sum, negotiation lies "at the heart of the (EU) policy process" (Wallace and Wallace 2000).

Conclusion

This chapter has given an overview of what happens during domestic-level EU negotiations: what are the challenges that confront national negotiators, and what are the trends and developments. It has been underlined that, with regard to the EU policy process, textbook manners are no match for reality. At times and in certain phases, governments have more and different ways to get to Brussels than a look at formal procedures would suggest. Instead of the dominant Council-oriented view on national interest representation, governments may provide an input at the Commission-dominated agenda-setting phase, at the high political level of the European Council, and also *bottom up* through the many administrative committees securing sound implementation of EU policy. Governments may even try to get MEPs to incorporate national positions into their voting lists. Even the sensitive second-pillar and third-pillar policy areas of foreign and security policy and justice and home affairs policy respectively, are subject to a slow but gradual *Brusselsization* as decision making is moved from the national capitals to various new committees and working groups at the EU level.

Moreover, and perhaps more seriously, member-state governments are often portrayed as unitary actors representing a coherent national interest in the Council phase of EU decision making. This chapter has illustrated that this classic intergovernmental image does not hold true in EU working practice. Representatives of national governments face constant competition, not only from newly engaged actors in the EU bargaining game but also with each other. At home this has forced a great deal of coordination effort on the part of national governments in order to get a grip on the broad scope of EU policy making. It is surprising, however, how slow national governments have been to date to adapt structurally to these new membership demands (Spence 1995, 353).

There are, however, two struggles that will continue to complicate the domestic management of EU affairs, particularly after the May 2004 EU enlargement to embrace ten or more new member states. First, there is the remaining tension between the administrative and the political level. Rather paradoxically, not only the EU departments but also the national experts at the lower administrative levels of government are generally quite "Europeanized" because of their frequent contacts with EU decision-making networks. These officials often complain about the lack of "European awareness" that they encounter in their superiors and at the political level (author interviews). National politicians tend to remain focused on what happens on the national political scene because they are generally not to be held accountable for what they do in Brussels. The lack of European *engagement* of national parliaments is a connected problem that will, one hopes, be tackled in the 2004 IGC.

Another serious complication for national governments in dealing with the demands of EU membership is the necessity of reconciling the task of "expert with in-depth knowledge" with the job of "skilled negotiator with oversight." In day-to-day European expert and working-group meetings the role of the diplomatic negotiator is being taken over by civil servant negotiators. The nature of the EU, however, implies that a combination of generalist knowledge and long-term overviews remains vital in securing compromises and package deals among negotiating positions. This has consequences for the recruitment and training of new diplomats. For a member state, the need to be present in the various networks that prepare and implement EU policy demands considerable manpower, expertise, and information, which member states do not have equally available (Börzel 2002). This forces national governments to prioritize and operate more strategically. This will be an especially demanding task for the new member states which should devote much of their limited human capital to institution building with regard to EU policy coordination. The direct and growing involvement of the private sector in Brussels committees and working groups (van Schendelen 1993) demands even more of national negotiators as they run the risk of being bypassed by sometimes conflicting private interests. This potential risk should be turned into an advantage by embedding private organizations in domestic EU policy cooperation procedures at a very early stage.

Last but not least, the interaction between Brussels and "home" is a two-way process with considerable implications for interest formation on both sides. The development of a transnational sense of community among those present in the Council has been called "a powerful illustration of the way in which the concept of national interest representation needs to be unpacked when studying the politics of the EU" (Christiansen 2001, 141). As officials become aware of the positions taken by other stakeholders and of the limits of emerging consensus, they will take these into consideration when revising a national position. This may mean that negotiators could end up telling national administrations at home what position they can take, rather than representing the position they should take (Christiansen 2001, 141). Regular and structured interaction in the EU can thus be expected to have a profound effect on the way national governments make policy.

Chapter 4

The Role of the Member States in the European Union

Pieter Langenberg

Introduction

To be able to clarify the role of member states and gain a better understanding of current negotiating processes in the European Union (EU), one must first have a good understanding of the procedures that are followed in a specific policy area. An interdisciplinary approach is required as it is often impossible to dissociate the legal aspects of a topic from the political or economic aspects. As member states are constrained to operate in a given legal (treaty) setting, there are varying limits to the influence they have. Strategic planning is important as there are only limited opportunities at the different stages of the legislative process to influence decision making. Furthermore, the influence of member states can differ substantially depending on the policy area and its corresponding legal basis. As more and more national policy areas are drawn into the scope of the European Union, the role of the Community is increasing in a broad range of policy areas. At the same time qualified-majority voting is becoming more and more the rule in the legislative process.[1] The role of the European Parliament (EP) as a colegislator has also increased through the codecision process. It has thus become more important to generate broad support to have one's views taken on board. It has also become more difficult for an individual member state to influence or even to block decision making as Community competences are increasing: consequently there is a growing need for coalition building and for an increasing willingness to accept compromises. The influence that member states exercise will be illustrated later in this chapter by a few recent examples from the negotiating process on the Framework Six Programme proposal for research and technological development as well as the Council decisions on the Specific Programmes that are necessary for its implementation.[2]

The less well known area of research and technological development (RTD) policy is a good illustration of the above-mentioned process in the still-developing area of Community research policy. It was the Single European Act of 1986 that created a separate chapter for the research area and also made scientific and technological research a Community responsibility, providing it with the status of a full-fledged Community policy area. The Maastricht treaty further widened the role played by the Community in research and technological development and highlighted its importance in upholding Europe's industrial competitiveness, fostering economic growth, and developing the research activities needed to implement other Community policies. Current policy initiatives by the Commission, such as the development of the concept of a European research area and the implementation of the so-called Lisbon process, endorsed by the European Council, which strives to make Europe more competitive in a global context, are in line with this thinking. The result, over the years, has been a strong impetus to increase budgetary allocations to fund research. Thus, the financial allocation within the European Union budget for research and development policy has strongly increased over the last years, rising to 17.5 billion euros for the four-year period from 2003 to 2006.[3] Few people realize that research and technological development ranks third after the better-known agricultural and structural funding policy allocations. This illustrates the increasing importance of RTD policy within the European Union and, consequently, the need for member states to be involved in it. Nevertheless, as the decision-making process becomes more complex because of the increasing number of member states, and with the European Parliament playing an equally important part in the deliberations, it is becoming more difficult for the member states to exercise influence. There are more institutional players, and the decision-making process is now based on qualified-majority voting.

A description will be given of how the RTD policy of the European Union is generally made and executed. The role of the three European institutions and the legal context must be mentioned before a description of the decision-making process and the role of the member states can be given. A few examples drawn from experience of the recent negotiations on the Framework Six Programme for research and technological development will be given while the processes and procedures, and the planning and position taking are being reviewed. The debate on the wording of restrictions regarding the bioethical dimension of research is a good example of the difficulties member states have in exercising influence: compromise is often unavoidable, even on issues that are nationally sensitive and therefore not really negotiable.

The Institutional Framework: The Players

It must be pointed out that research and technological development policy within the Community context takes place within certain legal parameters that limit the opportunities for changes by policy makers. First, all operations must take place within the context of the treaties on which the European Union is based and within the context of the European institutions. In establishing proposals for research and technological development policy, the Commission, the Council, and the European Parliament (EP) have their respective roles to play. Most of the procedures in the original treaties are comparable, although there are still differences in final decision making between the European Communities (EC) and Euratom treaties. There is, in both cases, a strong role foreseen for the European Commission—basically an initiating and executing role for the Commission alongside the two legislative institutions, the Council and the European Parliament.

Every four years a new European Communities RTD Framework proposal is prepared by the Commission which must be approved by the Council and the European Parliament. The Euratom RTD Framework proposal dealing with nuclear research programme activities has to be approved by the Council only, taking the opinion of the Parliament into account. The main difference between the EC Framework Programme proposal and the Euratom Framework Programme proposal lies in the decision making, the former being by qualified majority and codecision of the European Parliament, the latter by unanimity and merely consultation of the European Parliament. In the case of the Euratom Framework Programme, the role of the European Parliament is less influential, being only advisory and not based on codecision.

As the Commission has the right of initiating, it is more difficult for the Council or the European Parliament to have research activities included that are not taken up or are actually opposed by the Commission. The sequence of events in codecision is as follows:

1. Original Commission proposal.
2. Opinion of European Parliament.
3. Modified proposal of the Commission which may take up EP amendments.
4. Common position taken by the Council.
5. Transmission of the common position to the EP, and transmission of a separate communication by the Commission stating its position on the common position

of the Council. If the common position has been taken by qualified majority, it has legally become the Commission's proposal, and the Commission has then to explain the reasons why the modified proposal has changed again. If the common position has been adopted unanimously, the Commission can explain either why it accepts the common position or why it opposes certain elements of the common position that deviate from the Commission's modified proposal.

6. Second reading, European Parliament: the EP is confined to retabling those amendments from its first reading that were not taken up in the common position or to tabling new amendments on modifications introduced by the Council to the original Commission proposal on which the EP had based its first reading. Direct approval is possible if agreement with the EP is reached.

7. If no agreement is reached, conciliation becomes necessary so that a joint text can be adopted.

The influence of the Commission in the legislative process, however, goes much further than proposing new legislation on its own initiative or when requested by the Council and/or Parliament to include certain topics. First of all the Commission sits in on the Council deliberations and even on the debate in the European Parliament; here it can argue its case after tabling its initial proposal which is the basis for decision making. The Commission also has an important role as a moderator in the codecision process between the Council and the European Parliament, making this effectively a tripartite negotiating process. In the end, the three institutions have to agree on a joint text to make the process work. Time often becomes an important factor too, as illustrated in the case of the approval of the Framework Programme: there is a legal necessity to have the legislative package agreed upon in due time, as a new four-year Framework Programme must be prepared and must start on the first of January of each new four-year period. A codecision process can be lengthy (in practice often more than fourteen months) if conciliation has become unavoidable. In the end, therefore, the pressure increases on the member states and the European Parliament to compromise: no one wants to take the blame for blocking a reasonable compromise, and the general interest in approving the Framework Programme on time must also be taken into account

As the EU Council of Ministers can meet in different combinations, there is a Council of Ministers responsible for, inter alia, research policy, and this is composed of the ministers responsible for research and technology at the national level. Until recently there was a Council of Ministers for research (hereafter, Research Council) but this was replaced in the second half of 2002 by the so-called Competitiveness Council, dealing with research, industry, and internal-market policy matters. As most ministerial councils such as the former Research Council normally meet only once or twice during each Presidency (every half year), the daily business of the Council has been delegated to the Committee of Permanent Representatives (COREPER).[4] COREPER I is, inter alia, currently responsible for the area of research and technological development. As both COREPERs have an increasingly busy agenda, they have delegated the preparatory work to Council working groups dealing with specific policy areas. Research matters are normally discussed in the Council working group for research. As presidencies last only half a year, the permanent Council Secretariat assists the Council in its daily work. Its main task is to assist and advise the Presidency of the Council by preparing reports and text proposals. As the Presidency changes every six months, the Council Secretariat has considerable influence because of its collective memory; it has built the necessary legal and factual expertise over the years, and often prepares compromises on behalf of the Presidency. Generally speaking, presidencies operate neutrally as honest brokers, leaving it to the national delegates to argue the national positions. The main task of the Presidency is to chair the meetings, set the agendas, and try to enhance decision making by finding compromises. Presidencies operate as a go-between, not only among countries but also between the Commission and Parliament.[5]

The Commission implements Community policies, as in the field of research and technological development, and proposes multiannual research and technological development programmes such as the Framework Programme. The civil service of the Commission consists of different Directorates-General (DGs), one commissioner being responsible for each. There is a specific Directorate-General for research, but some of the research activities that take place within the context of the Framework Programme for Research and Technological Development are managed by other Directorates-General such as the DG Information Society or the DG Enterprise. Obviously, DG Research still has a leading role to play when the Commission, as such, is taking a position or preparing a new Framework Programme proposal. As mentioned before, the role of the Commission is more than an initiator or an executor of policy proposals. In the legislative decision-making process, although it has its own policy considerations, it often also plays the role of honest broker.

As well as the above-mentioned formal structure, the many informal advisory bodies, composed of experts in an individual or national capacity, should be mentioned. These bodies prepare reports and reviews for the different institutions and often have a great influence on opinion making. In the research and development field, mention should be made of the Scientific and Technical Research Committee (CREST),[6] established in 1974 by a Council resolution, which advises the Council and the Commission and is chaired by the Commission. CREST has traditionally focused on the technical and scientific content of Community research programmes and offers a discussion forum for the exchange of experiences between national and

EU research and development policies. As it is generally composed of high-level civil servants who advise their respective ministers at Research Council meetings, it has kept its importance. More specific research-related debate, at the level of experts in certain areas, generally takes place in the context of the programme committees that deal with the implementation of the EU RTD Framework Programme. A growing proliferation of high-level groups, initiated by the Commission, also advise on research matters. Generally, they are used to develop and test out policy proposals and are consequently of growing importance.[7]

The Legal Context

As indicated, the legal basis is decisive for the scope of activities proposed and the procedures followed, as well as setting limits to the ways in which member states and other players can operate in the decision-making processes. The funding of research and technological development activities is based on the EC and Euratom treaties, depending on the nature of the activities (nonnuclear or nuclear research). The majority of proposed RTD activities and the corresponding budget for the so-called multiannual Framework Programme is currently based on the EC treaty, Title XVIII, Articles 163–173, which are relatively recent and date back to the Single European Act of 1986. The First RTD Framework Programme was based on Article 235 of the EC treaty,[8] which gives the Council the power to initiate activities in the context of the internal market on the basis of a proposal by the Commission after consultation with the European Parliament. On the basis of the positive experiences with the First RTD Framework Programme, a separate chapter on research and technological development was included in the Single European Act,[9] making it a Community responsibility. The Treaty of Maastricht only marginally expanded its scope. Article 163 still underlines the importance of industry and its competitiveness as a major goal, although other types of research supporting other European policy areas are also included.

Article 164 describes the general outline of activities. The article indicates that the RTD activities of the Community should have a complementary nature to national activities (the principle of subsidiarity). In practice the successive Framework Programmes[10] have developed into an RTD programme in its own right, with almost the same level of ambition as some national RTD programmes. The current concept of a European Research Area (ERA), as developed and promoted by the current commissioner for research, Philippe Busquin, is therefore more in line with the intended spirit of this article. The current Sixth Framework Programme will be more instrumental in fulfilling ERA policy goals, the majority of which concern increasing European competitiveness. The underlying concept of Article 165, which deals with the necessity of coordinating national policies, has never been fully implemented by the member states and the Commission, as its interpretation is still open. The basic question remains: Should the Commission also try to coordinate national RTD policies to generate the required critical mass to compete globally, or should it act only if sufficient European value added seems assured? Must this be done on a voluntary basis, or are binding guidelines necessary? One could argue that the consultation process in the context of the high-level CREST committee and the programme committees already serves the purpose of this article. Article 166 is the basic article on which the current EU RTD Programme is founded and lays down the procedure to be followed (qualified majority, codecision).[11] The intended cycle of multiannual programming is four years.

The research activities foreseen in the context of the Framework Programme are elaborated in more detail by the Specific Programmes which are also based on Article 166(3). The Specific Programmes are elaborated further and implemented by separate, more detailed working programmes also based on the Commission's proposals.[12,13] Obviously, the general content must correspond to the already-agreed original Framework Programme proposal, the Council by qualified majority approving the Specific Programmes after consulting the European Parliament (advisory opinion) and the Economic and Social Committee. Article 167 deals with the implementation of the RTD Framework Programme by rules of participation.[14] Article 168, which permits participation in supplementary programmes by a limited number of member states, and Article 169, which permits joint programmes by member states in which the Community will participate, have not yet been used because only a limited number of member states take part in them. In the Sixth Framework Programme a proposal has been introduced on the basis of Article 169,[15] but as codecision would be obligatory the immediate financial and other benefits might not always be balanced by the necessary lengthy procedures that are foreseen. Article 170 deals with RTD cooperation with third countries and international organizations. The Framework Programme is open on the project level and also on the basis of mutual benefit; it is also open to participation by countries that have concluded the necessary association agreements. The procedure to be followed is described in Article 300; the Council authorizes the Commission first to start negotiations on the basis of approved negotiation directives; the Council would then approve the result of the negotiations by the Commission with a qualified majority and take a final decision in accordance with the opinion of the European Parliament. Articles 171 and 172, dealing with the establishment of joint undertakings or other structures to implement RTD programmes, have not yet been used in the context of the RTD Framework Programme, although Article 171 will be tried out for the first time with the establishment of a joint undertaking for the development phase of the

Galileo Project. Article 173 lays down the obligation for annual reporting by the Commission.

The Euratom treaty also deals with research in its Title II (Articles 4–11). The procedure to be followed can be found in Article 7, namely, a Commission proposal to be approved unanimously by the member states. The Commission is directly responsible for the implementation; this constitutes a slight difference from the way the activities in the EC Framework Programme are implemented, where the Commission must ask the opinion of the programme committees. Traditionally, the European Parliament gives its opinion on the Euratom Framework Programme, but it is only advisory in nature. The treaty text does not refer to the Framework Programme; the specific nuclear programmes are nevertheless presented as part of a joint Commission proposal for both the EC- and Euratom-specific programmes. Article 8 is of interest because it constitutes the basis for the Commission's network of Joint Research Centres. Initially the Joint Research Centres focused only on nuclear research, but they are diversifying more and more into nonnuclear research and participating in specifically nonnuclear programmes as the focus in Europe shifts away from the nuclear field. As mentioned above, the EC rules-of-procedure proposal is adopted in a codecision procedure with the European Parliament whereas, for the equivalent Euratom document, a unanimous decision is needed by the Council following consultation of Parliament.

As the Commission presents its proposals for the EC and Euratom Framework Programmes jointly, they are normally handled as an informal package. The same applies to the EC and Euratom proposals for the rules of participation and the individual Specific Programmes. Corresponding texts are normally brought into line. Formal adaptation takes place at a later stage only. The main focus is on the EC Framework Programme which forms the bulk of the package.

The indicative budget allocations for the EC and Euratom Framework Programmes are subject to the regular EU annual budgeting process (category III). The allocations, as politically agreed upon when the Framework Programmes are approved, are normally honored without modifications.

The Decision-making Process

This section will briefly describe how the Sixth Framework Programme and the Specific Programmes and rules-of-procedure proposals needed to implement it were negotiated, thereby illustrating the scope of the role of the member states. The process of deciding on new multiannual Framework Programmes is generally a lengthy one. Normally the last two years of a running Framework Programme coincide with the negotiations for the next one. The concept of rolling multiannual programmes requires continuity and the conclusion of the decision-making process in time for the new Framework Programme to start. Thus, in early 2001 the Commission had already presented the proposal for the Sixth Framework Programme,[16] while the Fifth Framework Programme continued until the end of 2002. This provided for the two necessary years of negotiating time as well as the adoption of the additional implementing legislation (rules of participation, Specific Programmes).

The scientific and technological aims and their respective priorities and, last but not least, indicative budget allocations, are set out in the Commission's RTD Framework Programme proposal. A break with the practice of the past was the prior introduction by Commissioner Busquin of the broader concept of the European Research Area.[17] As a consequence the Sixth Framework Programme was transformed into a major instrument for realizing ERA's goals. The Programme aims for more focus and concentration in a limited number of RTD areas,[18] where critical mass and European value added could result from increased European cooperation and integration of RTD activities. At the same time other instruments were proposed in line with the treaty chapter on RTD to stimulate European RTD activities more generally, for example, cooperation by a limited number of member states on the basis of Article 169. This broader, more conceptual approach was generally welcomed by the member states. As the Commission consulted a broad range of active RTD players in the member states, the priority setting resulted in a limited number of thematic research areas being funded from the Community budget. These research areas also turned out to be less controversial than might have been expected on the basis of past experiences. The scientific and technological content was also debated in CREST, but the main body of the text of the proposals was discussed first in the Council working group on research and then in COREPER I. The final decision was taken by the Council of Ministers.

Although the picture may seem complicated and the process is time-consuming, it is also quite straightforward. The original Commission proposal for the Sixth Framework Programme was presented to the Council and the European Parliament at the same time.[19] It was preceded by the Commission's more general communication on ERA. Normally, the Council does not enter upon a formal discussion of the Commission proposal until the Parliament's first reading is finished.[20] It generally uses the time to ask for clarifications from the Commission so as to better understand the proposal. After receiving the Parliament's opinion[21] the Council begins formal discussion (working group—COREPER I—Council level). The earlier Research Council of 30 October 2001 was able therefore to focus only on giving political guidance with respect to the fine-tuning of the priority areas and the corresponding budget allocations. It also discussed the relative weight to be accorded to the new and traditional instruments provided for implementation of the Sixth Framework Programme. During the ministerial Council meeting that followed on 10 December 2001 a political agreement was reached on the principles and main content of the Framework Programme proposal. This resulted in a revised proposal for a text rewritten by the Presidency of the Council, the so-called common position of the Council.[22,23] The Commission, which had been sitting in on the Council's deliberations, had already presented[24] a modified proposal of its own, which is of importance. To a certain degree the modified Commission proposal took into account opinions that had already been expressed by Parliament.[25] Reflecting this feedback meant, for example, changing the Programme budget. There were also changes to the thematic research areas. Genomics and biotechnology for health were split into two sections. The priority areas of sustainable development, global change, and ecosystems were extended in scope and split into three categories. The description of the new instruments to be used and their gradual introduction were also clarified in the text.

The divisive issue of ethics was already a previous source of disagreement among member states, and the Council had handled it by leaving it out of the Council's common position. The common position, in line with the Parliament and Commission, asserts only that fundamental ethical principles are to be respected in the conduct of research under the Sixth Framework Programme. It does not follow the Commission and the European Parliament, and it does not define activities that would be excluded from funding. It also expresses in principle the willingness of the Council to discuss the issue more extensively with the Parliament. The Commission tried to address this issue by appending a specific declaration to the minutes of the December Research Council in which it undertook not to finance any research involving genetic manipulation, human cloning, or the creation of embryos for research purposes.[26] Broadly the Commission endorsed the Council's common position, as it preserved the essential features of its original proposal and was, in overall terms, fairly consistent with the opinion of the Parliament.

After reaching its common position, the Council forwards the Commission's comments to the European Parliament for a second reading which, under the codecision procedure, the EP has the right of amending (by an absolute majority of members). The Parliament then gives it a second reading within a three-month period. In the trilogue process the three institutional players—Council, Commission, and Parliament—then try to reach agreement on a joint compromise text. Direct approval is possible if agreement with the Parliament is reached. Otherwise there are three months available for conciliation on a joint text which has to be approved within six weeks by Council and Parliament. This can turn into a time-consuming process, especially if agreement on a second reading fails and conciliation becomes necessary. Consequently, as time passes, the pressure to agree increases. This applies especially to the upcoming Framework Programme which has to be agreed before the current one expires. The institutional players know that they have to agree in due time before the end of the year to secure continuity and to give possible participants the necessary time to prepare for a new RTD Framework Programme. Time pressure is of great tactical value. During the Spanish Presidency the time pressure was further increased because of the political deadline to agree the RTD Framework Programme which was set for the summer of 2002 by the European Council of Stockholm. As the common position of the Council indicated a strong convergence of positions with respect both to the European Parliament and the Commission, the Commission endorsed it within the limitations expressed regarding the ethical issue.

It was not surprising, therefore, that in early June 2002 the Council and the Parliament came to an agreement in the second reading on the basic Framework Programme text without having to resort to conciliation and without further major changes to the Commission's proposal in terms of structure, content, budget, or operational arrangements. They managed to do so following an informal agreement not to introduce a number of controversial ethical amendments later and by giving a commitment that a number of detailed amendments to the Framework Programme proposal by the European Parliament would be taken on board in the Specific Programme proposals. On the ethical issues Parliament and the Council addressed their differences in opinion by opting to extend the Commission's declaration on ethical principles in which those areas that were not to be funded in the Sixth Framework Programme were listed. Thus, the potentially controversial details were taken out of the formal proposal but, as later transpired, the issue would rear its head yet again in the context of the Specific Programmes.

At the same time the other necessary additional proposals to implement the EC and Euratom Framework Programmes that still had to be agreed by Council and Parliament were also processed: the establishment of the rules of participation and the proposals for five Specific Programmes. As participation rules are generally very technical by nature, an agreement in the first reading of the codecision procedure with the Parliament was deemed feasible. The Specific Programmes are a more detailed version of the corresponding chapters of the Framework Programme and consequently less controversial because the main content has already been discussed in CREST and agreed upon in the Council during the Framework Programme approval of which they are an elaboration. As it turned out, this would not be the case because of the sections on life-science research where bioethical concerns still had to be addressed. Agreement on the Framework Programme proposal was reached by leaving out the more controversial parts on bioethical research; thus the debate was merely postponed, as the discussion on the relevant Specific Programme illustrated later. Tentative agreement on the Specific Programmes was reached by COREPER only at the end of July while formal adoption by the Competitiveness Council on 30 September was possible only after an elaboration of the controversial text in the form of a minutes' statement.

The Role of the Member States

Naturally, Commission proposals for the Framework Programme and the Specific Programmes have already been developed long before being formally presented to the Council. The proposed research activities have to be based either on existing research and technological development or on future research and technological perspectives. As stated, it is important for the Commission to sound out the research community through a consultative process before proposals are put together. This involves consulting advisory bodies, organizing seminars, and holding conferences to make an inventory of future scientific and technological needs. That way, the decision makers in the scientific communities are sounded out in advance and, if their advice is taken on board, acceptance by the Council at a later stage of the process becomes more probable. It is of course a two-way street: the Commission tries to influence the member states and the member states, during the consultative process, also try to influence the Commission. Some member states are better at guiding their experts in this process than others. They may also find it effective to approach the Commission officials involved in the initial drafting of the proposals. The draft proposal will be circulated within other involved Directorates after having been approved by DG Research. After that, the Commission must agree internally (decision of the College of Commissioners prepared by their respective cabinet staff members) before presenting the proposal formally to the Council, the European Parliament, and the Economic and Social Committee.

Only after receiving the opinion of Parliament can the Council start to discuss the text in depth and take positions. The Commission is present during the discussions and can be asked to justify or clarify certain issues. Based on member states' comments, if there is sufficient support or if there are no objections raised, the Commission draft text may be modified by the Presidency. This revised Presidency text will establish the basis for the so-called common position of the member states to be approved formally by the ministerial Council. Comments by the CREST committee on the scientific and technological content are also taken on board in the discussion in the Council working group on research. One example of this was the member states' broadening of the scope of the chapter on the environment into the domain of sustainable development by including energy and transport.[27] Normally the chair aims for consensus (avoiding a blocking minority of the other member states and objections on the part of the Commission) but if necessary a revised compromise text can be decided upon by noting a qualified majority in COREPER if the Commission goes along with this. Unanimity is needed if the Commission does not agree. Final formal approval of the common position is then needed by the Research Council. After the European Parliament's first reading, which results in the European Parliament's opinion, the Commission normally presents a modified proposal that embraces the European Parliament's proposals to the extent it agrees with these. In a supporting document the Commission will state its position regarding the Council's common position. Both texts are then forwarded to the European Parliament for a second reading.

It should be recalled that the European Parliament has already discussed the original Commission proposal and appointed a rapporteur to draft its opinion. The choice of rapporteur is a political matter; all parties have to take their turns at dealing with Commission proposals. The rapporteur consults with Commission officials and other interested parties, such as companies, associations, and pressure groups, before presenting his/her report with amendments. This process offers a good opportunity to lobby the Members of the European Parliament (MEPs), who have the right of amendment. As a result a first report with proposed amendments is drafted and voted upon in the competent committee (in the case of research, the Industry, External Trade, Research and Energy Committee [ITRE]) and the plenary of the European Parliament. In the second reading the European Parliament may only retable amendments from its first reading that were not taken up in the common position of the Council or table new amendments on modifications by the Council to the Commission's proposal on which the European Parliament had based its first reading. Afterwards, the member states have to decide if a compromise with the European Parliament is feasible by accommodating their proposed amendments while staying within the scope of the common position. Otherwise conciliation becomes unavoidable. The Presidency has to seek a formal mandate of the member states to negotiate with the Parliament on a mutually acceptable compromise text. In practice, most of the deliberations on the Framework Programme have taken place in an informal setting. Anticipating the known views of the Parliament is sometimes also an option for the Presidency during the establishment of the Council's common position, as this will later facilitate the codecision process. Normally most of the preparatory work is done by the Council working group on research. The formal positions are taken in the context of COREPER I (if necessary, by [noting] QMV). This formal common position constitutes the mandate for the Presidency to start negotiating. In the case of the Framework Programme negotiating process, the Council was not inclined to take on board amendments that would expand the proposed focus of the suggested RTD activities too greatly. There was a tendency to stick to the scope proposed by the Commission. Nonetheless the Parliament was successful in substantially adapting the focus and the corresponding budget allocation for the parts on the thematic research priority of life sciences and major diseases (cancer-related research). Basically there was a process of give-and-take, but the main structure, the focus of the research priorities of the Commission proposal, and even most of the budget allocations, remained more or less the same. Upon reflection this is not surprising, given the broad consultative process mentioned earlier. At the same time the process provides for checks and balances. It is difficult for one party (or member state) to substantially alter the Commission proposal unless there is convincing support generated. The same applies to Members of the European Parliament.

The finalization of the Specific Programmes is normally less controversial as they must reflect the content of the already-agreed Framework Programme proposal. As will be described below, this was not the case with the part of the Framework Six Programme proposal dealing with life sciences.

Case Study: The Divisive Issue of Stem-Cell Research

As indicated, the influence of member states is becoming more and more limited. A good illustration of this is the way the funding of bioethical-sensitive research was taken up in the legislative package. The proposal on the part of the Specific Programmes relating to life sciences was the only section of the Sixth Framework Programme package where agreement had yet to be reached. The diversity of opinion in the fifteen member states was wide. It varied—from some countries with fairly liberal attitudes that allow for much more far-reaching research on a national basis (in particular Finland, Sweden, and the United Kingdom [UK]) to countries that are far more restrictive (Austria, Germany, Ireland, Italy, and Portugal). The latter group hardened their opposition to the funding of embryonic stem-cell research.

The controversy was so divisive that some member states even considered opposing adoption of the Sixth Framework Programme. An equivalent split in opinion had already developed in the European Parliament.[28] The European Parliament also later voiced its concerns that it had not been thoroughly consulted during the process.

The problem is, of course, that is not feasible to reach an "average" ethical position especially if the topic is already so politically sensitive at the national level. The principle of subsidiarity naturally applies to nationally funded research, but what happens in the case of indirectly funded European research? It is difficult to agree to fund, in another country and from a common European source, research that would not be allowed at home but, one could also argue, why exclude it if it is allowed in some member states? It is interesting to note that in the end the decision making necessary to approve the necessary legislation for the Sixth Framework Programme was handled by taking out the most controversial parts on bioethical research. This made possible agreement with a qualified majority on the main part of the Sixth Framework Programme minus the small section on life sciences. Several member states added national statements to the minutes, reflecting their national positions, but they did not stop the decision-making process in the end.

The no-go areas did not figure in the Commission's initial Framework Six Programme proposal but were inserted into the Commission's modified proposal after the first reading by the European Parliament. This was a step in the direction of a corresponding European Parliament amendment without going through the whole amendment process. Although in its modified proposal the Commission had tried to exclude the more controversial areas of bioethical research from European funding by those member states where these practices were not allowed, this turned out still to be a step too far for a substantial minority of member states. But while for some member states it went too far, for others it did not go far enough. In the end, therefore, the member states were able to agree on a common position only by taking out the specific references to the three no-go areas in the Commission's modified Framework Programme proposal. The Commission made a separate declaration along the lines of the three no-go areas which would be binding but not an integral part of the Framework Programme proposal itself. The Council also made a declaration that it would come back to ethics at a later stage. The European Parliament, which was as divided as the member states, agreed subsequently to the Framework Programme proposal on the assumption that the issue would be dealt with accordingly in the context of the Specific Programmes. This was deliberately done to facilitate the decision-making process and to meet the deadline. In retrospect, rekindling the debate in Specific Programmes was unavoidable, as the issue was too controversial for a number of member states from the national political perspective.

When political agreement was being sought in the context of the Specific Programmes, it became clear that the only controversial issue left was—again—the establishment of the modalities and funding of certain sensitive areas of bioethical research. In the Specific Programme concerned, the Council reluctantly converged on the three no-go areas, as proposed by the Commission and not amended by the European Parliament, in its opinion on the Specific Programme. Although the general text of the Specific Programme corresponds to the Framework Programme proposal text, the Council had to add a minutes' statement dealing with specific implementation. This compromise placed a (temporary) embargo on European funding for human stem-cell research, cloning, and genetic modification until December 2003. At the heart of the compromise was the commitment to establishing detailed implementing provisions on the bioethical scrutiny of research activities within the life sciences involving the use of human embryos and human embryonic stem cells by 31 December 2003. Such activities would not receive Community funding before that time except in certain cases.[29] This was in addition to the earlier Commission pledge that no Framework Six Programme funding would support research in three no-go areas, namely, research aimed at human reproductive cloning, at modification of the genetic heritage of human beings, or at the creation of human embryos solely for the purpose of research on stem-cell procurement. After a long process of deliberation in COREPER a fragile qualified majority began to develop for the joint statement of the Council and the Commission in the minutes.[30] For this reason the Danish Presidency then sounded out the positions and the scope for compromising in COREPER. Any substantive change would force delegates to seek renewed approval at the political level in the capitals. Just before the summer recess of 2002 it became clear that the member states were in no position to agree among themselves other than by qualified-majority voting on the base of this compromise statement. In mid-August to get round the summer recess, the Presidency proposed a written procedure to adopt the Specific Programmes. As Italy objected, formal voting became necessary.[31]

To complicate matters the European Parliament subsequently protested about the contents of the minutes' statement, arguing that it went beyond the original agreement with the Council not to amend the text of the Framework Programme proposal agreement. In addition to the problem of content, there was the danger of a developing institutional power struggle taking the Framework Programme hostage: as the Parliament has no codecision rights in the Specific Programmes, it naturally wanted to agree on a package deal (Framework Programme, Specific Programmes, rules-of-participation proposal). The European Parliament even accused the Presidency of violating its codecision rights by introducing through the minutes' statement a temporary embargo on embryonic stem-cell research in order to reassure the more restrictive member states. When the Council adopted detailed procedures for establishing rules for the funding of bioethically sensitive research projects in COREPER, the Parliament felt that it had been left out of the final stage of the decision-making process. It argued, inter alia, that the Council had refused to honor earlier commitments not to take up more detailed procedures for bioethical research when the Council and the Parliament agreed to the Sixth Framework Programme proposal.[32]

In the end, agreement was reached to involve the European Parliament fully in the implementing measures, still to be worked out, for the possible funding of bioethically sensitive research.[33] The agreement reached stipulates that more-detailed implementing procedures and a more-comprehensive legislative act will be put in place in order to better regulate funding of any research under the European Framework Programme that involves the use of human embryonic stem cells. It foresees that, until the end of 2003, the Commission will not fund research projects involving embryonic stem cells with the exception of stem cells already banked or isolated in cultures. In early 2003 the Commission published a report on the evolution of stem-cell research that would form the basis of a public debate on the subject with the participation of the Council and the Parliament.[34] Following the seminar the Commission submitted a proposal to establish further guidelines;[35] the legislative procedure, based on Article 166(4) of the EC treaty, would have to be completed as soon as possible, and by December 2003 at the latest. This (politically agreed) moratorium would end on 31 December 2003. The minutes' statements were accordingly revised.[36] The European Parliament acquiesced in the compromise. A qualified majority in the voting in the Competitiveness Council took the final decision on the Specific Programmes. The formal adoption of the rules of participation followed before the end of 2002—a good illustration of procedural decision making in the European Union.

Conclusions

Within the Community legislative process there are only limited opportunities to influence the decision-making process. First of all, the leverage of individual member states is decreasing more and more as the number of players (other member states, Members of the European Parliament) increases. It is therefore essential to plan more strategically and to operate tactically. Building coalitions of the like-minded seems to be the key. From a longer-term perspective a member state has to participate as much as possible in the various consultative processes (advisory bodies) and to generate support from like-minded decision makers in the Commission services.[37] If certain propositions are already covered in the initial Commission proposal or, second best, if the Commission does not object, this makes honoring positions easier. The opportunities for successful lobbying decrease as the draft texts become more and more consolidated. From the legal perspective there are only limited opportunities to influence in the course of the decision-making process itself, as qualified-majority voting is decisive in the end. Tactically therefore, it is of importance to forge ad hoc coalitions with as many like-minded countries as possible on relevant issues.[38] If more member states support certain positions, the chance of those positions being honored is greater. It is, for example, quite feasible to support Scandinavians wanting to focus more on forestry research as long as they, in turn, support you in another area.

At the same time one must understand, from what has been mentioned above, the necessity of proper prioritizing. What is essential should always be stated clearly from the beginning (that a compromise is possible or that an issue is non-negotiable). Other member states may be willing to accommodate a member state on one or two issues as part of a package deal. It sometimes helps that there is a tendency to sympathize with certain known national positions, as people may find themselves in a similar situation on other topics. There is also an inclination to generate as broad support as possible and, if feasible, to take decisions by reaching political consensus. Stubbornly defending an isolated position, however, is often costly and ineffective in the end. Even a blocking minority often turns out to be only a temporary solution. Being outvoted or making national statements will not change the final decision.[39] There are, therefore, only limited opportunities for influencing certain outcomes unless these are part of a package deal that will generate majority support. The Sixth Framework Programme is a good illustration of a process of give-and-take that, in the end, did not make everybody one-hundred-percent happy. Taking out the more controversial parts and delaying controversial decisions to a later date, as was the case with the legislative Sixth Framework Programme package, turned out to be necessary so that its main parts could be finalized on time.[40]

Notes

1. In practice, most decisions are taken by consensus and without voting.
2. Official Journal L232, 29 August 2002 (Sixth Framework Programme), Official Journal L294, 29 October 2002 (Specific Programmes).
3. Representing an increase of 17 percent (nominal) over the Fifth Framework Programme.
4. In French, *Comité des Représentants Permanents.* COREPER meets up to twice a week as COREPER II (ambassadors) or COREPER I (ambassadors' deputies).
5. Community Research and Development Information Service (CORDIS) News and Events, 13 November 2000. Interview with François-Xavier de Donnea, chair of the Research Council during the Belgian Presidency.
6. In French, *Comité de la Recherche Scientifique et Technique.*
7. A good example is the European Research Advisory Board (EURAB), a high-level, independent, advisory committee created by the Commission to provide advice on the design and implementation of EU research policy. It is made up of forty-five top experts in a personal capacity from a wide range of academic and industrial backgrounds from EU countries and beyond.
8. Now Article 308 of the Treaty on European Union (EU treaty).
9. Title VI, Articles 130 F to 130 Q. In the enlarged EU treaty text they correspond to Articles 163 to 173.
10. The First Framework Programme started in 1984. To 2002 there have been five successive Framework Programmes.
11. See Article 251, EU treaty.
12. Decision making is based on the comitology procedures mentioned in the individual Specific Programmes, management procedure generally, regulatory procedure for life sciences (bioethical issues).
13. Programme committees (in different configurations) made up of national representatives and chaired by the Commission oversee the establishment and execution of the working programmes.
14. A separate regulation also demanding codecision with the European Parliament. The Framework Programme cannot be implemented without the approval of the rules of participation and the Specific Programmes.
15. Approval on 16 June 2003 of a clinical trials programme responding to the needs of developing countries.
16. Document COM(2001) 94 final of 21 February 2001.

17. Document COM (2000) 6 final of 18 January 2000.
18. Genomics and biotechnology for health; information society technologies; nanotechnologies and nanosciences, etc.; aerospace and space; food quality and safety; sustainable development and global change; citizens and governance in the European knowledge society.
19. Commission proposal, 21 February 2001.
20. Mention should also be made of the opinion of the Economic and Social Committee of 11 July 2001, and the opinion of the Committee of the Regions of 14 November 2001.
21. In the first reading six hundred amendments were introduced in the Industry, External Trade, Research and Energy (ITRE) Committee of the EP, of which 324 were voted through by the EP plenary on 14 November 2001. A vote of 248 was acceptable to the Commission.
22. It was formally adopted on 28 January 2002.
23. If the Commission rejects the revised proposals made by the Council, the Council needs unanimity, otherwise a decision can be taken by a qualified majority. Normally the aim is for consensus where possible.
24. See document COM(2001)709, 22 November 2001.
25. The Commission comments can be found in document, SEC(2002)105 final of 30 January 2002.
26. CORDIS News and Events: RTD beyond 2002, 17 May 2002. See also document SEC(2002)105 final of 30 January 2002.
27. This was in line with the recommendations of the European Council of Gothenborg of 15-16 June 2001. It also corresponded to recommendations by the European Parliament.
28. CORDIS News and Events: RTD beyond 2002, 30 November 2001. Parliament rejected at the end of 2001 a move to ban human cloning on the basis of the Fiori Report by the EP Committee on human genetics and other new technologies in science. There was a split between MEPs who supported research into therapeutic cloning and those who totally opposed the use of human embryos for any research purposes. Using therapeutic cloning, embryos are used to harvest stem cells, a potential cure for diseases such as Alzheimer's.
29. A number of countries (Sweden, UK) successfully insisted on the inclusion of existing banked stem cells or stem cells isolated in culture. For the more restrictive countries it was acceptable if the stem cells concerned already existed.
30. CORDIS News and Events: RTD beyond 2002, 1 August 2002.
31. CORDIS News and Events: RTD beyond 2002, 1 August 2002.
32. In a war of words, the European Parliament even threatened to take the Council to the European Court to block the budget of the Framework Programme or to stop the process of the already-agreed rules-of-participation proposal.
33. On 19 November 2003, the Parliament gave its opinion on Commission proposal COM 2003/390: see news report European Parliament, *EU funding of stem cells to be allowed under strict conditions*, 19 November 2003, report of 4 November 2003 by MEP Peter Liese: A5-0369/2003 final.
34. Document 8442/03 rech. 57. An interinstitutional seminar was held on 23 April 2003 covering scientific aspects as well as ethical and legal considerations.

35. Commission proposal document 11535/03 rech. 123 of 9 July 2003 for amending the Specific Programme with a view to establishing the envisaged implementing provisions concerning research activities involving human embryos and human embryonic stem cells eligible for Community funding.
36. The statement (document 12523/1/02 add. 1, rev. 1) was made by the Council and Commission at the time of adoption of Council decision 2002/834/EC on 30 September 2002 in relation to Article 3 thereof (application of ethical principles).
37. See, for example, the article by B.R. Bot in the International Spectator magazine dated 14 March 2002, *behartiging van de Nederlandse belangen in Brussel*, underlining the importance of good contacts within the Commission and of a sufficient representation of nationals within the Commission services. France and the UK, in particular, operate here with more success than other member states.
38. It helps, of course, if like-minded MEPs introduce equivalent amendments, which will facilitate revision during Council deliberations. It also reopens the possibility of including certain elements that failed to be taken on board by the Council.
39. This is often done because of domestic political considerations. A good example is the nuclear-specific (Euratom) programme where Germany abstained, or the stem-cell controversy.
40. A special meeting of the Competitiveness Council on 3 December 2004 again failed to deliver a political agreement on detailed implementing provisions for EU funding for human embryonic stem-cell research. However, the failure to adopt the Commission proposal for amending the Specific Programme, *Integrating and strengthening the European research area* (document 11535/03 rech. 123 of 9 July 2003) will not affect the existing right and obligation of the Commission to implement the already-agreed-upon Specific Programme. Projects will then be reviewed on a case-by-case basis by regulatory committees in which the member states are represented. In the case of less-controversial research using embryonic stem cells, it is feasible that some projects may be approved, as a qualified majority is needed to reject the proposal. See also press release, CORDIS website, dated 4 December 2003.

Chapter 5

EU Institutions and IGC Negotiations—How the EU Negotiation Process Affects Institutions' Ability to Gain Influence in IGCs

Derek Beach

Introduction

The European Union (EU) is a unique international organization. While internal policy making within the EU more closely resembles a federal polity than an international organization, the intergovernmental conference (IGC) negotiations that amend the EU's founding treaties are more traditional international intergovernmental negotiations.[1] IGC negotiations are held outside the institutional framework of the EU, and supranational institutions such as the Commission or the Council Secretariat[2] have a very weak *formal* role in them.

Yet despite not having formal voting rights, credible coercive threats, or formal control of the agenda, supranational EU institutions have been able to gain significant influence over IGC outcomes. The manner in which the IGC negotiation process is structured and conducted creates opportunities for supranational actors to translate their informational bargaining resources into influence over IGC outcomes that they otherwise would not possess.

This chapter demonstrates that IGC negotiation processes are not purely inter-governmental affairs. High bargaining costs grant supranational actors opportunities to intervene in the negotiation process, and depending upon the nature of the given negotiation, create various opportunities for them to use agenda-shaping and brokering strategies to translate their bargaining resources into influence over outcomes. It is argued that supranational institutions possess bargaining resources that can potentially be translated into influence over outcomes. Their ability to do so depends upon the negotiating context of the negotiations and whether they choose appropriate intervening strategies in the IGCs.

This chapter first discusses the common organizational features of IGC negotiations on treaty reform. Thereafter, the preferences of the two supranational institutions investigated are discussed. The chapter will investigate only the roles of the Commission and the Council Secretariat, and not other supranational institutions such as the European Parliament and the Court of Justice. Next, the bargaining resources of expertise and the reputation for impartiality possessed by the two institutions are described.

The chapter then investigates the impact of the negotiating context and the choice of stragegy for five IGCs: the 1985 IGC that concluded the Single European Act (SEA); the negotiation of the two parallel 1990–1991 IGCs that resulted in the Treaty on European Union (TEU); the 1996–1997 IGC that concluded the Treaty of Amsterdam; and the 2000 IGC that resulted in the Treaty of Nice.[3]

The concluding section first highlights the conditions under which supranational actors can influence IGC outcomes, and then relates these findings to more general findings of international negotiation theories.

The Importance of the Negotiation Process in Recent IGCs

In the following, first to be detailed are the common features of how the five IGCs in the period 1985–2000 were negotiated. Thereafter, the general preferences of the two supranational institutions are discussed, showing that they have not always overlapped with those of the member-state governments. The bargaining resources of the two institutions are then reviewed. Following this, the impact of the contextual variables across the five cases is discussed, pointing to the range of opportunities and constraints that these have opened for supranational actors in gaining influence in IGCs. Thereafter, the relative success of the agenda-shaping and brokering strategies employed are debated.

How IGC negotiations on treaty reform are conducted

IGCs are convened in order to review and revise the EU treaties. In effect, IGCs are "constitutional conventions" where, assisted by the Commission and Council Secretariat, history-making decisions are taken by national delegates that alter the competences and decision-making procedures of the EU (Beach 2004). Voting in IGCs is by unanimity in accordance with Article 48 TEU, and the final treaty must be ratified domestically in each member state. The European Parliament must be consulted prior to an IGC being convened, and, if appropriate, so must the Commission.

There are otherwise no formal provisions as to how IGCs should be negotiated, nor how the agenda should be prepared, but a set of negotiating norms has developed since 1985—the so-called *acquis conférenciel*. In practice both the Commission and the Council Secretariat assist the IGC, and the IGC is chaired by the government holding the Presidency. The European Parliament had no role in the 1985 or 1990–1991 IGCs but played an observer role on the sidelines in the 1996–1997 and 2000 IGCs.

IGCs since 1985 have been conducted at four levels. At the lowest level is the Friends of the Presidency, a forum used to prepare technical questions. The next level is composed of the personal representatives of the EU foreign ministers, together with Commission and Secretariat officials, who meet on average every week. Most of the negotiations are dealt with at this level, with discussions focusing on detailed and technical questions in a problem-solving environment (Stubb 2002). The third level of IGCs are the monthly meetings of foreign ministers, together with the President of the Commission and representatives and officials from the Commission and the Council Secretariat. While this level was intended to have overall control of the negotiation process, in reality it is sandwiched between levels, lacking as it does the informational skills to follow the lower-level discussions as well as the political weight of the heads of state or government to strike key deals (McDonagh 1998, 20). The highest level of the IGC are the heads of state or government[4] meeting within the European Council, joined by representatives of the Commission and the Council Secretariat. It is at this level that the key deals are brokered, and that the final treaty is concluded.

The Preferences of the Commission and Council Secretariat

The Commission

The Commission enters an IGC with publicized preferences[5] and, in that respect, resembles a national delegation. Based on its perception of its role as the guardian of the treaties and the common European interest, the Commission is partial to the strengthening of EU-level competences and particularly to the prerogatives of supranational institutions such as the Commission, European Parliament, and European Court of Justice (Dinan 2000b; Ross 1995; Rometsch and Wessels 1997). During IGCs the Commission also attempts to push the outcome toward the highest possible level of European integration, sometimes admonishing national delegates for their lack of ambition as Delors did after the failure of the integration-friendly Dutch draft treaty in late September 1991.

The Council Secretariat

While, formally, the Council Secretariat has only a secretarial function, there are many indications that it also has its own pro-integration agenda that does not merely reflect member-state preferences. The Secretariat has strong institutional interests in increasing the strength and scope of policy areas dealt with at the European level, but only if the role of the Council of Ministers in EU policy making is strengthened in the process.[6] Institutional issues are especially important to the Secretariat as it has intimate knowledge of what works and what does not work in the EU through its daily work in the Council. It is also quite pragmatic in its views, this in contrast with the Commission which believes that an incremental first step is often a better way of achieving a final goal than a single "big-bang" decision that might not be accepted by the member states.

The Bargaining Resources of the Commission and Council Secretariat

As neither the Commission nor the Council Secretariat have formal bargaining resources such as voting rights, the only relevant bargaining resources they have are comparative informational advantages and a reputation for impartial interventions.

Looking first at the informational advantages of the Commission and Council Secretariat, these primarily result from their roles in the daily EU policy-making process and prior participation in IGCs. The Commission's role in EU policy making is well known and does not require extensive elaboration here. Suffice to say that its central role in both the legislative and implementation processes at EU level provides it with detailed insights into the practical and legal aspects of the workings of the EU treaties that are not possessed by any other actor. Additionally, despite the small number of policy-making civil servants in the Commission in comparison with the larger member states' foreign ministries, there is a relatively low turnover in Commission staff; moreover, these officials focus exclusively upon EU matters, whereas there is often a much higher turnover in officials working on EU matters in national foreign ministries. Member states are therefore often dependent upon the Commission for substantive information on the actual working of provisions of the EU treaties—information which is, of course, vital when the EU treaties are being revised in an IGC.

The Council Secretariat plays a lesser-known role in the EU policy-making process. As its name suggests the Council Secretariat officially provides administrative and technical assistance to the Council of Ministers and the national Presidency chairing the Council. Despite not being a treaty-based institution of the European Union in the manner of the Commission or European Parliament, it does play a very important role in the day-to-day policy-making process by: a) providing authoritative technical and legal advice to the Council itself and to national representatives therein; b) playing the role of *confidant* and advisor to national delegations (Westlake 1999, 318); and c) stepping in and brokering compromise solutions in difficult impasse situations in the Council. The role of being a "vital cog" in Council decision making provides the Secretariat with detailed knowledge of the workings of the EU treaties, the preferences of member states, and extensive experience of brokering compromises (Westlake 1999; Metcalfe 1998). It is especially in the latter that the Secretariat has a comparative advantage over all other actors in an IGC.[7]

Turning to look at the perceived acceptability of the two institutions among EU governments, despite the Secretariat's role having changed from that of a "*notaire*" to the "right-hand man" of the Presidency during the 1980s (Westlake 1999, 313), most national delegates saw (and still see) the Secretariat as a relatively neutral institution that can be trusted to produce issue briefs of the highest quality, formulate fair compromises, and in general help the member states achieve their wishes.[8] In contrast, while governments accepted that the Commission played a central agenda-setting role in the 1985 IGC because of the increasingly activist line of the Delors Commission in the late 1980s and the conduct of the Commission in the 1990–1991 Political Union (PU) IGC, member states have become increasingly wary of trusting the interventions of the Commission in IGC negotiations.

The Impact of the Negotiating Context

Contextual variables, such as the institutional position occupied by the supranational institution, the nature of the issue, and the level of negotiations, define the range of opportunities and constraints involved in attempts by supranational actors to translate their bargaining resources into influence. The following section compares the contextual conditions across IGCs and their impact on the ability of supranational actors to translate their bargaining resources into influence.

The impact of the institutional structure of the negotiations

Based upon negotiation theory, it is expected that a privileged institutional position will give actors more opportunities to shape the agenda and broker key deals, and vice versa (Pollack 2003; Zartman 2002). *Table 5.1* illustrates the findings for the five IGCs.

Table 5.1. Institutional role played by the supranational actors in the five IGCs

	Commission	Council Secretariat

1985 IGC	• Privileged institutional position
	  –drafter of treaty texts
	  –asked to put forward set
	   of proposals
	  –provider of legal advice
	   together with Secretariat
		(not investigated)

1990–1991 IGCs	• Privileged position during
	  agenda-setting phase of
	  EMU IGC
	• Weaker position during
	  actual IGC negotiations
		• Privileged institutional position
		  –drafter of treaty texts
		  –advice to Presidency
		  –center of communication
		  –provider of legal advice

1996–1997 IGC	• Weak institutional position –
	  "16th member state"
		• Privileged institutional position
		  –drafter of treaty texts
		  –advice to Presidency
		  –center of communication
		  –provider of legal advice

2000 IGC	• Weak institutional position –
	  "just another member
	  state," though privileged
	  in discussions on
	  juridical reform
		• Less-privileged institutional
		  position due to the role that it
		  was allowed to play during
		  the Portuguese and French
		  presidencies

If we look across the IGCs the Commission's role has become increasingly peripheral over time, creating a less favorable context for Commission attempts to actively gain influence in IGCs. In the 1985 IGC the Commission played a very central role. The member states and the Luxembourg Presidency accepted that the Commission played an agenda-controlling function similar to its daily European Communities (EC) policy-making tasks—drafting texts and putting forward authoritative proposals—although in the IGC the Commission did not have a monopoly on policy initiation as it has in daily policy making. In the two parallel 1990–1991 IGCs, the Commission was able, through successful institutional politics, to secure a central role for itself in the agenda-setting phase of the Economic and Monetary Union (EMU) IGC (Dyson and Featherstone 1999, 712–3).

Yet, during the two IGCs, the Commission surprisingly withdrew from the drafting group in which it had participated in the 1985 IGC, attempting instead to play a higher-profile initiating role—with little success, as we will see below. The Italian, Luxembourg, and Dutch presidencies effectively controlled the agenda, though with some assistance from the Secretariat. The role of the Commission further declined in the next two IGCs, with the low point coming during the 2000

IGC, where the Commission was all but excluded from the proceedings because of a combination of poor tactics, advocacy of extreme policy positions, and resistance on the part of the French Presidency to allowing the Commission to play a significant role. The notable exception to this decline was the role played by the Commission in the negotiation of judicial reform in the 2000 IGC, where the Commission succeeded in creating a favorable forum within the Friends of the Presidency group that helped push outcomes closer to its own preferred outcome.

In contrast, the Council Secretariat had a privileged role in all the IGCs investigated, though with some variations. Although it had a privileged position in the 1985 IGC, it did not have as central and important a role as it had in later IGCs (Beach 2004). In the 1990–1991 IGCs, the Secretariat had a central role in the PU IGC, especially through its roles as drafter of treaty texts and sole legal adviser to the conference, thereby opening many potential opportunities for Secretariat influence. These opportunities were even greater in the 1996–1997 IGC, as two of the presidencies (Irish and Dutch) were very dependent on the informational resources of the Secretariat, and the third Presidency (Italy) was unable to provide leadership or brokerage because of a political crisis. In the 2000 IGC, the Secretariat had similar functions, although it was not allowed to play such a central role during either the Portuguese or French presidencies.

The impact of the nature of the issue being negotiated

We ought to expect supranational actors to be able to translate informational advantages into influence in issues of relatively low salience and technical complexity. *Table 5.2* illustrates the nature of the issues being negotiated in the five IGCs and the opportunities and constraints that this has imposed on the strategies employed by supranational actors in the IGCs.

In the 1985 IGC the implications of many of the issues under discussion were very complex and difficult to discern, creating opportunities for the Commission to translate its policy experience regarding economic integration into influence over outcomes. In contrast, in the negotiation of foreign policy, the member states guarded their prerogatives and did not allow the Commission to step in and assist the negotiations. The Commission proved influential in many high-salience issues during the IGC. These, however, were all issues with complex institutional implications that dealt with the core of the EC, while most of the issues in the 1985 IGC were what can be termed integrative issues, where all actors were interested in some form of integration over the no-agreement alternative.

The 1990–1991 IGCs dealt with complex and sensitive issues. The issue of European monetary union was complex and sensitive, although the level of political salience of several issues was lowered significantly because of the institutional context in which these were settled (the Delors Committee). On the Political

Table 5.2. The impact of the nature of the issues being negotiated in the five IGCs.

	Nature of the issue being negotiated
1985 IGC	• Many complex issues were on the agenda, with the full long-term implications of certain changes difficult to discern; • Several of the issues were politically salient, such as foreign policy and the free movement of persons; • But the overall picture was one of perceived low salience, as most of the issues dealt with negative integration/integrative issues; • Empirical results (only for the Commission in this case): −not strong correlation between salience and influence; −correlation between complexity and influence, especially as regards core subject matters of the EC.
1990–1991 IGCs	• Central issues such as EMU and the structure of the treaty were quite complex; • Many of the central issues were politically very sensitive, dealing with questions that can be regarded as matters of "high politics"; • Empirical results (only for the Commission in this case): −not strong correlation between salience and influence for the Commission, although partly due to Commission success in shifting many EMU issues to a nonpoliticized institutional forum prior to IGC; −some correlation between complexity and influence for the Commission, especially as regards core subject matters of the EC and the prerogatives of the Commission.
1996–1997 IGC	• Most of the issues in the IGC were quite complex, such as flexibility and the communitarization of JHA, although the most salient issues dealing with the so-called "institutional triangle" were relatively simple issues; • Most issues were low salience, with the exception of CFSP and JHA, and the "institutional triangle," which were issues of "high politics" and/or distributive issues; • Empirical results: −strong correlation between both level of issue salience and complexity and influence for the Commission, especially within core subject matters of the EC (first pillar); −not strong correlation between salience and influence for the Secretariat; −correlation between complexity and influence for the Secretariat, especially as regards core subject matters of the EC.
2000 IGC	• Most of the issues were relatively simple; • Most of the issues were very sensitive as they dealt with distributive issues; • Empirical results: −correlation both between level of issue salience and complexity and influence for the Commission, especially within core subject matters of the EC (first pillar); −no correlation between salience and influence for the Secretariat; −some correlation between complexity and influence for the Secretariat, especially as regards core subject matters of the EC.

Union IGC's agenda were many issues that can be termed high politics, that is, core sovereignty issues such as foreign policy or military affairs (Hoffman 1966).

There was little correlation between the level of salience and the influence of the Commission, although this was affected by the success of the Commission's efforts at shifting the agenda setting on EMU into a relatively nonpoliticized institutional forum. The Commission proved most successful in complex and technical issues that were at the core of EC competences, especially matters dealing directly with the internal market.

In the 1996–1997 IGC, most of the issues were low-salience and quite complex—creating many opportunities for supranational actors to translate informational advantages into influence. Pointing in the other direction, however, were the extensive preparations prior to the start of negotiations by national governments within the Reflection Group, where the agenda was well prepared.[9] Further, there were sensitive issues on the agenda, such as the negotiation of changes in the second pillar, common foreign and security policy (CFSP), and the institutional triangle that dealt with reweighting of Council votes, number of Commissioners, and the extension of qualified-majority voting (QMV). In these sensitive institutional issues, "Compromises did not lie in skillful drafting or the gradual refining of texts. These were points of gut difference and fundamental importance such as cannot be resolved until the end of any negotiation" (McDonagh 1998, 155).

We would expect therefore that supranational actors would be strongly constrained in these types of "high-politics" issues (Hoffman 1966). Looking at the empirical results, there was a correlation between Commission influence and both issue salience and the complexity/technicality of the issues. In comparison, the Secretariat was influential in both low- and high-salience issues, but its relative influence varied according to the complexity of the issue, with high Secretariat influence in complex, first-pillar institutional issues such as flexibility.

The issues dealt with in the 2000 IGC granted fewer opportunities for supranational influence. There were only a few highly salient issues on the agenda, including the sensitive institutional triangle of reweighting of Council votes, number of Commissioners, and the extension of majority voting—issues that were either distributive issues and/or that dealt with sensitive matters of national prestige. Several of the sensitive issues were, however, quite complex, such as reforms of the provision on social security coordination (Article 42) and the common trade policy (Article 133 EC treaty), which created some opportunities for supranational actors to gain influence. While Commission influence varied according to both issue salience and technicality/complexity, the Secretariat had influence in both high- and low-salience issues, its influence varying only according to the complexity of the issue. In simple issues such as the reweighting of votes, the Secretariat had little influence, and vice versa.

The impact of the level of complexity of the negotiating situation

Based upon multilateral negotiation theories, we would expect that as the number of parties and issues increases in the IGCs and the number of cleavages increases, the demand for supranational intervention to help the member states find a mutually acceptable outcome would also increase.

Table 5.3 depicts the complexity of the negotiating situation for the five IGCs. Both the 1985 and 2000 IGCs were relatively simple situations, with one or two primary cleavages. National delegates were aware of the zone of possible agreement, thus lowering the demand for supranational brokerage. In contrast, the PU IGC and the 1996–1997 IGCs were, in particular, extremely complex negotiations with dozens of cleavages on a variety of issues, which created a strong demand for brokerage and agenda shaping to find and/or create zones of possible agreements. Yet we must also take into account the strength of the cleavage. In the 2000 IGC for instance, the very sensitive small-large member state cleavage created a strong demand for brokerage, which was supplied partially by the French Presidency and partially by the Secretariat and individual member states.

Table 5.3. The level of complexity of the negotiating situation in the five IGCs.

	Level of complexity of the negotiating situation
1985 IGC	• Simple negotiating context, with one primary cleavage.
1990–1991 IGCs	• EMU IGC – relatively simple context, with two main cleavages. • PU IGC – highly complex situation, with numerous different cleavages.
1996–1997 IGC	• Highly complex situation, with numerous different cleavages.
2000 IGC	• Simple negotiating context, with two primary cleavages.

The impact of the choice of strategy

What factors determined the success of the strategies used by supranational actors in translating the opportunities created by the context of the IGC negotiations into influence over IGC outcomes? What types of tactics proved most successful? Why?

There will first be a discussion of the empirical findings for agenda-shaping strategies, showing that low-profile agenda-shaping tactics coupled with a reputation for trust and a central institutional position were the most significant factors allowing supranational actors to translate their informational advantages into influence over outcomes. Following this the findings for supranational brokering strategies will be reviewed, with the study pointing again at the impact of the level of acceptance of the interventions of the supranational actors and their institutional centrality as being vital for their success in brokering key deals. Given the difficulties in obtaining sufficient and reliable information on supranational brokerage during the IGCs, this section will be considerably shorter and the empirical conclusions more tentative in comparison with the agenda-shaping section.

Agenda shaping by supranational actors

The Commission

The results for the Commission showed that across the five IGCs the level of Commission influence decreased in each IGC because of a combination of structural factors and an inappropriate choice of strategies. While the context in the 1985 IGC opened up many opportunities for Commission influence, the context in subsequent IGCs was increasingly unfavorable for Commission attempts to shape the agenda. Furthermore, the Delors Commission in the 1985 IGC skillfully exploited the window of opportunity available to it by putting forward both a White Paper and a series of proposals in the IGC that shifted outcomes closer, though *within* existing zones of possible agreement, to Commission preferences.

In subsequent IGCs, the Commission increasingly advocated extreme policy positions. The poor choice of strategies was perhaps most evident in the 1990–1991 IGCs where the Commission gave up its influential behind-the-scenes drafting role in favor of a stronger but more risky open advocacy of its position.

1985 IGC

In the negotiation of the SEA, the Commission exploited its privileged institutional position, first by helping to open a window of opportunity and then by capitalizing on the open window to substantially influence the final outcome. Crucial to this ability were the strong comparative informational advantages possessed by the Commission, given that most of the issues dealt with were core policy areas of the EC. Further, the Commission was widely accepted as an intervening actor in the IGC, with member states expecting the Commission to play an initiating and brokering role similar to the one it played in daily EC policy making, which led the Luxembourg Presidency to grant the Commission an accepted agenda-setting role (Dinan 2000b, 261; Budden 2002, 90).

The Commission successfully created a window of opportunity by lobbying the member states to take seriously their commitment in the Treaty of Rome to create a functioning internal market. Once a window of opportunity opened, the Commission exploited its institutional position to expand the zone of possible agreements by first publishing the White Paper on the internal market which linked numerous issues together. Thereafter the Commission helped the Italian Presidency convene an IGC and widened the scope of the IGC agenda by linking IGC issues with the

White Paper. According to most reports, the Commission played a "determining role" in the IGC negotiations, writing 60 percent to 70 percent of the final SEA (de Ruyt 1987; Ross 1995, 32; Grant 1994, 75; Beach 2004). In the process the Commission shifted outcomes closer to its own priorities in areas such as the scope of the definition of the internal market (de Ruyt 1987), where it secured a wider definition than member states would otherwise have agreed upon, the inclusion of foreign policy cooperation within the treaties, and the strengthening of the common elements of the treaty (Grant 1994, 74; Corbett 1987, 254).

Yet despite this considerable success, the final SEA was *not merely* the product of Commission entrepreneurship. While the Commission was able to shift the agreement closer to its own preferences, this Commission influence was broadly within the bounds defined by the member states. This was clearly illustrated in the negotiation of the monetary union provisions where, despite its best efforts, the Commission was able to achieve only a vague reference to EMU in the SEA. Most of the areas where the Commission shifted outcomes were *within* zones of possible agreement. But this is still analytically significant as it created a higher level of integration than the member states would otherwise have agreed upon in the absence of Commission intervention; and when we look at the SEA as an aggregate whole, the small shifts add up to a significant increase in the scope and depth of integration agreed in the treaty.

The 1990–1991 IGCs

The success of the Commission's agenda shaping was radically different in the two IGCs, for while the Commission succeeded in shaping significant points of the EMU IGC's agenda through its participation in the Delors Committee which set the IGC agenda, the Commission failed spectacularly in the PU IGC, antagonizing the member states and thereby substantially weakening its own position both in daily EU policy making and subsequent IGCs.

In the EMU IGC the Commission was able to significantly influence the agenda-setting phase, primarily in the Delors Committee that helped prepare the EMU IGC agenda. Through institutional politics, the Commission lobbied to create a nonpoliticized forum for the development of the EMU agenda, and as it was able to coopt key actors into the process, the final report proved to be an authoritative focal point for the ensuing negotiations, given that it was signed by all the central bank governors (Dyson and Featherstone 1999; Ross, 1995; Verdun 1999; Christoffersen 1992, 61 and 72). Delors was able to shape the agenda by first skillfully using his role as chair to broker a unanimous final report (see below for more on brokerage by Delors) and second by exploiting his drafting role in the Committee to shift the developing agenda closer to his own preferred outcome, though within the overall bounds of what the *Bundesbank* would accept. Commission agenda shaping was most evident in the inclusion of a stronger economic pillar of EMU in the final report than was wanted by the *Bundesbank* (Dyson and Featherstone 1999, 719; Grant 1994, 123–24) . The Commission then put forward a draft EMU treaty prior to the start of the IGC that also helped shape the EMU agenda. Yet during the actual negotiations the Commission played a much less important role and notably proved unable to shape the agenda after the publication of its draft treaty.

The PU IGC, in contrast, turned out to be a nightmare for the Commission. The Commission proved unable to shape the agenda, and even found itself fighting a rearguard battle to maintain its institutional prerogatives against repeated attempts to weaken its powers. However, the Commission was also partly responsible for its own lack of success as, early in the PU IGC, Delors decided to pull out his officials from the Presidency drafting group and instead chose to openly advocate increasingly extreme and unrealistic proposals. Additionally, the first series of Commission proposals to the PU IGC were only relatively vague suggestions, and when the Commission started to put forward proposals in legal text, they were for the most part tabled too late in the negotiations.

The lack of Commission influence was particularly notable in the "high-politics" issue areas where Commission proposals were all but ignored. Worse was to come for the Commission, for after supporting the failed first Dutch draft treaty in September where the Dutch had broken an unwritten rule that the Presidency should not act in a manner that was excessively partial to its own interests, the Commission found its perceived acceptability falling dramatically, and it found itself sidelined during the remaining IGC negotiations.

The 1996–1997 IGC

The relative decline in Commission influence continued during the 1996–1997 IGC because of its weaker institutional position and its choice of inappropriate negotiating strategies. While the Commission was influential in several low-salience and complex institutional issues, the overall picture was one of low Commission influence. This was exacerbated by the low level of acceptability of the Commission's interventions.

The Commission did have close connections with several of the presidencies during the IGC, and appeared to have learned from its mistakes in the PU IGC by attempting to play a lower-profile role in this IGC. For example, the Commission's representative to the Reflection Group, the Spanish commissioner, Oreja, had relatively close contacts with the Spanish Presidency which chaired the preparations of the IGC agenda in the Reflection Group (Gray 2002; Dinan 1997, 209). There are indications that the Commission was able to influence the final Reflection Group report which formed the basic agenda for the IGC (Gray 2002). During the IGC, when the Commission was asked by presidencies for assistance, some opportunities were created for the Commission to shape the agenda. For example, the Irish Presidency asked the Commission to table a set of provisions for "communitarizing" a hard core of justice and home affairs (JHA) policies. This proposal shaped the agenda and outcome (den Boer 2002, 519). Yet in general the Commission's attempts to shape the IGC agenda were unsuccessful, and the proposals put forward by the Commission were, for the most part, far outside the zone of possible agreements and therefore had little impact in most issue areas. This was most evident in the negotiation of CFSP provisions.

The 2000 IGC

If anything, things became even worse for the Commission in the 2000 IGC. A variety of factors came into play, including a low level of perceived acceptability and poor negotiating tactics, with top Commission officials blundering on the negotiation of several important dossiers.

The Commission did have good contacts with the Finnish Presidency which prepared the IGC agenda and it was able to shape the IGC agenda in questions such as the categorization of articles to be transferred to QMV (Gray and Stubb 2001, 16.) But once the negotiations of QMV got under way the agenda shifted away from the Commission's position to a case-by-case approach, and the final outcome was closer to the lowest common denominator than to the Commission's position (den Boer 2002, 519). During the IGC itself the Commission had poor relations with the Portuguese Presidency which perceived the Commission to be following a large-member-state agenda. The Commission had even worse relations with the French Presidency which seemed to go out of its way to alienate and exclude the Commission.

Yet this picture of low Commission influence contrasts sharply with Commission influence in the negotiation of judicial reforms within the Friends of the Presidency group. Here clever institutional politics by the Commission ensured the creation of a favorable institutional forum for the negotiations. An "epistemic" community of like-minded actors was created by the Commission, first in the working group prior to the IGC and then in the Friends of the Presidency. The Commission was interested in having the negotiations held in this forum; it believed that these actors would be much less critical of the European Court of Justice (ECJ) and its strongly pro-integrative role, and would therefore agree upon an outcome closer to the preferred outcome of the Commission. Further, the Commission succeeded in securing a privileged position in the group; for example, the Commission drafted the agenda for the discussions in both groups.

The Council Secretariat

The Secretariat was overall quite successful in its attempts to translate its bargaining resources into influence in the IGCs investigated, although with some notable exceptions. The key to the success of the Secretariat was its use of low-key tactics such as agenda shaping, through behind-the-scenes drafting and informational tactics, and mediating key deals. In the PU IGC in 1990–1991 and in the 1996–1997 IGC, these tactics enabled the Secretariat to significantly shift outcomes closer to its own preferences, to push the outcome toward a more integrated but also more Council-based Union. When the Secretariat departed from these behind-the-scenes tactics, and attempted to pursue its own interests more openly by using more politicized agenda-shaping tactics such as open advocacy, this damaged the perceived acceptability of the Secretariat's interventions (independent variable), which then through a feedback loop affected the role that the Secretariat was allowed to play in the negotiations (contextual intervening variable). This was most evident in the 2000 IGC, where the Portuguese Presidency excluded the Secretariat from many of the traditional roles that it had played during small-state presidencies, as the Portuguese perceived that the Secretariat's interventions were excessively biased toward the interests of the larger member states. The impact of Secretariat strategies during the 1985 IGC has not been investigated because of lack of adequate information.

The 1990–1991 IGCs

The Secretariat had few opportunities to shape the agenda in the EMU IGC, as it did not take part in the drafting of the pre-IGC agenda within the Delors Committee; and once the IGC was under way, the agenda was formed primarily by draft EMU treaties tabled by the Commission, France, and Germany (Dyson and Featherstone 1999, 727; Christoffersen 1992, 33–34).

In the PU IGC, on the other hand, the Secretariat had a central role and proved successful in exploiting several windows of opportunity through agenda-shaping strategies. The member states had relatively vague ideas about what they wanted out of the IGC, and the agenda was poorly prepared prior to it. During the IGC itself the Luxembourg Presidency was very dependent upon the resources of the Secretariat (Ross 1995, 90).

The best example of Secretariat influence during the PU IGC was the Secretariat's ability to exploit the window of opportunity regarding finding a workable legal formula for the pillarization of the treaty. A suggestion that the treaty be pillarized had been put forward by France, but this metaphor needed to be translated into concrete legal reality—something that the Secretariat was uniquely positioned to do given both its expertise and its trusted institutional role in the IGC. The Luxembourg Presidency did not have the informational resources to produce the formula, and if France, for instance, had put forward the formula, other more pro-integrative member states would have reacted more negatively than they did to the Secretariat's draft text. The Secretariat's legal formula therefore created a focal point around which member state preferences converged, leading to an outcome that arguably would not otherwise have been reached.

The contingent nature of supranational influence was clearly demonstrated during the PU IGC. The Dutch Presidency cut the Secretariat out of the loop during its first three months (July to September) as the Dutch attempted to introduce a pro-integrative, single-pillar treaty formula in competition with the Secretariat's pillarized formula. But after the other member states resoundingly rejected the Dutch draft, the Dutch relied increasingly upon the resources of the Secretariat in the final months of the IGC, which created opportunities for the Secretariat to gain influence. The Secretariat exploited this position to shape the agenda and outcomes for example, by providing the winning legal formula for codecision.

The 1996–1997 IGC

While the "high-water mark" of Commission influence was the 1985 IGC, the Secretariat's "high-water mark" was the negotiation of the Treaty of Amsterdam. The context of the IGC opened up many opportunities that were then skillfully taken by the Secretariat. During the Spanish Presidency which prepared the IGC agenda, the Secretariat exploited its privileged drafting position to insert several of its own priorities into the Reflection Group report—but toward the end of the preparation of the report, the Spanish Presidency became wary of using the Secretariat as it perceived it to be acting in an excessively partial manner. The Spanish then took full control of the drafting process (Svensson 2000, 56) demonstrating again the contingent nature of supranational influence upon the acceptance of the formal parties to the negotiations, especially the Presidency.

The political crisis in Italy during its Presidency in the spring of 1996 gave the Secretariat carte blanche to manage the IGC agenda, enabling it to insert into it several of its priorities (Svensson 2000, 83). The Secretariat was also closely associated with the Irish Presidency in the second half of 1996, but was not given the free hand that it had enjoyed during the Italian Presidency. In complex institutional matters throughout the IGC, however, there was a strong demand for the interventions of the Secretariat, providing opportunities for it to step in and shape the agenda using advocacy and informational tactics, most notably in the negotiation of flexible integration.

The Dutch Presidency in the first half of 1997 was also dependent upon the resources of the Secretariat, although it did not use it in certain issues as the Dutch believed that the issue briefs and draft texts the Secretariat produced were excessively partial to its own interests in these issues. This was most manifest as regards the incorporation of the Schengen Agreement into the EU, to which the Secretariat was strongly opposed. Yet in issues where the Dutch did not have strong interests that clashed with Secretariat priorities, significant Secretariat agenda shaping was produced which was most evident in the issues of flexibility and the legal personality of the Union.

Overall Secretariat fingerprints can be seen throughout the Treaty of Amsterdam. This influence was naturally contingent upon the acquiescence of the Presidency and, as was seen in both the Spanish and Dutch presidencies, when the Presidency perceived that the Secretariat was advocating its own positions too openly, it had the final say and was able to exclude it from further agenda shaping in those particular issue areas.

It is also important to underline that in most of the issues where the Secretariat was able to influence outcomes, a skewing of outcomes resulted *within* the zone of possible agreements among the member states (type 1 influence). The most significant exception to this was in the negotiation of flexibility where the Secretariat shifted the zone of possible agreements itself (type 2 influence). At the start of the IGC, based upon national preferences, we would have predicted that the final outcome in flexibility would have been the creation of a form of "hard core" dealing primarily with CFSP. The Secretariat shifted this zone to create a complex legal formula that included many institutional safeguards and even excluded CFSP (Stubb 2002).

The 2000 IGC

The negotiation of the Treaty of Nice clearly showed the impact of the contextual variables upon the level of Secretariat influence. All three contextual variables placed the Secretariat in a weak position. Yet despite this difficult situation, the Secretariat was able to step in and shape the IGC agenda in several cases. For instance, during the Finnish Presidency which prepared the IGC agenda, Deputy Secretary-General de Boissieu "chopped up" the draft Finnish Presidency conclusions, using managerial agenda-shaping tactics to exclude issues that were unwanted by the Secretariat.[10] Additionally, the Secretariat was able to successfully utilize advocacy tactics to insert several of its "pet projects" into the IGC endgame.

But these negotiations also illustrated that the Secretariat is clearly not a unitary actor. While lower-level officials provided valuable assistance to the Portuguese Presidency, Deputy Secretary-General de Boissieu was all but excluded from the deliberations by the Portuguese as they believed him to be following a large-state (French) agenda in his interventions. This situation was reversed during the French Presidency which concluded the negotiations with de Boissieu acting as President Chirac's "right-hand man" during the Nice summit, a position on which he was able to capitalize to gain influence in several issues.[11] In contrast, the French Presidency prevented the Secretariat from playing its more traditional behind-the-scenes drafting and brokering roles in most dossiers.

Brokerage by supranational actors

The Commission

As there is little information available for Commission brokerage in the 1985 IGC, there will be no discussion of the 1985 IGC here. In the 1990–1991 IGC, the Commission played a key brokering role in the agenda-setting phase of the negotiations. Delors, in his role as chair of the Delors Committee, succeeded in brokering a unanimous report using a variety of tactics. One method was ensuring the acceptability of his interventions among central bankers, which involved a series of confidence-building measures prior to and during the work of the Committee (Dyson and Featherstone 1999, 708, and 714–16; Verdun 1999, 318). Another was to use Wim Duisenberg to mediate among the views of most other delegations and those of the *Bundesbank* in order to find a compromise formulation (Dyson and Featherstone 1999, 717). By achieving a unanimous report, which by no means could be assumed a priori, Delors ensured that a form of monetary union would be in the final treaty.

During the IGCs the Commission for the most part proved unable to play a strong brokering role, particularly because of its lack of acceptability following its intervention in favor of the Dutch first draft treaty in September. Yet in the endgame the Commission was able to utilize its informational advantages and assisted the Dutch Presidency in brokering deals on economic cohesion and social policy—both issues where a no-agreement outcome could have jeopardized the whole treaty itself (Christoffersen 1992, 126–28; Forster 1999, 92–93). The Commission was successful in mediating a deal on economic cohesion as it was able to use budgetary commitments as a side payment for the poorer member states (Moravcsik 1998, 446; Grant 1994, 200). In social policy, the Commission's interventions were accepted as it was advocating an outcome that eleven other member states wanted, and as the policy area was directly linked with the internal market.

In both the 1996–1997 and 2000 IGCs, the Commission was relatively unsuccessful in its attempts to broker key deals, primarily because of its lack of acceptability as an intervening actor. Based on the available information, there were no examples of successful Commission brokerage during the 1996–1997 IGC. In the 2000 IGC the Commission was able to broker a deal on Article 133 of the Treaty Establishing the European Community (TEC) in the IGC endgame, utilizing its comparative expertise in the issue and the strong demand for brokerage to mediate a compromise together with the Finnish delegation that both France and other member states could accept.[12]

The Council Secretariat

Given the lack of research on the subject there is unfortunately only sufficient information available to analyze the brokering actions of the Secretariat in the 1996–1997 and 2000 IGCs. In general though, the Secretariat proved successful in its brokerage attempts, given in particular its trusted and accepted intervening role, its extensive experience of brokering compromises in daily EU policy making, and its institutional position at the center of a web of communication in the IGCs. In the 1996–1997 IGC, when it was allowed to do so by the presidencies, the Secretariat stepped in and supplied brokerage in the negotiations using a variety of brokering tactics. The Secretariat mediated compromises regarding Article 133 TEC, and the new post of High Representative for CFSP. In both instances, the Secretariat not only ensured that a compromise agreement was reached but also skewed outcomes closer to its own preferred outcome. Tellingly, the final deal brokered by the Secretariat placed the new post of High Representative for CFSP within the Council Secretariat itself by significantly upgrading the post of Secretary-General of the Council, thereby also strengthening in the process its own institutional prestige.

During the 2000 IGC, the French Presidency attempted to undertake most of the brokering functions itself—with somewhat predictable results given its strongly partial behavior. Further, the Secretariat had no relative informational advantages regarding the state of play of most of the issues being negotiated, as the most salient were simple, zero-sum, or distributive issues. Despite this the Secretariat, in the endgame, did assist the French Presidency by brokering deals in several salient questions, most notably in finding a compromise formulation for the venue of European Council summits. By mandating that after 2002 at least one European Council summit per Presidency would be held in Brussels, and that after the EU expansion to eighteen members, all summits would be held in Brussels, Belgium was able to swallow being given fewer Council votes than the Netherlands.

Conclusions

The central argument of this chapter is that despite not having a strong formal role, supranational institutions can and do play a significant role in EU intergovernmental conferences on treaty reform. IGCs are not always purely intergovernmental affairs, but, because of the often-high bargaining costs, they grant supranational actors opportunities to translate their bargaining resources into influence over outcomes through agenda-shaping and brokering strategies. The argument was not that supranational actors were always influential in IGCs, nor even that IGCs were always necessary in order for the member states to reach an agreement. The chapter did, however, find that the context of the negotiations and the strategies employed by supranational actors in a given IGC can grant supranational actors opportunities to successfully intervene in the negotiations and thereby gain influence over outcomes.

Supranational actors were found to have significant influence upon IGC outcomes, with especially the Council Secretariat being influential because of its combination of a high level of expertise, a reputation as a trusted intervening actor, a privileged institutional position, and a skillful use of pragmatic and behind-the-scenes agenda-shaping and brokering strategies. This combination allowed the Secretariat to skew final IGC outcomes closer to its own preferences on numerous occasions. In contrast, the Commission had a weaker institutional position, did not have the trust of national delegates, and increasingly resorted to strongly advocating extreme policy positions—in effect, acting like an unwelcome extra member state with the added disadvantage of not having a vote. That the Secretariat has been a more influential actor than the Commission in most IGCs highlights a significant empirical oversight in the existing literature on the EU which has almost exclusively focused upon the role of the Commission and the European Parliament.

These findings point to the conclusion that we cannot simply explain IGC outcomes based upon actor preferences and relative power prior to an IGC, which is what most theorists on European integration do. What is necessary to move theoretical work on European integration forward is to attempt to incorporate the analytical significance of negotiations into our models to better explain which actors "won" in an IGC and why—in effect opening up the IGC "black box" to bring the study of negotiations back into theorizing on European integration.

Turning to look at the implications of this study for international negotiation theory more generally, this chapter substantiates the general claim that negotiations matter. However, in contrast with many of the studies in the negotiation literature that make this claim but then do not provide empirical documentation, this chapter has put forward hard empirical evidence backing the claim and has shown that how negotiations are structured and conducted plays an important intervening role between actor resources and influence over final outcomes.

The finding that third parties can gain significant influence in complex, multilateral negotiations has broader implications than the EU itself. As international negotiations increasingly move away from classic bilateral, power-based negotiations, and become increasingly complex, multilateral, and institutionalized, significant opportunities are opening up for actors that possess comparative informational advantages to influence international outcomes.

Naturally, there are differences between IGCs and other types of international negotiations. Among the main differences are the substantially higher level of institutionalization and formalization of IGCs in comparison with most international organizations and the intensity of interaction among participants, the EU perhaps being the penultimate iterated game, with delegates in IGCs working with each other on a day-to-day basis within the EU policy-making process.

However, the conclusions of this chapter underline the basic point made by supranational entrepreneur theory,[13] namely, we should expect negotiation processes to become increasingly important intervening variables as the nature of international politics and negotiations becomes increasingly complex, multilateral, and institutionalized within the World Trade Organization (WTO), the North American Free Trade Agreement (NAFTA), and other international organizations. This will open up significant opportunities for actors possessing relative informational advantages to gain influence over outcomes, contingent upon the conduct and context of the given negotiation. Instead of being relegated to being mere assistants without influence that help lower bargaining costs by providing administrative assistance, as argued by Keohane and Nye, (Keohane 1983; Keohane and Nye 1989). Centrally placed secretariats and other intervening actors such as small states that possess informational advantages will have increased opportunities to gain influence in future international negotiations. But this influence is contingent, as was demonstrated in, for example, the 2000 IGC; intervening actors can be cut out of all influence by governments. As the Nice summit in December 2000 demonstrated, the death of interstate politics has been greatly exaggerated.[14]

Notes

1. The EU is an amalgamation of four different major EU treaties: the original European Coal and Steel Community Treaty (which expired in 2002), the Treaty Establishing the European Community (Treaty of Rome), Euratom, and the Treaty on European Union (Treaty of Maastricht). Since 1985 five intergovernmental conferences have been convened that have conducted major revisions of the treaties. In these, both the EU's policy scope has been widened and the EU's institutional structures have been substantially strengthened.

2. While it can be debated whether the Council Secretariat is an intergovernmental or supranational institution, I argue that as the Secretariat plays an increasingly important role of "coguardian" of the treaties alongside the Commission in the day-to-day work of the EU and in IGCs and as it possesses institutional preferences that are more pro-integrationist than most member states, the term supranational can also be applied to the Secretariat. For another discussion of this point that reaches a similar conclusion, see Christiansen (2002).

3. For further empirical documentation of the findings of this chapter, see Beach (2004).

4. France and Finland are represented by their heads of state (presidents), whereas the other thirteen member states are represented by their prime ministers.

5. See, for example, European Commission (1996), for the Commission's opinion prior to the 1996-1997 IGC.

6. See Lipsius (1995) and Charlemagne (1994), for the Secretariat's preferences in the 1996-97 IGC. See Piris (1999) for the 2000 IGC. See also Beach (2004); Christiansen (2002); and Westlake (1999) for more.
7. One former Secretariat official in an interview appropriately called the Secretariat the "Council Negotiating Secretariat."
8. Interview with former Council Secretariat official, January 2002.
9. For more on this, see Beach (2004).
10. Interviews with national civil servants that took part in the 2000 IGC, Brussels, May 2001 and April 2002.
11. For more see Beach (2004).
12. Interviews with Commission official, Brussels, April 2002; and national civil servants, London, February 2002.
13. Most prominently, Young (1991) and Young (1999).
14. Earlier versions of this chapter were presented at the 4th Pan-European International Relations Conference in 2001, the 2001 annual meeting of the Danish European Community Shipowner's Association (ECSA), and at the 2002 ISA annual convention. The author would particularly like to thank the contributors to this volume, together with Finn Laursen, Thomas Christiansen, Ole Elgström, Jonas Tallberg, Morten Greve, Markus Jachtenfuchs, Alexander Stubb, Thomas Pedersen, Susanne Boras, and Anders Wivel for valuable feedback in various stages of this research. I would also like to thank the national and EU civil servants that I have interviewed for their insights on the informal politics of IGC negotiations.

Chapter 6

What Kind of Negotiation Does "Consensus Decision Making" Involve?[1]

Dorothee Heisenberg

Decision making in the European Union (EU) is complex: not only does the legislative process seem to change with every treaty revision but proposals are subject to very different requirements depending on the issue area. Moreover, historically, the process has been cloaked in secrecy, and only recently have certain statistics become available. It is difficult for all but the most committed EU analysts to fully understand the formal process by which the EU makes decisions.

The arcane decision-making process and the various changes to it have been the subject of scholarly analysis and hypothesizing for more than twenty years. What is more, with so much of the empirical information about the process being unavailable, the rationalist paradigm has been especially prominent in analyses of the legislative process, with assumptions being made about strategic actor behavior that were based on the formal rules of the game (Garrett and Tsebelis 1996; Hosli 1993). Most important among the rationalists' assumptions was the idea that qualified-majority voting (QMV) required the Commission to make proposals that would meet the "median voter" criterion in order to pass the Council of Ministers. Fundamentally, the rationalists' ideas about the decision-making processes in the EU rested on the assumption that formal rules were, in fact, followed.

This assumption, however, is problematic in the light of statistics showing that only a small minority of proposals are actually voted on by the members of the

Council: most legislative proposals are passed by consensus among the Council members. In the 2002 legislative year 81 percent of the acts were passed by consensus, down from 97 percent in 2000 but not significantly different from the average (see *Table 6.1*).

In the light of these data this chapter proposes to examine the institution of "consensus" as the prime decision-making mechanism in the Council of Ministers. The purpose of the chapter is to examine what the label of "consensus" could mean in terms of negotiation theories that have been explored elsewhere. There have been few studies to date that examine the EU decision-making process from this vantage point, not least because the process is informal and changes from vote to vote. Thus, the discussion here is more of a theoretical than empirical analysis of the EU's consensus decision making. The final section of the chapter discusses the concrete results of this informal process; unless voting becomes the norm and consensus is abandoned, the EU will not be able to make progress on the difficult issues facing it today, nor will its institutions be perceived by the public as being democratically accountable and legitimate.

The Role of Consensus in the Legislative Process

This section briefly details the formal decision-making mechanisms in the EU legislative process.[2]

Formally, legislation in the EU begins with a proposal by the Commission that is then generally passed to the Council of Ministers and European Parliament (EP).[3] The choice of decision-making procedure depends on the legal basis of the initiative, which is determined by the Commission when it drafts a proposal. Depending on the decision-making procedure determined by the Commission, the Council votes by qualified-majority voting or unanimity. Although the EP has evolved and now has a much more important impact on the decision-making process than at its creation (Scully 2001; Scully 1997), most analysts of EU policy focus on the Council as the most important decision-making institution of Europe.

Thus voting is the treaty-prescribed decision-making process, and there has been a deliberate attempt to shield the decision makers from the potential wrath of individual member states' citizens by mandating secrecy of the voting and process.[4,5] For this reason it is difficult to understand the reluctance to vote observed in this institution.

An explanation of this reluctance is more likely to be found in the historical legacy of the Luxembourg Compromise (1966) and its partial reversal in the Single European Act of 1986. As any student of EU history knows the Luxembourg Compromise represents the first major informal norm in EU decision-making procedures. The compromise between de Gaulle's antisupranationalism and the Treaty

Table 6.1. Consensus as Dominant Pattern in Legislative Acts

	2002	2001	2000	1999	1998	1997	1996	1995	1994	Average
Total Abstentions	30	25	12	9	34	17	14	14	29	20
Total Votes Against	28	27	22	30	60	56	55	62	37	42
Total Legislative Acts with Dissent[a]	37	31	5	30	56	48	44	76	65	44
Total Legislative Acts	194	187	191	199	219	218	229	344	261	227
Legislative Acts passed by Consensus	157	156	186	169	163	170	185	268	196	183
Consensus legislation (%)	81%	83%	97%	85%	74%	78%	81%	78%	75%	81%

Source: General Secretariat of the Council of the European Union: DG F III: Information, Transparency, Public Relations

2002 legislative acts Formal rules:	total acts	dissented acts	percent dissented	percent consensus
Unanimity rule (29%)	57	4	7%	93%
QMV rule (71%)	137	33	24%	76%
Total (100%)	194	37	19%	81%

[a]This number is not the sum of abstentions and votes against because some legislative acts have both abstentions and votes against.

of Rome's mandated evolution to QMV typified many decisions made by the member states to paper over significant differences about the formal application of EU treaty obligations by means of informal ad hoc agreements between elites. As Nugent (1999, 168–69) describes the situation:

> After 1966 the norm became not one of unanimous voting but of no voting at all, except in a few areas where decisions could not be indefinitely delayed or postponed, such as during the annual budgetary cycle and on internal staffing matters. Most decisions, even on routine issues, came to be made by letting deliberations and negotiations run until an agreement finally emerged. As a result, there was rarely a need for the veto to be formally invoked, and it was so only very occasionally—no more than a dozen times between 1966 and 1985.

Although the Single European Act curtailed the already limited use of the Luxembourg Compromise and extended QMV into many other areas of EU legislation, the informal norms spawned by the Luxembourg Compromise persist. Most decisions continue to be made by consensus rather than by voting. In the light of this almost thirty-five-year experience with consensus decision making, it is rather difficult to understand the member states' often acrimonious debates about the reallocation of Council voting weights in conjunction with every accession of new members.[6] Moreover, it is also difficult to understand the reluctance of member states to increase the use of QMV when, in practice, consensus is the norm.[7] It is this paradox that is explored in the next section.

What does "Consensus" Mean?

The American Heritage Dictionary defines consensus as "an opinion or position reached by a group as a whole," which is rather unsatisfactory in the context of this chapter because the word describes an outcome rather than a process. For those who study negotiation the outcome is causally related to the process but less relevant than the process itself. It is, however, possible to discern what consensus is not: consensus in the EU is not synonymous with unanimity, although it may include it.

Most theoretical studies of EU decision making, especially the rational choice analyses and those constructing power indices, approach the decision making as represented accurately by the formal rules (Hosli 1993 and 1995; Garrett 1995; Garrett and Tsebelis 1996, 2000, 2001a, 2001b). They justify this simplification on the grounds that a threat of a vote can coerce a "consensus" opinion (the so-called shadow of the vote) and thus QMV essentially is used in practice and can be analyzed accordingly. In reality, however, this simplification overlooks the fact that because a culture of consensus exists in the decision-making forum, the range of decisions that can be made overall is truncated. To quote Nugent (1999, 173):

> Majority voting is thus significant and has certainly increased in importance over the years, but its impact should not be overstated. Consensual decision-making remains and can be expected to remain a key feature of Council processes... (T)here is still a strong preference for trying to reach general agreements where "important", "sensitive", and "political" matters, as opposed to "technical" matters are being considered.

Structural Factors in Negotiations

In order to attempt an analysis of what kinds of negotiating relationships "consensus" in the Council may include, it is important to note the structures in which the decision-making process is embedded. The EU structures are unique and display some of the characteristics of both international negotiation and domestic legislative bargaining. This mix means that the metaphor of joint construction of the future (Sergeev 2002) is perhaps the most apt. An emphasis on involving all participant member states in this context and avoiding secrecy vis-à-vis the other Council members are indeed the hallmarks of Council decision making. As Sergeev notes, "The existence of optimal joint choice is a presumption of the process," meaning that the common understanding of all participants is that decision making in the EU is a non-zero-sum process. In EU parlance this common understanding might be considered an informal component of the *acquis communautaire*, the body of EU law, rules, and decisions that each member state agrees to when it joins the EU.

A second difference between EU decision making and international negotiation is the role of the Commission as agenda setter. Zartman (2002) indicates that successful negotiations between symmetrical partners come about because both sides realize that their position is not Pareto-optimal and that negotiation is the only alternative to an otherwise stable equilibrium. Therefore, as a necessary prerequisite to successful negotiation, all players must have exhausted all unilateral possibilities to move to the Pareto frontier and have recognized that negotiation is the only way to achieve that objective. In the EU's case the Council does not set the agenda for what will be negotiated—the Commission does. There is obviously a degree of consultation between the Commission and the member states about what items to move on to the agenda but it is not clear that all the players have necessarily concluded that a coordinated solution is better than the status quo or unilateral action.

A third difference between EU decision making and international negotiations is that there is an enforcement mechanism in the EU that does not exist under international law. The existence of the European Court of Justice (ECJ) means that the bargains struck in the Council will actually need to be implemented by all member states, with the result that agreement based on the assumption of shirking one's commitments later on is not an option.

These common understandings are the result of the forty-year history of negotiations among the same partners and the acculturation of new members to those norms. This means that the negotiations are structured in a formal framework where, because of the iterated nature of the negotiations, trust is very high and reputation matters a great deal. Over time the "evolution of cooperation" can be seen in this structure, and noncooperation among member states is rare.[8] Thus, negotiations are also more "personalized" in the EU than in other multilateral settings because the frequency of meeting is so much higher and many of the member-state elites have had the opportunity to interact in earlier positions. It is telling that the history of EU integration is replete with examples of "good chemistry" between two decision makers being the catalyst for achieving new initiatives.[9]

Another structural factor is that negotiations are held behind closed doors. Thus, although occasionally there may be two-level game (Putnam 1988) dynamics, if the ministers are negotiating something that the member states will ultimately have to ratify (such as the EU constitution) in general, there is less public posturing and little political payoff for obstruction. This creates a structure in which the substance of the issue can be isolated and negotiated without the distraction of "spinning" the issue to an electorate. Of course, there may be spin involved after the Council and EP's decision but by then the issue is generally presented as a "European" initiative, and constituents' ire is directed at Brussels rather than at another member state.

Finally, the information gathering and interactions between member states in the Council have the effect of creating a "common frame of reference" for understanding the issues. Social theory, under the label of constructivism, has made significant contributions to the theory of international relations (Wendt 1999). Its emphasis on ideas and actors' perceptions, as opposed to the hard structural constraints and opportunities stressed by realists, was overdue and, more than the earlier theories of international relations, focused on the process of international interaction. From the perspective of interpreting consensus in the Council, it is important to recognize the common understandings that facilitate negotiations, such as the common understanding of the historical importance of the European project, the necessity of having either France or Germany supporting an initiative, and the lack of an exit option or the threat of force.[10]

In addition to informal norms that structure the character of bargaining, there are also informal power asymmetries that impact negotiation. Although there is formal symmetry between member states in all the bargains, informally it is large countries, countries that joined earlier, and countries that have long-serving ministers that have a bargaining advantage. Thus, for example, the years when Germany's long-serving foreign minister Hans-Dietrich Genscher acted in the Council proved extremely important to the making of significant decisions there. Perhaps his most historically important decision was to put monetary union on the agenda in early 1988, without which monetary union could never have gotten off the ground.

The decision-making structures play a significant role, but it is also the ability to link bargains in different issue areas that make efficient decision making possible (Moravcsik 1991). Here again, there is a difference between Council decision-making processes and international negotiations, in that one of the central aspects of international negotiation is secrecy:

> An important feature of understanding negotiations through the bargaining metaphor is the necessity for total secrecy regarding one's own position, both resources and the limits of possible concessions. Any leak of information promises losses in results and gives partners the background for tough behavior (Sergeev 2002, 66).

In the Council there is significantly less secrecy about positions, reservation prices, and potential concessions than in international negotiations because the open dialogue can facilitate bargains, and states do not fear being outvoted. In fact, one could make the analogy that Council decision making resembles transactions more than bargaining in the sense that each participant knows what the other is demanding and the main questions revolve around how best to accumulate the currency to meet the requirements.

It has been suggested that the level of openness in Council deliberations represents a competitive disadvantage vis-à-vis third-country negotiators because the Council's positions are known in some detail to the EU's negotiating opponents (Paemen and Bensch 1995, 95). Here again, the Council's negotiations resemble more closely the bargaining in domestic legislatures than in international organizations. Bargaining between member states can involve informal vote trading within the existing legislative agenda ("logrolling") or intertemporal vote swapping because the number of interactions between Council members is so high and the negotiations are conducted in an atmosphere of mutual trust. Moreover, the iterated negotiations over time create conditions where reputations matter a great deal. Finally, although the structure of the Council institution would seem to mitigate bargaining across issue areas by organizing along functional lines, there is in fact a great deal of coordination (the General Affairs Council [GAC], COREPER, and even the European Council) so that, in practice, any number of cross-issue bargains can be struck. Moreover, the draft EU constitution reduces the number of Councils to only two, with the potential to establish further formations as necessary. Thus, assuming this provision remains intact in the final version of the constitution, the number of Council formations would decrease relative to the present situation of nine Council formations. One consequence of such a change would be to increase the number of potential bargains in the Council. Thus consensus in this context is shorthand for "selling" preferences that are not strongly held for advantages in other issue areas or in future negotiations (the "favor bank"[11]).

The characteristic of consensus that is particularly valuable in the EU is its ability to utilize a country's *intensity* of preferences. The informal decision-making system allows states that have very strong preferences on a specific item to keep negotiating until that states' objectives have been met. There is, of course, a constraint that the states' interests must be acknowledged by the others, and that states cannot perpetually "cry wolf." However, in the EU where sovereignty issues remain difficult, the consensus method presents an emergency exit which makes EU joint decision making more palatable to all.

It is possible to make the case that consensus is actually a more efficient market mechanism in the Council than QMV because it creates more of an opportunity to generate new bargains (the outvoted minority demands some limited consideration in other bargains) and it gives preferences different weights that can be empirically observed and satisfied. The logic here is somewhat neofunctionalist, but the mechanism would be the following: in their search for agreement on one issue, member states need to meet the demand of another member state in a different issue area which creates demand for another legislative act on that issue. In QMV, if that member state is not needed in the majority, its requirements are ignored. To use a financial market analogy, it creates a liquid market in which each transaction does not necessarily have to find one counterparty.

Pfetsch (1998, 297) has termed this characteristic of the Council "network" negotiation, where networks are defined as "formal or informal interactions between actors, mostly organizations or individuals with different but reciprocal interests; the participants in a network are exposed to a common problem or issue; they work toward its solution together in a decentralized, not a hierarchical arena." The metaphor of a network is clearly useful in describing the interactions with the various levels of government and member states. But perhaps its most interesting characteristic has been ignored: the existence of "network effects." Network effects have been defined as a change in the benefit, or surplus, that someone derives from a good when the number of other agents consuming the same kind of good changes. For example, as fax machine use becomes more widespread, fax machines become increasingly valuable as each individual will have more opportunities to use them. Thus part of the value of the network is derived from the number of participants. In the context of the EU these network effects not only explain why countries want to join at a growing pace but also why Council decision making has not broken down despite the increase in Council participants. As countries join, the number of potential deals rises exponentially, and as long as the Council ministers are free to negotiate, the Council acts as a large clearinghouse for potential bargains across issue areas. This network charactersistic may explain why EU widening has not been antithetical to deepening, as many had feared.

On this point, it is important to note that although the bargaining across issue areas within the Council may be Pareto-optimal in the aggregate, on the individual issues there are losers that must pretend to go along with the consensus. From a democratic transparency standpoint this deception of the public may be problematic because it creates an informal market of IOUs about which only the insiders are knowledgeable and that may not correspond to the preferences of the insiders' constituencies. Thus, to the extent that in their voting calculations voters use governments' revealed preferences (using votes cast in favor or opposed to a policy as a proxy for a government's preferences) and actually hold governments accountable for those preferences, the practice of consensus obscures a valuable source of information.

Although the transparency and democracy issues are important and will be discussed in the final section of the chapter, the difficulties they pose are distributed symmetrically among all member states; thus one could argue that they are the price to be paid for a well-functioning supranational level of governance in Europe. There are other interpretations of consensus, however, whose benefits may not be symmetrical, nor even Pareto-optimal.

Literature on negotiations is filled with references to asymmetrical bargaining relationships (Zartman 2002). In the EU's case, the Treaty of Rome deliberately attempted to compensate for the power asymmetries associated with country and population size and therefore overweighted the representation of small countries in the EU's decision-making forums, including the Council. The most extreme case of overweighting is in the governing council of the European Central Bank (ECB) where Germany and Luxembourg each have the same single vote (although after Eurozone enlargement, Germany will be rotated into a voting position more often than Luxembourg). It is probable, however, that a culture of making decisions by consensus rather than QMV reverses that "fix" and accords greater power to the EU's four large states to the detriment of the small states.[12] Thus, while small member states can demand compensation for their minority position, their rights are less protected under a system of consensus decision making than in voting (with the exception of very intensely held preferences). Thus, at least in theory, one could find systematic "losers" whose preferences are systematically ignored.

The Council Data, 1996–2002

Looking at the historical data on voting in the Council raises many more questions, and this chapter proposes some possible interpretations. *Table 6.2* breaks down the abstentions and votes against in legislative proposals by country.[13] Perhaps the first question to examine is the role of abstentions in a system of consensus. Why make a statement to abstain from a consensus? One can think of the various EU decision-making options on a continuum:

veto – minority vote against – abstention – consensus,

where veto in the Luxembourg or Ioannina style leads to a joint decision not to proceed. These options correspond roughly to the "exit–voice–loyalty" typology of Hirschman (1970), with similar behavior patterns. Hirschman asked "under what conditions will the exit option prevail over the voice option and vice versa?" To the extent that decision making in the EU involves mostly joint choice from among different alternatives, understanding why a member state would abstain should be viewed more as a "voice" device: a permanent record of dissent from the dominant direction the legislation takes. Establishing a minority vote against a legislative act is thus a stronger version of voice, but with similar consequences. These responses should be viewed as signaling devices to the other member states to alert them to the strongly held alternative preferences. The institution of publishing dissents exists in the United States (U.S.) Supreme Court and in the U.S. federal reserve open market committee. In both cases, the underlying logic is to signal the strength of preferences and reasoning in order to allow others observers and colleagues to gauge the trajectory of the institution in the future. As one U.S. Supreme Court justice observed:

> Dissents speak to a future age. It's not simply to say, "my colleagues are wrong and I would do it this way." The greatest dissents do become court opinions, and gradually, over time, their views become the dominant view. So that's the dissenter's hope, that they are writing not for today, but for tomorrow.[14]

Thus the data on contested legislative acts in *Table 6.2* suggest which countries are sufficiently concerned about the direction of the legislative agenda of the EU to vote against and be in the minority or to abstain from the vote. Put differently, these are indications of member states with strong preferences and ones who want to record their differences with the majority. Seen in this light, it is perhaps not surprising that the large member states are more likely to vote against or abstain from a legislative act than the smaller member states. While we would expect *ceteris paribus*

Table 6.2. Council Voting in Historical Perspective

| | Abstentions | | | | | | | | % of | % of Contested Legislative |
Country	2002	2001	2000	1999	1998	1997	1996	Total	Abstentions	Acts
Germany	3	5	0	1	7	2	4	22	15.60%	8.76%
France	6	3	0	0	2	3	1	15	10.64%	5.98%
Italy	0	3	2	1	5	1	1	13	9.22%	5.18%
Spain	1	2	0	2	7	1	0	13	9.22%	5.18%
Portugal	3	1	0	1	4	2	2	13	9.22%	5.18%
United Kingdom	4	2	1	3	0	3	0	13	9.22%	5.18%
Belgium	1	1	5	0	3	1	1	12	8.51%	4.78%
Denmark	4	1	2	0	1	1	0	9	6.38%	3.59%
Luxembourg	1	2	0	0	2	1	2	8	5.67%	3.19%
Netherlands	1	1	1	1	1	0	2	7	4.96%	2.79%
Austria	0	4	0	0	0	1	1	6	4.26%	2.39%
Sweden	5	0	0	0	0	0	0	5	3.55%	1.99%
Greece	0	0	0	0	2	0	0	2	1.42%	0.80%
Finland	1	0	1	0	0	0	0	2	1.42%	0.80%
Ireland	0	0	0	0	0	1	0	1	0.71%	0.40%
Total Abstentions	30	25	12	9	34	17	14	141		
# Legislative acts	194	187	191	199	219	218	229	1437		
# Acts with abstentions or votes against	37	31	5	30	56	48	44	251		
Abstentions/legislative acts	19%	17%	3%	15%	26%	22%	19%	17%		
Acts passed by consensus	81%	83%	97%	85%	74%	78%	81%	83%		

Source: General Secretariat of the Council of the European Union: DG F III: Information, Transparency, Public Relations

Table 6.2. Council Voting in Historical Perspective (continued)

Country	Votes against							Total	% of Votes against	% of Contested Legislative Acts
	2002	2001	2000	1999	1998	1997	1996			
Germany	2	3	4	2	11	9	14	45	16.19%	17.93%
Italy	2	2	1	8	8	6	6	33	11.87%	13.15%
Netherlands	5	1	2	4	12	2	2	28	10.07%	11.16%
Denmark	2	3	3	4	7	6	2	27	9.71%	10.76%
Sweden	6	4	2	0	3	7	4	26	9.35%	10.36%
United Kingdom	1	2	2	0	2	7	7	21	7.55%	8.37%
France	0	3	1	3	3	3	3	16	5.76%	6.37%
Greece	2	1	3	1	2	4	2	15	5.40%	5.98%
Belgium	0	2	1	2	4	0	5	14	5.04%	5.58%
Austria	1	1	2	1	3	2	2	12	4.32%	4.78%
Spain	1	3	0	1	1	2	4	12	4.32%	4.78%
Ireland	2	1	0	1	2	1	2	9	3.24%	3.59%
Finland	2	1	1	0	0	4	1	9	3.24%	3.59%
Portugal	1	0	0	1	2	2	1	7	2.52%	2.79%
Luxembourg	1	0	0	2	0	1	0	4	1.44%	1.59%
Totals	28	27	22	30	60	56	55	278		
# Legislative acts	194	187	191	199	219	218	229	1437		
# Acts with abstentions or votes against	37	31	5	30	56	48	44	251		
Abstentions/legislative acts	19%	17%	3%	15%	26%	22%	19%	17%		

Source: General Secretariat of the Council of the European Union: DG F III: Information, Transparency, Public Relations

Table 6.3. Correlations with Votes Against and Abstentions

	Votes Against	Abstentions
Years of EU membership	0.38	0.50
Population	0.63	0.80
Pre-Nice population per Council vote	0.68	0.79
GDP per capita	−0.14	−0.09
EU contributions per capita	0.43	0.40

abstentions and votes against legislative acts to be evenly distributed among members, or perhaps that the smallest members would vote against the tyranny of the large, it is the large countries that vote against and abstain from proposals. In fact, the smallest members hardly ever vote against or abstain: between them, the five largest member states account for 48 percent of the votes against and 56 percent of the abstentions. Thus, one could construe the propensity to contest a vote as a measure of voice in the future direction of the EU. Abstentions are strongly correlated with size (correlation coefficient of 0.80) and votes against are moderately correlated with population per vote in the Council (0.68). Thus, Germany has a much higher propensity to vote against legislative proposals than the other member states. To put the "size matters" argument into perspective, correlations to other variables corresponding to other explanations were done (see *Table 6.3*). There is no correlation between abstentions or votes against and gross domestic product (GDP) per capita (−0.09 and −0.14 respectively). It is not the case that rich countries or poor countries vote against or abstain more often. And there is only a very weak correlation between membership years of the EU and abstentions or votes against (0.50 and 0.38 respectively), showing that newer members are not more likely to keep the consensus nor will older members be more inclined to break the consensus. Finally net payers are not more likely to dissent: here the correlation is 0.43 for voting against and 0.40 for abstentions.

Consensus, Efficient Decision Making, and Democratic Accountability

Arguably, consensus decision making is the answer to many of the inherent contradictions of the Monnet method of integration: it facilitates bargaining, it compensates losers, and it acknowledges intensely held preferences. There are, however, potentially deleterious consequences to the practice of consensus, and this section briefly examines them.

The first concern speaks to the question of efficient decision making. Although the bargaining within the existing range of issues is efficient, that range is artificially truncated, and there is therefore only a subset of EU issues that can be decided in this fashion. Any of the serious issues that would significantly change the workings of the EU are rejected because of the uncertainty about the new institutional dynamics. Thus, to the extent that the EU faces new challenges that create the need to act despite uncertainty about the outcomes, consensus decision making in the Council will prevent the timely resolution of these issues. It is this element of the EU's future to which Romano Prodi referred, when he said:

> From a much broader standpoint, we must carry through to completion the process whereby consensus is replaced by voting, the normal procedure in a democratic system. What we must do is evolve towards a system of decision-making that is based on voting, a system that is both effective and can be understood by everyone. . . [W]e must come to embrace a majority voting culture, in which decisions reflect the will of the largest number but apply equally to each and everyone. All too often, we aim for consensus even when there is none to be found, and progress grinds to a halt. To overcome reservations in some quarters, there is only one solution: to put the matter to the vote.[15]

Prodi also obliquely refers to the lack of democratic accountability of community decision making. He would like a system, he said, that is "understood by everyone" and reading between the lines more democratically legitimate. Paradoxically, the main justification for having consensual decision making rather than hard voting has always been to solidify the legitimacy of the EU in the eyes of its citizens by not making the losers apparent.[16] In national domestic contexts consensual decision making has been very successful in shoring up support for political decisions despite large internal differences (Lijphart 1999). The causal mechanism, however, is not the opacity of the process nor the lack of information about winners and losers. Anderson and Guillory (1997, 66), building on the concept of Lijphart's consensual–majoritarian typology, showed that consensual democratic institutions differentially and systematically affect citizen satisfaction with the way democracy works. Specifically "losers in systems that are more consensual display higher levels of satisfaction with the way democracy works than do losers in systems with majoritarian characteristics." In Anderson and Guillory's theoretical perspective, however, this additional satisfaction from consensual decision making is due to mechanisms for procedural justice and opportunities for input into the decisions made by government. The perception that the minority can have an impact on legislation is the primary legitimation mechanism. This is not a whitewashing of political conflicts in a consensus. Thus, while the label "consensus" is used to describe both systems, the political legitimacy that attaches to the domestic consensual systems is mostly absent in the EU context because of a lack of information about the process of resolving conflictual decisions.[17]

It may be that a culture of making decisions by consensus rather than QMV accords greater power to the EU's large states at the expense of the small states. Steinberg (2002, 360) argues that invisible weighting is the hallmark of the GATT/WTO decision making and that "sovereign equality rules [consensus] are more likely than weighted voting to confer legitimacy on . . . outcomes." Moreover, the "legitimizing effect of sovereign equality rules on outcomes may be particularly pronounced for domestic audiences, as opposed to . . . negotiators who have witnessed invisible weighting first-hand." Thus, while small member states can demand compensation for their minority position, their rights are less protected under a system of consensus decision making than in voting. However, the decision-making process obscures this reality from the public.

At the Council level decision making has been shrouded in secrecy in order to avoid nationalist characterizations of the voting. Although member states can choose to make public their loser status with abstentions and votes against specific proposals, there is no EU-wide obligation to do so. Some of the smaller states (e.g., the Netherlands) must give their national parliaments information about the votes they have cast in the Council; but again, this is a domestic practice that is not obligatory in all states.

The practice of negotiating away from the public eye also results in states agreeing to a developing consensus but leaving with an informal "opt out" or watering down of the measure which is noted in the minutes. The Council's legal service was sufficiently worried about this practice to issue an internal study on publishing statements for the minutes.[18] Although admitting that "statements in the Council minutes. . . have always been a handy negotiating tool," the report concludes that those statements "contradicting or adding to the enacting terms of legislation must absolutely not be made."[19] Noting that these statements would create "legitimate expectations" on the part of the public despite having no force of law in the European Court of Justice, the Council's legal service foresaw an enormous legal liability.

The practice of allowing democratically elected decision makers to reach secret deals with their counterparts that are binding on their citizens is quite rare internationally. In most domestic and international negotiation scenarios, the outcomes of the negotiations are known, as are the individual decision makers' preferences and roles in those outcomes. Indeed, it is often the democratic national parliaments that must approve the negotiation mandate of the decision maker, either beforehand ("fast-track authority") or subsequently (ratification). Moreover, an essential requirement of democratic accountability is the availability of information on the decision maker's deals to allow the voter the opportunity to censor the decision maker at the ballot box.

Thus, both in domestic and international scenarios, consensus thwarts many of the essential elements of democratic decision making. Steinberg (2002, 342) calls consensus decision making in the General Agreement on Tariffs and Trade/World Trade Organization (GATT/WTO) context "organized hypocrisy" because the informal norms make it possible to "formulate legislative packages that favor the interests of powerful states, yet can be accepted by all participating states and can be generally considered legitimate by them."

Similarly, Gruber's (2000) analysis of why states join supranational institutions when the latter are not perceived to be superior to the status quo shows that the fear of being outside the supranational institution (in this case, the consensus that is developing) leads states to decisions that are not necessarily Pareto-optimal. Moreover, in a skillfully handled Council the chair may attenuate information asymmetries and obtain a vote in favor of a legislative act even if a blocking minority exists. In the Council, a decision to go along with the Council's consensus despite reservations must not even be justified to the voters. It is not difficult to see why any models of democratic process that rest on a notion of agent control break down in the context of the Council.

In the final analysis the institution of consensus in the EU is a mixed bag: on the one hand it has created the tremendous integration of the past forty years, but on the other, it holds the EU back from a new level of international governance. Consensus has proved extremely difficult to eradicate, as its effects are seen as benign. The May 2004 enlargement may, however, be the catalyst for changing the negotiation style of the EU in a fundamental way. The willingness of Poland and Spain to defy the consensus on new voting rules and to stymie approval of the EU constitution in December 2003 was a signal to all that standing up for the national interest was more desirable than the "construction of a joint future." If this negotiation style filters down to the Council of Ministers, the institution of "consensus" in the EU may become an historical artifact.

Notes

1. An earlier version of this chapter was published in the *European Journal of Political Research* 2004.
2. More detailed accounts can be found in Nugent (1999); Dinan (2000a); Peterson and Bomberg (1999); Hayes-Renshaw and Wallace (1997); van Schendelen (1996); Raunio and Wiberg (1998); and Westlake (1995).
3. As outlined on the EU website, "The *assent* procedure was introduced by the Single European Act 1986. It means that the Council has to obtain the European Parliament's assent before certain very important decisions are taken. Parliament can accept or reject a proposal but cannot amend it. The *codecision* procedure was introduced by the Treaty on European Union (Treaty of Maastricht) 1992, and is governed by Article 251

of the Treaty establishing the European Community. It was simplified and its field of application extended by the Treaty of Amsterdam 1997. It provides for two successive readings, by Parliament and the Council, of a Commission proposal and the convocation, if the two colegislators cannot agree, of a "conciliation committee," composed of Council and Parliament representatives, with the participation of the Commission, in order to reach an agreement. This agreement is then submitted to Parliament and the Council for a third reading with a view to its final adoption. Under the *consultation procedure* the opinion of the European Parliament is sought. Once it has received this opinion the Commission can amend its proposal accordingly. The proposal is then examined by the Council, which can adopt it as it is or amend it first. However, if the Council decides to reject the Commission proposal, this must be a unanimous decision." See <http://europa.eu.int/institutions/decision-making/index_en.htm>.

4. The EU's attempts to create greater transparency in the Council in light of criticisms of democratic deficit have been only marginally successful in creating a greater awareness of, and satisfaction with, the EU legislative process. For a discussion of the transparency problem in the Council, see Dinan (2000a).

5. Note that the European Court of Justice which is similarly situated with respect to non-transparency and handing down judgments unanimously, *does* in fact vote by majority rule.

6. By far the most acrimonious negotiations were those on the European constitution in December 2003. At the summit Poland and Spain refused to give up their advantageous voting position obtained in the Nice treaty, resulting in a stalemate on the entire constitution. Before that, the EFTA accessions in 1994, when Spain and the UK threatened to veto the enlargement because of the calculations of their weighted votes in the total Council votes, also almost caused a negotiation breakdown.

7. The Nice summit was also noted for the member states' unwillingness to increase QMV despite many hours of negotiations to do just that by the French Presidency.

8. Axelrod (1984) suggests that the primary decision rule that produces optimal cooperation patterns in an iterated prisoner's dilemma framework is "tit for tat." The fact that the Council does not seem to utilize this decision rule in practice suggests that the coordination game in the Council does not have prisoner's-dilemma (PD) payoffs.

9. For example, the famed friendships of Adenauer and de Gaulle, Schmidt and Giscard d'Estaing, and Kohl and Mitterrand.

10. Indeed, it has been suggested that one risk to a "big-bang" enlargement of the EU is the reduction of these common understandings and of the ability of the 15 to acculturate the 10 new states to the existing informal norms of negotiation.

11. Intertemporal bargains are more likely to be made retroactively than prospectively, as in, "remember when I voted for your proposal even though. . ." (Author's interview with the chief of cabinet of a foreign affairs ministry, 3 May 2002).

12. This is true unless one equates consensus with unanimity, in which case the rights of the smaller countries are significantly enhanced vis-à-vis QMV.

13. The data available are only on "definitive legislative acts" (i.e., acts adopted after the second reading by the EP). The transparency DG chooses to omit so-called other acts from its publicly available statistics. These can be any nonlegislative—but nevertheless political—acts, including antidumping duties and regulations. Occasionally a member state may make its vote public, as the Netherlands did, for example, with a

Council resolution to impose antidumping duties on zinc oxide from China in February 2002.

14. Ruth Bader Ginsburg: "Ginsburg Interview, Part 1" *Morning Edition*, 2 May 2002.

15. *For a Strong Europe, with a Grand Design and the Means of Action.* Speech by the president of the European Commission, Romano Prodi, at the *Institut d'Etudes Politiques*, 29 May 2001 in Paris. Available at <http://europa.eu.int/comm/commissioners/prodi/speeches/index_en.htm>.

16. Author's interview with member of COREPER, 14 June 2002.

17. Bogaards and Crepaz (2002, 367) indicates that even national consociational politics have been subject to democratic critiques.

18. Legal Service of the Council of Ministers. 1995. *Study of Council Practice Regarding Statements for the Minutes in Connection with Openness*, 3 May. See also *The Independent*, 23 June 1995.

19. Legal Service of the Council of Ministers. 1995. *Study of Council Practice Regarding Statements for the Minutes in Connection with Openness*, 3 May.

Chapter 7

Negotiation and Mediation in the EU Council of Ministers

Ole Elgström

Introduction

The Council of Ministers of the European Union (EU) has been described as a site for consensus building and as "concession-making machinery." Observers regularly note that this is the place where the compromises and package deals that shape EU policies are forged. It is also an arena for brokerage and mediation where several actors compete in their efforts to "move things forward" and to construct "yesable" proposals (author interviews; Hayes-Renshaw and Wallace 1997; Spence 1995; Kirchner 1992; Sherrington 2000).

In this chapter the aim is to highlight some of the characteristics of Council negotiation and mediation and to explain these traits with reference to a number of institutional mechanisms. I use neoinstitutional theory to analyze the impact of, inter alia, agenda-shaping rules, decision-making procedures, and voting rules, as well as to emphasize the importance of informal norms guiding actor behavior. I focus particularly on the institutionally assigned roles played by the Commission and the Presidency in agenda setting and mediation and on how procedures and rules influence the bargaining strategies of both member states and institutional actors.

Although my main focus is on the Council itself, many of the points made are also relevant for negotiations in working parties and in the Committee of Permanent

Representatives (COREPER). My findings on Presidency behavior should be compared to what is reported by Guggenbühl (in this volume). My remarks primarily concern first-pillar negotiations although at certain points, I shall also refer to other contexts and underline the situational particularities of negotiating strategies. The conclusions I draw are partly based on a large number of interviews with officials in Brussels and Stockholm representing the Commission, the Council General Secretariat, and several permanent representations and foreign ministries. The findings from these interviews have been compared with existing EU literature and with results from my previous case studies of EU negotiation processes (Elgström 2001; Bjurulf and Elgström 2004).

I start by detailing some of the general characteristics of EU negotiations that also have a major bearing on Council bargaining. One such feature is the highly institutionalized nature of the negotiation game. Neoinstitutionalism is the theoretical platform for my analysis, and some key elements of this approach are highlighted in the next section. The analytical part of the chapter begins with a scrutiny of the agenda-setting powers of the Commission and the Presidency and with an analysis of how procedural mechanisms related to the Commission monopoly of initiative influence actor strategies. I will then show how voting rules and the "shadow of the vote" impact upon coalition and negotiation behavior. The final analytical section is devoted to a comparison of the mediator roles played by the Presidency and the Commission, emphasizing the informal norms that inform their actions. I conclude the chapter with a brief discussion on the effects of prevailing institutional mechanisms on EU policy.

General Features of EU Negotiations

The EU may be described as a "multilateral inter-bureaucratic negotiation marathon" (Kohler-Koch 1996, 367) or as a "permanent negotiation institute" (Bal 1995, 1). The continuous nature of EU negotiations, with no endgame and no exit options in sight, tends to facilitate cooperative solutions (Jönsson *et al.* 1998). The "shadow of the future" (Axelrod 1984) is large, allowing the actors to count on future reciprocal concessions if they concede in a single negotiating game. In the words of Adrienne Héritier (1996, 157), "participants know that their relationship is not merely a temporary one, but meant to be durable. They therefore think twice before ruthlessly seeking to maximize their individual interests." That all EU members have entered the Union voluntarily, expecting that collaboration will produce efficiency gains on all sides, and that all members share the same basic values, are both phenomena that reinforce this cooperative tendency. The result is consensus-seeking behavior and a problem-solving approach to negotiations (Elgström and Jönsson 2000; see Walton and McKersie 1991; Lax and Sebenius 1996). There are, however, islands of conflictual bargaining in the seas of problem-solving behavior: evidence exists that competitive, tough strategies are frequently encountered in highly politicized settings and when negotiations concern redistribution and constitutional matters (Elgström and Jönsson 2000, 690–99).

Negotiations in working parties, in COREPER (especially COREPER I) and the Council are typically text negotiations. Participants focus on a written proposal, initially produced by the Commission and sometimes amended later by the Presidency, and scrutinize each sentence, word by word. "Negotiations are all about formulations," in the words of one interviewee. Text negotiations ordinarily imply that the original text becomes very important as actors tend to be bound by the structure and wording of the first draft and react to this text. Text negotiations are quite special, and give skillful formulators a particular potential for influence.

Another prominent characteristic of EU negotiation is its high degree of institutionalization. Not only is the institutional setup of the EU extremely complex, with a large number of participating actors at different levels (Peterson and Bomberg, 1999) but there is also a plethora of legal rules and informal norms that surround the actors and condition their behavior. These institutional mechanisms, that leave their distinctive mark on EU negotiations, are suitably examined using neoinstitutional theory.

A Neoinstitutionalist Theoretical Framework

I will in this chapter rely on a basically rationalist neoinstitutionalist approach (Hall and Taylor 1996; Aspinwall and Schneider 2000). Rationalists perceive humans as rational utility maximizers who behave strategically to reach their preferred goals. Institutions, defined as "legal arrangements, routines, procedures, conventions, norms, and organizational forms" (Norgaard 1996, 39), provide a context or a strategic operating environment, within which individual decisions are taken. "Political struggles are mediated by prevailing institutional arrangements," as Simon Bulmer (1994, 355) formulates it. Institutions provide a framework that constrains or empowers the actors, shapes their expectations, and determines what alternatives they see as possible. In these ways they structure relationships and decision-making processes and combine these with preferences to produce outcomes (Shepsle 1989, 135–37). They may decide, inter alia, who has the right of initiative and the right to submit and alter text proposals as well as where, when, and how decisions are made. Rules therefore privilege certain actors and disfavor others; they also proscribe certain alternatives from being considered and facilitate others coming to the fore.

From this perspective formal and informal rules are viewed mainly as intervening variables and are not seen as influencing actor preferences. I do not include just formal rules and procedures in my consideration of institutions. Attention to informal norms is, in my view, essential for a deep understanding of Council negotiation processes (see Eising 2002). Such norms guide behavior by influencing the cost-benefit analyses of the actors involved. Expectations of what is acceptable or appropriate behavior enter into the strategic calculations of rational actors and lead them to select the most cost-efficient actions inclusive of these criteria. Moral approval or shaming, rather like material incentives and disincentives, influence strategic choice (see Johnston 2001).

Institutional Arrangements and Council Negotiation

Agenda-setting powers and rules on how to effect changes in proposals

According to formal rules the Commission enjoys the monopoly of initiative in the first pillar (Pollack 1997; Schmidt 2000). When the Commission has submitted a proposal, the Council has to decide by unanimity if it wants to enforce changes. As under qualified-majority voting (QMV), it is often easier to accept the proposal by a majority vote than to alter it, the Commission is claimed to have considerable agenda-setting powers. "Put simply, the Commission enjoys agenda-setting power when the Council can adopt a Commission proposal by a qualified-majority vote but amend it only by unanimity" (Pollack 1997, 102; see Schmidt 2001,126; Tsebelis and Garrett 2000; Crombez 2000; Steunenberg 2000). Furthermore, the Commission has the right to withdraw its proposal if the member states do not accept its provisions (Spence 1995, 383), a fact that can also be used as a threat to members that are eager to reach a decision (Pollack 1997, 124). Therefore, it is argued, an astute and cunning Commission can draft proposals that are close to its own interests and simultaneously acceptable to a majority in the Council. This obviously demands correct information about member-state preferences.

In real life, the situation is more complex. Based on a number of case studies, Susanne Schmidt (2001, 129–31) argues that the Commission not infrequently resigns its formal powers by not defending its initial proposal. Instead, it takes an "approach of least resistance" and leaves the floor open for Presidency initiatives. Even when the Commission has theoretically had a good chance of pressing through its own proposal by standing firm and relying on coalitions with like-minded member states, it did not, Schmidt reports, object to Presidency compromise proposals, although these severely diluted its main objectives. An in-depth case study on processes leading up to the regulation on public access to EU documents (European Parliament and Council Regulation 1049/2001) confirms the results offered by Schmidt (Bjurulf and Elgström 2004). This study also demonstrates, however, that the Commission's proposal in fact functions as a single negotiating text (SNT), around which expectations converge. The tabled text becomes the "standard" and other actors have to argue for changes in relation to the Commission formulations (see Hayes-Renshaw and Wallace 1997, 187). This could in some cases be a decisive advantage. Similarly, Pollack (1997, 125) argues that the Commission may exert informal agenda-setting power by providing focal points for bargaining and by framing its proposals in an attractive way.

Our interviewees tend to emphasize the formal powers of the Commission, while at the same time admitting that in concrete cases the Commission is often "flexible." Many observers emphasize that it is up to the Commission to initiate changes to its text if the Council cannot enforce alterations by unanimity and they see this as a major power resource of the Commission. Furthermore, the Commission may enjoy considerable leverage over member states as a provider of funds and other resources. Member states (and not least the Presidency) are also dependent on the Commission to initiate legislative proposals that they dearly wish to see on the table and may therefore hesitate to go against the Commission in other fields. Therefore, Commission drafts are often accepted "if properly handled" (author interview), especially in technical and apolitical issue areas.

Resistance against Commission proposals ordinarily leads to negotiations between Council and Commission representatives. One basic trait of Council negotiations is *continuous consultations between Presidency and Commission*; "the Presidency has to cooperate with the Commission, as only the Commission itself can enact changes in its proposal"; moreover, "its main concern should be to have the Commission on board" (author interviews). In theory, the Commission needs only one ally in the Council (to be able to block proposed changes) but in reality it strives to "find a balance" and as a rule accepts most of the changes proposed by the Presidency. In the first pillar the Commission is thus often "modest and flexible" and highly consensus-oriented. It is "loathe to block decisions," as it ordinarily wants to reach a conclusion in the file at hand (author interviews). In most cases Garrett (1992, 552) suggests, the Commission is more eager than the member states to secure the passage of legislative acts, inducing it to bring forward new proposals that are closer to the preferences of Council majority. In many cases final texts are negotiated and drafted by the Presidency and the Commission together. In other cases, however, the Commission plays a much more withdrawn role and does not interfere with the efforts of the Presidency. It is in such cases that it "cedes its formal agenda-setting powers" and loses its initiative to the presidencies, according to Schmidt (2001, 135 and 131).

The Commission seems more prone to play a low-key role when files are politicized and when member-state interests are strong, for example, when the distributional consequences of a policy proposal are significant (Elgström and Jönsson 2000; Pollack 1997, 126). Conversely, the Commission is more apt to meet success when its proposals are perceived as apolitical, when it enjoys an advantage of information and expertise, and when it can exploit differences in member-state preferences (Pollack 1997, 123–26; Sandholz 1992). The likelihood of Commission concessions diminishes if there is a minority of member states that support the original Commission proposal, if the Commission can be accused (for example, by the European Parliament) of abandoning ideological principles, and if the legal base of a document is questioned. In such cases, the Commission can be extremely stubborn and refuse to withdraw its proposal. In the psychological game that ensues, there is the unspoken threat of a unanimous vote that would make the Commission lose face. If fighting for principles, the Commission may anyway choose to insist on its text, even if facing certain defeat by unanimity. This is especially likely if the Commission thinks that its standpoint will be backed by the European Court of Justice (ECJ).

The almost consensual view is that the Commission is today a less powerful actor in the Council than it was under the leadership of Jacques Delors (author interviews; Hayes-Renshaw and Wallace 1997, 147; Schout 1998, 2; Sherrington 2000). The winner is often claimed to be the Presidency. The Presidency's agenda-shaping powers consist of its ability to prioritize among dossiers, to increase the tempo in some files while holding back others (Tallberg 2001), but also of its position to offer "Presidency compromises." The Presidency is expected by other member states to try to come up with compromise proposals that reflect broad majorities and that are acceptable to all. Furthermore, the Commission is, as explained above, apt to agree to changes that mirror widely held member-state concerns. I will return to these issues in my discussion on mediation.

In this section, I have made three major claims about the impact of institutional arrangements on Council negotiations:

1. The formal monopoly of initiative and the institutional rule that amendments by member states can be decided only by unanimity gives the Commission strong formal negotiation powers.
2. In reality, these arrangements necessitate constant negotiations between the Presidency and the Commission; these are basically psychological games involving assessments of existing correlations of forces and considerations of credibility and resolve.
3. Quite often, the Commission resigns its power of initiative to the Presidency, which has a norm-based obligation to offer Presidency compromises.

The shadow of the vote

Bargaining dynamics differ in situations with or without the so-called shadow of the vote. Under unanimity all member states need to be on board, and search processes aim to find least-common-denominator solutions, that is, compromises that even the most reluctant member state can accept. The effect is likely to be gradual and cautious, not-so-radical change. The decision-making calculus of more ambitious members then consists of weighing the pros of having an agreement (that might improve the situation, although marginally) against the cons of it being a highly watered-down agreement (with the risk that this will lead to domestic criticism). Under unanimity one or a few members can block decisions—though whether this actually happens in reality seems to depend on who is the potential blocker: it is much easier for a large member state to unilaterally stop processes than it is for a smaller state. When vital national interests can credibly be argued to be at stake, however, small members too are ordinarily "allowed" to prevent decisions.

Majority voting is often considered beneficial to the effectiveness of the Council. The possibility that there may be a vote "makes constructive negotiations imperative" (author interview). The result is ordinarily broad compromises "which everyone can live with." Negotiations are therefore primarily of a problem-solving nature (Elgström and Jönsson 2000), aiming to find solutions that everyone can accept rather than constructing minimal winning coalitions (Kirchner 1992, 107; Metcalfe 1998, 418). If possible, votes are avoided. According to our interviewees minorities usually give in if they realize that they face a solid majority, most often without a vote. "There is no point in obstructing if you are sure you will be outvoted" (author interview). Exceptions exist, however, especially if it is felt to be domestically wise to be seen as struggling to the bitter end. The minority is also often offered small but visible face-saving concessions in the endgame of a negotiation in order to persuade its members to accept the compromise at hand.

The Presidency has to decide when the time is ripe for announcing that a majority exists. Thus, the Presidency at any given moment faces a twofold choice (see Iklé 1967, 59–75): Should it propose an agreement (with the implicit threat of a vote) or should it continue negotiations? The ideal is to offer a compromise that is certain to be accepted without a vote and that is as close to the Presidency's own preferences as possible. It does happen that a Presidency announces that it has a majority for its proposal when, in reality, it does not, hoping that the hesitant member states will still find it "minimally satisfactory" (author interview). In such cases the Presidency uses the informal powers of its office to press for a deal that is relatively beneficial to its own interests. The Presidency seeks to work on members of blocking minorities; as member states do not want to stand alone against the rest, "it is important for them to jump sides at the right moment" (author interview). This dynamic can be exploited by the Presidency to dissolve blocking coalitions. If the preferences of some country representations are unclear the Presidency has to decide "whether to flush out the silent blocker or to leave a likely abstainer undisturbed" (Hayes-Renshaw and Wallace 1997, 148). In general, the task of the skillful Presidency is to search for "yesable" compromises and to create situations "where it is impossible to say no" (author interviews).

Rather few decisions in the Council are taken by vote. Mattila and Lane (2001, 40–42) report that during the time period 1994 to 1998, the proportion of unanimous decisions was between 75 percent and 80 percent in all legislative decisions by the Council. Roll calls in which negative votes are given are quite rare, hovering between 12 percent and 19 percent (the difference being abstentions). Furthermore, a fairly similar pattern is found in policy areas that exclusively use QMV: the percentage of decisions in which negative votes were given was 28 percent in the internal market sector and 21 percent in agriculture. In the common commercial policy there are almost no votes. One reason for this preference for unanimity has already been given: minorities tend to concede well before a vote is called if they are sure to be outvoted. There is also a long-standing Council *norm* stressing consensus decision making (Westlake 1995, 110–11; Kirchner 1992, 107–9). The consensus norm implies that member states avoid riding roughshod over minorities and that it is better to reach a broad compromise than to force a majority decision. Group dynamics in the Council strengthen the tendency toward consensus decision making. In the words of one interviewee, "We are more pals than enemies." Consensus is thus "the working hypothesis" and taking a vote is seen as "a last resort" (author interview). Exceptions occur, but mostly when a situation is considered urgent (for example, when external events create a need for instant decisions) or when a deadline is looming. As described above, the consensus norm has an enormous impact on negotiation and mediation behavior. The goal is to construct acceptable texts rather than majority coalitions. The frequent recourse to package deals and linkage politics and the existence of crosscutting cleavages in the Council (see Hopmann 1996, 254–57) facilitate such efforts.

Still, coalition building is a vital part of Council negotiations. The emphasis is on process coalitions rather than on voting coalitions (although the latter also play an important role, especially in some issue areas). An actor will strive to demonstrate to its coplayers that it is not alone and can indeed form either a majority coalition behind its position or at least a blocking minority coalition that prevents a majority decision. It does this to reach a better bargaining position: if you can credibly show that you can block a decision and the majority is more eager than you are to have a decision, then you stand a good chance of extracting significant concessions. That is why presidencies try to unravel minority alliances, as shown earlier. At times, however, a Presidency may also attempt to forge a blocking minority itself—as happened in the case of the transparency regulation where the Swedish Presidency confronted a much more secrecy-oriented majority in the Council and had vital national interests to defend. The Swedish strategy was to form a strong minority alliance in the Council, at the same time taking advantage of the codecision procedure with its requirement of Parliamentary consent, to use the protransparency stance of the European Parliament as a lever to force the Commission majority to concede.

In this section, I have underlined four key effects of institutional mechanisms related to voting rules, norms, and institutional roles:

1. Negotiations in the Council are primarily of a problem-solving nature because of the constructive influence of the shadow of the vote.
2. In a vast majority of Council decision-making processes, the member states seek broad compromise agreements, because of small-group dynamics and the prevalence of a consensus norm.
3. The Presidency plays an influential institutional role in seeking to promote consensus, using a multifaceted toolbox of tactics and strategies.
4. Actors utilize process coalitions, trying to construct majorities or blocking minorities in order to increase their bargaining strength.

Mediation in the Council

The Commission and the Presidency as mediators

The mediator function in the Council is not formally regulated. On the other hand, it is a function that needs to be fulfilled: the strong consensus norm in combination with an equally strong wish, both from the Commission and the Council, to produce results and to "move things forward," ensures that there is a high demand for a compromise broker. There are two main contenders with a potential desire to fill this niche: the Commission and the Presidency.

While some observers stress the need for symbiotic cooperation between the two institutions (Spence 1995, 383; Metcalfe 1998, 418), others underline the importance of competition between them (Hayes-Renshaw and Wallace 1997, 147). A shared mediator role seems to be the ideal, attainable under certain circumstances (primarily, where there are similar preferences and a shared and equal desire for results), but in other cases not. Several interviewees portray the situation as one where the Presidency first seeks a compromise among the Council members and then negotiates with the Commission to induce it to accept changes in its proposal (see my previous discussion on the impact of the institutionally based need for Commission approval of any amendment to its text).

It is also possible to see the two actors as complementary in their mediation efforts. First, the Commission is more likely to act as a broker in the early stage of the decision-making process (author interviews). When preparing its proposal, the Commission is regularly approached by other actors who want to influence the draft. As the Commission officials want their proposal to be accepted and implemented, they are wise to listen to suggestions from member states and to include such elements in their text so as to ensure there will be a majority behind it. This anticipatory activity may in itself be perceived as a type of mediatory behavior, as *preventive mediation*. The Presidency is better suited to act as a compromise maker in the actual decision-making phase in Council negotiations (although the Commission is also inclined to aspire to a role at this stage) when its negotiators— with the often invaluable help of the Council Secretariat—are in control of the best information on member-state preferences. This could be labeled *facilitative mediation*.

Second, the Commission might be expected to be better placed for *long-term mediation* as it is a constant factor (together with the Council Secretariat) in Council negotiations (see Hayes-Renshaw and Wallace 1997, 189). The Commission is well placed to plan and mediate for decisions in the next few years to come; it commands an institutional memory and has an institutionalized responsibility to plan for the future of the Union. It may utilize linkages across time to achieve its goals. The Presidency is more of an *ad hoc mediator*, as its six-month term at the helm not only prevents the country holding the office from directly influencing processes beyond its mandate but also necessitates instant brokering to achieve results during the short time span at its disposal. The fact that every Presidency needs substantive results during its Presidency period in order to be considered a success creates an impetus for short-term, result-oriented mediation.

Both actors possess advantages and disadvantages as mediators. The Commission has an advantage as "the deviser and owner of the text tabled" (Hayes-Renshaw and Wallace 1997, 187). It has the sole right to modify its own proposal and may use this institutional arrangement to broker a compromise. Up to the mid-1960s, the Commission was seen as "detached" and as standing outside the bitter interstate conflicts, a position that encouraged the member states to use the "good offices" of the Commission (author interviews). However, the Commission's role as a mediator has weakened (author interviews; Kirchner and Tsagkari 1993, 19; Wallace 1985, 15). It has acquired vested interests and is increasingly perceived as a defender of its own ideals and texts, and is therefore today seen as less well placed to behave impartially (on the importance of impartiality, see below). Today the Commission is treated by the member states as "yet another member" with its own interests (author interviews). To this might be added that Commission proposals are at times rigid and difficult to unravel as they are themselves the result of internal compromises within the Commission itself. Inflexibility is not a positive asset for a potential mediator.

A pervasive and strong norm has developed that ascribes to the Presidency the role of a mediator and package broker. Other member states and Community institutions expect the Presidency to act in this way: "The ability to offer successful compromise has become the touchstone of a Presidency's effectiveness" (Nicoll 1998, 6); "A Presidency is, or ought to be, an honest broker, a cobbler of agreement and an architect of coalition" (Ludlow 1993, 249). To this may be added the equally decisive *effectiveness norm*, which stipulates "effectiveness"—in terms of accomplishing a large number of decisions—as a major criterion for Presidency success and which stimulates others to expect the Presidency to energetically try to conclude negotiations and achieve results. Both these informal norms vouch for active mediation efforts on the part of the Presidency

Presidencies are claimed to be more flexible than the Commission, partly because of the aforementioned norms and especially if the Presidency is held by a member state with few vested interests in the issue at hand. The latter point implies, according to several observers, that smaller member states are more effective than bigger ones in performing the mediator role (author interviews; Kirchner and Tsagkari 1993, 29; Wallace 1985, 16–17). As will be detailed in the next section, the highly institutionalized *impartiality norm*, which prescribes that the Presidency should be an evenhanded and disinterested compromise maker, is believed both to be deeply entrenched in the office and to enhance its effectiveness. Some analysts, however, explicitly question the possibility for any Presidency to be impartial and therefore tend to evaluate their chances of acting as successful mediators in a less-sanguine way (Schout 1998; see Elgström 2001). According to this view it is exceedingly problematic for actors with vested interests in a file to credibly change their role for six months and act as "neutral brokers"; not to mention how difficult it is for other actors to believe that they are sincerely impartial. Empirically, events during the Dutch Presidency of 1991 and the French Presidency of 2000 are often cited as examples of presidencies that have abused the mediator role.

Presidencies have a raft of instruments and tactical devices at their disposal. Among these, the confessionals (confidential and private discussions with individual member states who are supposed to reveal bottom lines and other secret information to the Presidency) are among the best known, but the toolkit also includes informal lunches, *tours de capitales*, indicative votes, appeals for solidarity and the imposition of time pressure (Westlake 1995, 113–120; Nicoll 1998). The "Presidency compromise" is the final, lethal weapon: when a supposedly impartial broker presents what is claimed to be the best possible compromise, it is extremely difficult for other member states to say no (author interviews; see Nicoll 1998; Wallace 1985, 16).

In this connection, three essential claims have been made with a bearing on institutional mechanisms:

1. Powerful informal norms exist that create a need for mediation in Council negotiations.
2. Competition exists between two institutional actors, the Commission and the Presidency, to fulfill the mediator role. Because of basic institutional characteristics, the Commission tends to work best as a preventive, long-term mediator, while the Presidency is more of a facilitative ad hoc mediator.
3. Impartiality is considered an essential element of mediation in the Council, as expressed by the strong impartiality norm. Today, the Presidency is better placed to act as an evenhanded broker than the Commission.

Impartiality—the essence of mediation?

According to conventional wisdom in mediation theory, impartiality is seen as a necessary feature of successful mediation (Carnevale and Arad 1996, 40–41; Young 1967, 309). A third party is ideally "not connected to either disputant, is not biased toward either side, has no investment in any outcome, and does not expect any special reward" (Wehr and Lederach 1996, 57). These traits are believed to increase the credibility of the mediator and the trust of the conflicting parties in the inherent fairness of its compromise proposals. Impartiality is also supposed to facilitate agreement by enhancing the mediator's chances of acquiring sensitive information from the parties, thereby improving its chances of offering well-balanced, realistic proposals (Carnevale and Arad 1996, 41; Kleiboer 1997, 29; Stenelo 1972, 33–35). Trust in the mediator is considered by many EU practitioners as an essential prerequisite for success (author interviews). Efforts to hear everyone's opinions, to give all a fair chance to speak, and not to isolate any delegation are tactics meant to build trust in the impartiality of the chair.

As mentioned above, the importance of impartiality is strongly supported in the EU. The Presidency Handbook of the Council Secretariat asserts that "the presidency must, by definition, be neutral and impartial." The impartiality norm is almost uncontested among practitioners as well as among academic writers. "A Presidency can only be an important player if it is seen as fair and evenhanded," is a typical quote from our interviews. The scholarly literature mirrors such views, with few exceptions. The Presidency is described as a "neutral arbitrator" (Wallace 1985, 16) or a "neutral broker" (Schout 1998, 3). Kirchner and Tsagkari (1993, 20) stress the Presidency's efforts to produce "objective compromises." The Commission's decline as a mediator is often associated with a perceived transition from detachment to active involvement. The success of Presidency confessionals depend on the extent to which the Presidency is perceived as impartial.

Some authors, however, argue that the impartiality norm in fact allows a rather large latitude for Presidency initiatives, and that it is not always strictly "neutral." Metcalfe, for example, notes that the most important thing for a mediator is to be seen as evenhanded during the negotiation process. Results that favor a majority position are often accepted if the mediator is seen to have been impartial and fair (Metcalfe 1998, 420–21). Likewise, Elgström (2001) makes a distinction between process and outcome partiality and argues that there are opportunities for a Presidency to push for its own interests as long as these are supported by a Council majority and as long as its process behavior, especially as regards procedural aspects, is considered unbiased.

The proposition that presidencies do, and indeed must, sometimes push the other actors is supported by our informants. Some voices from the interviews: "it is not possible to be totally neutral—then you would never achieve results"; "if the other member states trust the chair, it is possible to drive hard deals"; "it is the insistent and active presidencies that have the best track record, not the traditional diplomats." Active assertion of self-interests should, however, be avoided if it cannot be cloaked in the guise of European interests. If you openly pursue narrow national interests, other states punish you immediately. This is especially true when money or institutional questions are concerned (author interviews).

That presidencies are permitted to speak in favor of their own concerns—within the limits mentioned—is partly explained by the institutional fact that member states take turns as chairs. "We will all get the chance," as one observer put it. The knowledge that the time will eventually come when you yourself will have the chance of making an impact inclines you to let others have their "day in the sun."

From a comparative, empirical perspective it is clear that the degree of Presidency impartiality varies. At one extreme we have the "great-power presidency," exemplified by the French Presidency of 2000. Such presidencies clearly prioritize important national interests before impartiality concerns. On the other extreme we have the "small-state presidency," illustrated by Finland 1999. Finland regularly abandoned its national positions as soon as it discovered that there was a majority against the Finnish proposal. In the middle, we have the "pragmatic presidency," that takes the chances it gets to promote self-interests but avoids doing so openly: ". . .we try to be the honest broker, but without being masochistic," as a Portuguese representative put it.

Expectations that stress the mediator role compete with expectations emphasizing leadership. The leader is expected to have a vision and to move the integration process forward. The active leader promotes its vision by putting pressure on others—perhaps not always listening to advice from them. Assertive leadership is preferred to impartial mediation. The French Presidency of 2000 has been characterized in such terms. Other presidencies, for example, the Swedish Presidency of 2001, put more emphasis on achieving broad consensus. This may be time-consuming but it leaves more room for impartial mediation efforts.

In this final part of the section, I have proposed that:

1. Although the impartiality norm is predominant, there is still room for pursuing self-interests within certain limits, especially if these can be framed as also being "European" interests.
2. Empirically member states have varied in the extent to which they a) prioritize impartiality or national interests, and b) prioritize a leadership or a mediator role.

Conclusion: The Importance of Institutionalized Negotiation and Mediation Mechanisms for European Integration

In this chapter, several outstanding traits of Council negotiations have been highlighted:

- The potentially important role of the Commission as agenda setter;
- The need for ongoing negotiations between Presidency and Commission;
- The prominence of a problem-solving mode of negotiations and of a search for consensus solutions;
- The existence of two mediators: the Commission as a preventive, long-term mediator, the Presidency as a facilitative ad hoc compromise broker; and
- The constant balancing, not least for the Presidency, between protecting self-interest and playing mediator or leadership roles.

I have explained these characteristics with reference to institutional arrangements; both formal rules and informal norms. I have paid particular attention to rules on agenda setting and on how to enact changes in proposed texts, to voting rules and procedures, and to the norms surrounding Council negotiation and mediation.

It remains only to discuss briefly what impact these characteristic features may have on EU policy making and on the European integration process. The most noteworthy effect is a tendency for the Council to produce ever more decisions, to "move things forward." The agenda-setting role given to the Commission, with its inherent interest in furthering deepened integration, is one contributing factor; the norms emphasizing "effectiveness" and "achieving results" are another. Both the Commission and the Presidency feel a strong pressure to be perceived as successful, and finalizing files under negotiation is considered one important element of reaching this goal. We can therefore expect a continuous stream of new decisions, presumably pushing the integration process forward.

On the other hand, the need for compromise—among member states and between Council and Commission—which is an integral part of the system, tends to result in solutions that are rather conservative. Fritz Scharpf's discussion on the "joint-decision trap" (Scharpf 1998) still seems relevant despite the change to an increased use of QMV. In a system where consensus is encouraged by rules and norms, dramatic reforms are not to be expected.

Enlargement will probably lead to a more frequent actual use of majority voting, and this could result in less concern for minorities and thus facilitate effective negotiations. Still, more members, and members with a wider variety of cultural backgrounds, will also complicate decision making. Coalition building will prove essential but may produce blocking minorities as well as clear majorities. The need for a package broker and a finder of compromise formulations will probably increase. Whether this role will be occupied by the Presidency or the Commission remains to be seen: much depends upon the assertiveness of coming Commissions, but also on the results of the constitution-changing processes that are underway. Institutional developments will have a substantial impact on future Council negotiations.

Chapter 8

Member States Operating in the EU Council of Ministers: Inside Impressions[1]

Leendert Jan Bal

The complexity of the European Union (EU) is often seen as one of its stumbling blocks. The many variations in the decision-making rules, the lengthiness of the procedures, the variety of players and institutions—all these individual aspects constantly attract adverse attention. Put them all together within a framework, however, and it is no wonder that "lobbying Brussels" has become such a popular EU pastime.

The number of lobbyists working in Brussels and their public-affairs activities is impressive. However, the actual negotiation process between member states—which is only a part of what influences decision making in the EU institutions—remains hidden in the shadows. Within the Council of Ministers as an institution, negotiations take place at three levels: the working group, the Committee of Permanent Representatives (COREPER), and the Council (ministerial meetings). Of these three, most people have heard of the European Council summits and perhaps of COREPER, the standing committee of ambassadors; but the overall image of the Council is quite negative; indeed, it is sometimes described in newspapers such as the Financial Times as the most powerful and most uncontrolled group of negotiators in the European Union. This stereotype almost makes the Council sound like an "organized crime" syndicate, but this is not very helpful in elucidating the multilateral negotiation characteristics of the European Union. This chapter offers a modest stepping stone, based on sector experience, to a better insight into the daily negotiation processes among member states within the Justus Lipsius building in Brussels.

Some "Mechanics" of the Negotiation Process among Member States

As a practitioner I would like to present some observations that are difficult to find in academic studies, but, first of all, I must introduce a disclaimer. Within the Council, there are numerous small variations in working methods and slightly differing traditions. For example, in some working groups experts from the capital are in charge; in other working groups the representatives in Brussels are normally the spokespersons; and in other cases there is a mixture of the two. The positions of member states may also differ. A member state may be strong within one Council grouping and weak within another. These variations may lead to somewhat different observations by others in different parts of the Council.

Before going into the negotiation approaches of member states, some general observations are needed to define the negotiating arena. My observations, as a practitioner, may differ from those of other colleagues and/or put the "mechanics" of EU negotiations into a fresh perspective. I hope that this may encourage other practitioners also to record their experiences. The observations I make have to be seen in a framework of the Council dealing with average *classic* first-pillar European Commission proposals. To partly counterbalance the academic opinions expressed in this book, I would like to focus on: perception of time; the qualified-majority voting system in practice; packages and linkages; and fixed and flexible coalitions. Other elements, such as an extended description of the role of the Presidency, are dealt with in other chapters of this book.

Decision making in the Council: "slow" and "fast" working

Unlike in the European Parliament, where there is a fixed time frame for preparing a dossier that always ends with a final plenary vote, in the Council there is no time limit imposed for formulating a first opinion; after a common position is agreed in the Council, however, the codecision procedure does prescribe a fixed timetable for negotiations between the Council and the Parliament.

Thus, there is no time limit to the duration of the first deliberations in the Council. Indeed, when a topic is very controversial or when—because of a stalemate— no qualified majority can be found, it may take some time. In such a case a topic may be repeatedly discussed in a working group, but it can also go up and down through the other levels (working groups, COREPER, and Council of Ministers). This may sometimes take years, and dossiers have even been known to end up on a shelf because no political solution could be found among two or more opposing camps.

Discussions in the Council are also able to proceed very quickly. This may happen when there is no controversy at all—for example, when a topic is a straightforward, simple technical proposal—or where there is enormous political pressure. Conclusions of the European Council are used to put pressure on ongoing negotiations. The European Commission and/or the Presidency insert language into these conclusions to urge Council groupings to take a decision within a certain period of time. However, ministers of a Council formation are not always impressed by these deadlines. Frequently, more time is needed for objective reasons. *Time* as such is not a burden for the EU negotiation process. *Time* is an indispensable instrument, allowing the capitals to get used to certain topics being dealt with at the European level or for finding a proper political solution that will enjoy sufficient support among member states. Within the Council there are more complaints about speed than about lack of progress. In particular, the final rush toward a decisive Council meeting may cause problems. In only a few days the working group and COREPER may meet several times to clear up the last outstanding issues. Documents with the latest compromise proposals may be handed out by the Presidency or by delegations only hours before a meeting or even during meetings. It is a major challenge for national coordination processes to keep up with the latest developments and to deliver a coordinated national point of view on time. Capitals may lose track of events and have to depend fully on their negotiators in Brussels.[2] Member states who have given their negotiators too little flexibility will lose out considerably in this phase of the negotiations. If a state's Brussels-based representatives are not able to participate in formulating compromises (because their mandate does not allow it) and if, therefore, they can enter only a scrutiny reservation, the opportunity of being heard is lost and the only option left is to accept the outcome.

A ghost called "qualified-majority voting"

If an observer were to attend Council meetings he or she would notice next to no evidence of qualified-majority voting. It is very unusual for presidencies to ask delegations to vote. The official explanation is that presidencies will seek consensus around the table and will thus avoid isolating colleagues. This expression of *noblesse oblige* is, of course, very welcome but is only part of the explanation. Qualified-majority voting is like the sword of Damocles hanging above the negotiation table. It is in the mind of everyone. The Presidency, Commission, and delegations assess the state of negotiation—almost permanently and automatically—in terms of whether there is a qualified majority or a blocking minority. Delegations try to prevent themselves being outvoted in the open; thus, during the negotiation process, delegations will look for coalitions, and will offer compromises to make a gain when there is a threat of being outvoted. If nothing has worked and all fallback positions have failed, delegations often prepare unilateral statements to explain to the people at home what went wrong or to provide their own interpretation of the outcome of negotiations. One could say that working in a world of qualified-majority voting helps to stimulate convergence. Delegations, as shown by their behavior during negotiations, anticipate a possible vote. There are, in general, only two reasons for an official vote (against or abstention) in the Council of Ministers. Most of the time a vote will take place when a political solution acceptable to all delegations has not been found and delegations voting against were not able to convince others that crucial national interests were at stake and had to be taken into account (negotiation failure or lack of leverage). Sometimes an official vote against is needed for domestic political purposes. The latter occurs when, for example, member states are satisfied with the final result but acknowledging it as such in public could have repercussions at home. An example in the field of transport is the position of Belgium, France, and Luxembourg concerning the second railway package; although these member states helped to build an acceptable compromise within the Council they nevertheless voted against it. All in all, voting is never *l'art pour l'art* but has to have a particular political reason, as mentioned above. A lack of official voting, however, does not mean at all that the qualified-majority system is absent, nor does it mean that finding consensus is the general rule.

Packages and linkages

A stubborn myth has to be dismantled: many people are convinced that the European Union can take decisions only on proposals that are part of a larger package deal that extends beyond individual dossiers. The author is not aware of many trade-offs between different policy fields within the European Union at the Council of Ministers level. However, such a situation may sometimes be true of the broad political guidelines of the European Council which command a great deal of attention in the media. Within formations of the Council there are—if one wishes to use the word "package"—two kinds of packages. All outstanding questions regarding a legislative proposal are connected when a final deal is being made; thus, there has to be a balance in the final outcome. Here, we are just talking about a single dossier. Second, if Commission proposals are linked because of their content, the Council may want to treat them as a package. This means that a decision has to be taken regarding all the proposals in the "package" at the same time. These proposals will be dealt with in parallel. Examples in the area of transport are the first and second railway packages, maritime safety packages "Erika I" and "Erika II," and the Single European Sky proposals.

To complete the picture, political trade-offs and linkages between member states do occasionally play a role when controversial issues are being discussed; these are constructed "in the corridors." Although it is hard to provide scientific evidence, (large) member states sometimes make package deals on a bilateral basis that may involve different policy fields and/or different issues (deals regarding seats, appointments, and other matters). Deals of a purely political magnitude will override specific "technical" interests. Such packages, which are exceptional, are concluded at the highest political level. Examples are the famous Franco–German cooperation, which is quite intense, and gaining importance, and the British–Spanish deals as a consequence of political support for Iraq or as part of a "cease-fire" deal regarding Gibraltar. These linkages may change the outcome of the multilateral negotiation process because a large member state changing position alters an existing majority or minority. An unwritten rule should also be mentioned here: large member states will help each other not to be outvoted by small member states. In a classical multilateral setting it is very difficult to anticipate or counterbalance such political—often last-minute—package deals.

Flexible and fixed coalitions

Because of qualified-majority voting, the building of coalitions is important. There is, in practice, a pattern of flexible and fixed coalitions. As a rule one could say that the factual interests of a member state are decisive for its choice of coalition. During negotiations coalitions can vary constantly. Dealing with a legislative proposal, every article, part of a text, or even sentence, brings about different *coincidental* coalitions. There are, therefore, all sorts of configurations of member states supporting and opposing each other. This does not mean at all that all member states are part of one coalition or another. Normally two (coincidental) coalitions appear at each end of the spectrum. (The word "coincidental" is used because there has been no special effort or action taken to build the coalition.) In the middle there is a large group of indifferent member states. Although their indifference may have various reasons, it is often due to lacking a specific interest in the issue at stake (or the power to change the dominant opinion).

Fixed *underlying* coalitions are well known. They appear when horizontal issues are being discussed. Regarding financial issues, there is a North–South divide and therefore two coalitions. Regarding institutional matters there may be a group of member states in favor of a Community approach and another group in favor of an intergovernmental approach. There is a group safeguarding the interests of small member states versus a group safeguarding the interests of large member states. There are also member states that are ambitious in the field of environmental standards and member states that are not. Of course, many other issues can be added to this list of classical dividing lines or classical coalitions between member states.

When political important issues are at stake "corridors" and bilateral contacts will be (frequently) used to check whether coalition partners are still of the same opinion and whether a blocking minority or qualified majority still exists. Uncertainty prevails. Opponents, but in particular the Commission and the Presidency, will continue to look for the weakest link. The European Commission is regularly involved in this process as it wishes to avoid a blocking minority against its own proposals. The Presidency wants to have as many results as possible during its term in office. Sometimes, making a concession to one of the member states of a blocking minority will be enough to split the opposition. In general, therefore, only one member state from a blocking coalition will gain from this in terms of getting something in return for its *nuisance value.* Timing, tactics, and concessions are essential ingredients for winning in this situation. Others will lose and may only vote against. In this context it should be mentioned that a combination of power and muddling through normally wins out over adherence to principles. In practice, it is very difficult to stop Commission proposals being adopted even by considerably watering them down. A total rejection is not really feasible. Sometimes delegations argue that topics fall under the subsidiarity principle (e.g., that a topic can be better dealt with at a national or even regional level). This is conceived as saying "no." Normally this argument does not work if there is no blocking minority to back it up. Thus, it is crucial to know when to sacrifice your own position and to go for a second-best option. Concessions and compromises will lead to—by definition—a suboptimal average of all interests. The main challenge is to get the most you can out of it.

The "Software" of Negotiations

Interrelated factors. PIP: People, Interests, and Power

The most difficult part of analyzing negotiations within the Council of Ministers is describing what is happening without repeating the procedural steps of the decision-making process. Some mechanisms are already described in the first part of this chapter, such as the way the qualified-majority voting system works in practice. In reality the outcome of multilateral negotiations in the Council is a result of an interaction of people, interests of member states, and sometimes individuals, and the (institutional) power of all players (including the Commission and the Council Secretariat).

The European Union, and the Council of Ministers in particular, may look like an overregulated setting for negotiations. A dark forest of procedures hides the importance of the human factor. Within the Council of Ministers there are different social circuits. Every working group, COREPER, and even the ministerial meetings has its own social dynamics. People representing their member states in a working group or in COREPER actually meet more than once a week, every week. Sometimes during peaks (for example when a ministerial meeting is approaching) they may meet almost every day. At working-group level, participants are a mixture of experts from the capitals and Brussels-based representatives from a permanent representation. At every level there is a "pecking order" that influences the outcome of the negotiation process. This fact, unsurprisingly, is sometimes part of negotiation tactics. A member state may well focus on the level where it is being best represented to secure its national interests and to make the deal there.

The personal capacity of negotiators can be of crucial importance. One could very cautiously argue that, in general, the bigger the member state and/or the bigger the interests involved, the better the negotiators will be. In all honesty, this is almost impossible to prove. There are examples to support this thesis but there are also some that will prove the contrary. The quality of the negotiators depends on various factors, such as the quality of the civil service of a particular member state, the policy regarding sending people to work abroad (providing a further career perspective, helping a working partner to find a job), and many more. Interests are an element as well. In an average working group Greece and Cyprus may be modest participants, but in the working group on shipping, where there are huge national interests at stake, they are outspoken and play an active role in negotiations. Individuals' personal qualities may also change the balance of power. For example, in the transport working groups, the influence of Portugal far exceeded what one would have expected it to be in EU negotiations because it included a Portuguese national who had worked in Brussels for twelve years and whose character made him very influential. Too often it is the structures of EU negotiations that are emphasized in studies, which strengthens the tendency to underestimate the influence of individuals and social processes on their outcome.

Negotiation "Styles" of Member States

This will be probably the most perilous part of this chapter. A description of negotiation styles or approaches can only really be indicative when it is based on experience within a certain period of time and within a limited context. This aspect cannot, however, be neglected as so many people ask for information on the performance of individual member states within the European Union.

France seems to be the best member state of the European Union as far as negotiation is concerned. Power is often the convincing argument in Brussels, and France really knows how to use it. The general features of France are well known: the *Ecole Nationale d'Administration* (ENA) system delivers skilled and motivated civil servants, while the hierarchical setup of the administration strengthens coordination ability and enables France to use different levels to communicate its position. What is less known, but very interesting, is the freedom of maneuver the French negotiators have in Brussels. Strong coordination with "up-front" flexibility is a very strong combination. Negotiators can act: they are able to propose alternatives during negotiations and normally they are backed up by their capital. Their assessment of the situation will be taken into account in the strategy indicated by Paris. France will not settle for 80 percent or 90 percent of its demands. If something is important France will try to get all the concessions approved by the other member states. The strong image of France, and the way its political leaders can be mobilized to support demands made during negotiations as well as to exert political pressure, strengthens its position even further: the self-fulfilling prophecy continues. In difficult situations the Paris–Berlin axis is used to overrule German experts, where needed. This is a strong asset in terms of changing the balance of power to its own advantage. Delegations are even hesitant to resist French demands openly.

In a few cases where France is not able to conclude negotiations in a satisfactory manner, it uses a clever policy of withdrawal and, in these situations, is able to avoid a loss of face. It will delay negotiations in order to surrender on its own terms and to be able as much as possible to adapt on the national level to the new unwanted outcome. A good illustration of this process are dossiers concerning the liberalization of markets: "surrendering" will take place after domestic politics have become used to the outcome of negotiations and French industry has been able to prepare itself for new competition. Unlike any other member state, France is able to use the European Union as an instrument that supports and is interlinked with domestic politics. For example, it is able to export social problems to the EU level. National concessions to the unions that may undermine the level playing field of French companies are neutralized by upgrading "social standards" to the EU level, thereby diminishing the industrial lead of other member states.

The United Kingdom is also at the forefront of EU negotiations. Although there is difference between "Eurospeak–English" and "English–English" it is an advantage to be able to conduct negotiations in your own language. The United Kingdom is a large member state and in general able to produce good negotiators. Like France it has a large administration able to provide decent technical input for negotiations. British negotiators are given enough flexibility to get the best result from negotiations. Sometimes because of an "anticontinental mood" the UK proclaims subsidiarity and a desire to avoid Community legislation. Unfortunately—

as already explained—in Brussels, high principles are seldom part of the winners' strategy.

Germany undermines the thesis—which is almost true—that the bigger a member state is, the better it performs. For this author, the—in relative terms—suboptimal performance of Germany is one of the biggest surprises of Brussels. Germany pays one quarter of the Community budget and has many interests at stake. However, a cumbersome coordination system undermines the operational abilities of the German administration. The German Permanent Representation does not receive a sufficient mandate from its capital to allow it to operate as efficiently as it could. Experts are too dominant in the instructions (*expertenkultur*). Therefore, the political dimension of the operation is often neglected. In addition, coordination with the federal states take too much time, which make it impossible to follow quick rounds of negotiations in the final stage of decision making. Germany's important position in the European Council is only occasionally reflected in lower settings of the Council. When Germany operates "top down" it can be very powerful, but normally not the other way around. Unfortunately for Germany, there is no indication that a rethink of its own system of coordination is coming. Of course, Germany is still one of the biggest member states and therefore it is a power that "matters"; it could, however, gain much more from the EU negotiation process.

It is not easy to describe Italy in this context. The quality of its people in Brussels and in the capital vary from poor to excellent. Although it appears that working as a civil servant does not have as high a standing in Italy as working in industry, there are nevertheless some excellent Italian negotiators. The evolving performance of Italy can be seen as proof that negotiation approaches are slowly converging in the European Union. The argument of social and economic cohesion in the European Union and support for peripheral regions is still heard (for example, from Greece), but it is less dominant than in the past. Northwest Europe believes in a market approach, while southern Europe often believes that government has a large responsibility for organizing society. Here as well, a less clear-cut picture emerges than a decade ago. If one looks at the liberalization in public transport in Italy and Spain (it is not generally well known that they have advanced systems with concessions and competition), a simple North–South divergence no longer exists. There are, however, underlying differences in culture and administration. In southern Europe a *political* (top-down) approach prevails, while in northern Europe, there is a *policy* (bottom-up) approach. I would like for a moment to elaborate on this phenomenon. Although the French language is losing ground in the EU institutions (this process will be strengthened after enlargement), the way of doing business is still based on the French system. This dates back to the setting up of the EU institutions in the late 1950s and early 1960s, which means that in the EU institutions, politics, and power are more important than policy and implementation. Southern European administrations have greater familiarity with this system than administrations from northern Europe. Nevertheless, sharp differences between member states that are geographically far apart are disappearing. The process of making legislation jointly is slowly creating common attitudes by introducing or implementing approaches in national law that originate elsewhere in the European Union. Because of this matrix of differences and convergence, the European Union is more of a patchwork, which leads to a greater number of different coalitions in EU multilateral negotiations.

In general Spain's performance in the negotiation process is above average without being overexposed, and it usually has skillful experts and negotiators operating in Brussels. When Spain has a strong political desire to get things done in its own way, it is extremely difficult to say "no" to it. It was, for example, rather impressive how Spain—in conjunction with a Spanish Commissioner—was able to dictate conclusions to the Transport Council—setting a (legislative) road map for EU martitime-safety actions—in the aftermath of the disaster with the oil tanker *Prestige* off the coast of Galicia. It refused to accept any watering down of its proposed measures. Almost all member states were unwilling to hinder any of the Spanish intentions because they were afraid of attracting media blame for being "environmentally unfriendly" and not showing enough solidarity with victims in Spain. In this particular case Spain also utilized the European Council very well as a political instrument to put pressure on member states and the Commission. Both Spain and Portugal are willing to use "power" in order to emphasize their positions. Portugal has relatively strong personalities working in Brussels backed up by a rather weak administration. An excellent knowledge of the relevant procedures helps them to use the interpretation of the "rules of the game" to support their position in negotiations. Politically speaking Portugal does not have a tradition of outspoken politicians to give their blessing to the position taken by its representatives in Brussels and, of course, this does not help in creating a credible and strong position.

As a general remark I must mention that many of the smaller member states do not have large administrations, which has several implications. With small administrations it is not always easy to provide detailed input for negotiating legislative proposals. The absence of instructions makes it very difficult to participate actively in meetings. How such member states behave on a day-to-day basis will depend, case by case, on the availability of experts and expertise. Moreover, it is not easy for such member states to find skilled negotiators within their small administrations to represent them in Brussels. Some of these member states focus in practice on a limited number of topics, depending again on their own concrete national interests at stake. These member states may be called "single-issue states."

Greece is a modest participant in negotiations. As already explained this is not so much the case when it comes to shipping. It is not always easy for the Greek administration to follow negotiations and to give instructions. Unfortunately, hierarchy is strong in the Greek administration, and this does not allow for a great deal of flexibility for the negotiators in Brussels. The Brussels-based negotiators generally have to operate on their own. The small administrations of Greece, Luxembourg, and Portugal are not able, for various reasons, to send experts to the working groups on a regular basis.

The Scandinavian member states are also quite modest within the negotiation process. They are not very outspoken and not very demanding. Although in some of these states the general feeling of society is euroskeptic, this is not overly reflected in Brussels. Denmark, for example, until two years ago favored international standards in maritime affairs above a European approach, but with their Presidency (second half of 2002) this changed completely, and the political focus became more European. Sweden has some horizontal "evergreens" that are presented at every suitable occasion. For instance, it always makes a plea for public access to documents: openness and transparency are national values that are exported to Brussels. In general the Scandinavians also have a proenvironment approach. Finland is in favor of international maritime standards as it is confronted with a great deal of transit traffic from the Russian Federation that cannot be bound by EU legislation. The Finnish "hobbyhorse" is to promote support for icebreakers wherever they can; and in several cases the Finns have asked for understanding for their remote location in Europe, a kind of "underdog argument." Scandinavian member states also raise these typically national issues at a political level in the EU.

Ireland and Luxembourg are two member states that monitor negotiations and only become active when their own direct interests are being discussed. Luxembourg has a very small administration and is not able to attend all meetings in Brussels. It has developed a "pick-and-choose" approach. In general representatives of Luxembourg will attend the working group only when "interesting dossiers" are on the agenda. (This does not apply to COREPER where all member states are represented all the time.) In not trying to pursue every issue and intervening only where necessary, Luxembourg has chosen a successful model, albeit with constraints. When national interests are threatened Luxembourg has a very firm position that it will not allow to be watered down because it is a small member state. Ireland (always present) as a traditional net receiver naturally has a positive reaction to Commission proposals. Strengthening the position of the Commission or the Community at large is conceived as an Irish interest. Ireland is always present to underline territorial cohesion as a key to more Community funding and to explain the special needs and characteristics of an island member state, and how this should be reflected in Community legislation.

Belgium benefits a great deal from the presence of the European institutions in Brussels. Belgium has a traditional pro-European approach. The effectiveness of the Belgian delegation in negotiations is often watered down by the complex political structure of its nation. On the one hand it is sometimes difficult to keep a consistent line in negotiations because of its weak federalist administration and large, strong cabinets of ministers, and on the other hand there are many variations in coordination between federal and regional bodies. Almost every issue has a political connotation and has to be judged in light of the balancing act between different regions and political factions.

Austria is another example of a "single-issue state." The position of the transport sector in Austria is weak, and economically speaking transportation is not an important sector. Every element of the Austrian position is related to the problem of transit traffic through Austria. The federal government is, by definition, under criticism from the powerful regions. The entire government is (therefore) involved in backing Austrian interests in this dossier. Austria tries to survive by using power play and harsh negotiation tactics, attacking everyone who stands in its way. This approach is only partly successful; it does not create friends in the long-term perspective. As a side issue, Austria strongly supports all environmental measures for transport and wants to have the label of "sensitive region" bestowed on itself so that is has more room for maneuver in terms of securing measures against transit traffic.

Regarding the Netherlands it is difficult for this author, being Dutch, to sketch an objective self-portrait. The Netherlands has a strong transport and logistics sector. Thus transport is a relatively important field, in which the Netherlands is quite active. Good preparations and a flexible mandate for negotiators in Brussels make it possible to put Dutch interests across reasonably well, but this cannot be taken for granted in the long term. The serious budget cuts for ministries under the current government endanger the availability of good expertise. This element, in combination with an enlarged European Union (fewer votes in the Council, fewer representatives in the EP and doubts as to whether the Netherlands will have a [senior] commissioner), will make it very difficult to maintain the same level of influence in the Brussels decision-making process after enlargement.

One of the most important players in the Council is not a member state, but the European Commission. The right of initiative of the Commission has many implications. In general, the Commission has a powerful role in negotiations. As author of the legislative proposals it is able to give a firm direction to discussions in the Council. The Commission is always present during negotiations (in the working groups, at COREPER, and at the Council of Ministers). It has a central role in explaining its proposals. It evaluates the modifications proposed by delegations and—something that may come as a surprise to the reader—it sometimes operates as a ghost writer of Presidency compromise proposals. The extent to which the

Commission is able to be a ghostwriter depends of course on what Presidency is in office. "Nationalistic presidencies" have been very reluctant to allow this, but refusal is exceptional. If the Council wishes to change elements of the Commission's proposal and the Commission does not like this, the member states must be unanimous. This can be achieved in only clear-cut cases where member states all have similar interests. The Presidency normally gives the Commission the opportunity to react to all proposals put forward by member states during the negotiations. If the first reaction of the Commission is negative, it is not very easy for delegations to pursue modifications.

The remarks about the Commission are without prejudice to the vital role of the Council Secretariat. Keeping a record of the state of negotiations by producing an "outcome of proceedings," the legislative texts annotated with delegations' footnotes and containing new compromise proposals on behalf of the Presidency, is not the only task of the Council Secretariat. It is also the institutional memory of the Council that supports the Presidency in so many ways. The Secretariat prepares speaking notes for COREPER and the Council (and even for speeches in the European Parliament [EP]); it also has contacts with the European Parliament regarding codecision dossiers. By preparing speaking notes and writing compromise proposals the Secretariat helps to outline Council compromise packages and may suggest decisive elements for solutions. The extent to which the Council Secretariat is able to play a strong mediating role depends on various factors, such as the strength of the Presidency and the Commission (and the quality of the people working at the Secretariat).

At this stage it is impossible to give an impression of the accession states that became full members of the European Union on 1 May 2004. As observers they were concerned with organizing themselves. In the months preceding full membership their missions in Brussels were being strengthened, and working arrangements with capitals were being established and tested. Where negotiations touched upon their interests they naturally intervened, but such occasions were infrequent. In a couple of years, this chapter will need to be extended to include the operational characteristics of the newcomers.

Council Performance as Colegislator

At the end of the negotiation process, it is up to the Presidency to make the final deal with the European Parliament. The influence of individual member states is rather limited at this stage and may cause frustration. Even after a couple of years the codecision procedure is still a challenge to the Council. After the Council has taken a political decision, it has to agree first-pillar legislation with the European Parliament. Ground for negotiations is explored in informal and formal trilogues (meetings between the Presidency, EP rapporteurs, and the Commission), followed by an official conciliation meeting or meetings. Both institutions will have to find a common solution within fixed deadlines (six plus two weeks) and both institutions have a right to reject the final outcome. In this process the member states are fully dependent on the Presidency. The Presidency, supported by the Council Secretariat, represents the Council. Individual member states no longer sit at the table as part of the negotiation process. They have to rely on the Presidency and have to wait to see what will come out of its consultations.

In the case of controversial dossiers, finding a solution in the Council has been difficult, and member states have had to go to the last fallback position in order to be able to reach an agreement. Such a political agreement or common position may be a very fragile and sensitive compromise. This internal process within the Council can be so intense and difficult that member states are unable to countenance further negotiations with European Parliament. They are not capable of building additional room for concessions into the next stage of negotiations. Therefore, member states normally wish to stick to the common position. Although the Parliament may explain this as an unwillingness to compromise on the part of the Council, it is in fact caused by the difficult process of aligning the opposing views of member states.

When the Presidency is going to represent the member states, there is a general feeling of concern and even distrust. During COREPER meetings the member states give a mandate to the Presidency (the chair of COREPER is the head of delegation; it is only at official conciliation meetings that the minister comes and leads negotiations). COREPER is also used for debriefing after talks with the Parliament and for further adaptations of the mandate. During this stage of the negotiation process, member states are fully dependent on the Presidency. They want to know where it wants to give in and where it wishes to stand firm. The choice made by the Presidency may harm some member states more than others. Concessions may be sought in the wrong domain of the dossier. Of course this situation does not occur when the views of member states are more similar.

It is very difficult for individual member states to intervene in this process. For example, during the negotiations with the EP about the "Erika" package on maritime safety, the Council and the Parliament discussed two directives; one on port state control (PSC) and one on classification societies. The Netherlands, as one of the member states in the Council, was willing to compromise on the classification societies and to stay firm on the PSC directive. At that time, however, the French Presidency, together with some other member states, had opposing interests and constructed a deal containing a compromise on PSC while maintaining the Council's position on the classification societies. In such a situation a member state may try to influence (one or more of the fifteen) MEPs who are part of the conciliation delegation. (However, in this case, the Netherlands was not successful.) This is not an easy route to follow, but occasionally a member states can achieve "small corrections" via the European Parliament.

The role of (individual) member states is becoming smaller in cases where the codecision procedure does apply. More and more, the Presidency, together with the European Parliament and with support of the Commission, is looking for compromises during the first or second reading. By so doing they can avoid the cumbersome conciliation procedure. The number of formal and informal trilogues is growing rapidly. There are two sides of this coin as far as the Presidency is concerned. The Presidency has a stronger position in determining the outcome of negotiations, but at the same time these meetings and the preparations for them are a growing burden on it. A clear sign of this development is the growing number of points every week on the COREPER agenda regarding the preparation and debriefing of trilogues. This tendency undermines the formal involvement of member states. A reserved seat at the table of the Council is not enough. When vital interests are at stake, member states have to put additional energy into influencing the Presidency, the Commission, and the Parliament in the corridors.

Conclusion

It will continue to be a challenge to cope successfully with decision making within the European Union. A slow process of convergence against a background of structural differences among EU member states, will be put to the test now that the European Union has been enlarged from fifteen to twenty-five member states. A situation will emerge with even more players and a broader range of national interests and opinions, and thus a fair risk of being outvoted. At the same time, federalists may be pessimistic about the supranational process of European integration; the Commission and the European Parliament have gained considerably with the codecision procedure. As already explained, member states are still struggling with preparing conciliations. Thus there are intergovernmental and Community developments proceeding at the same time, changing the scope of operation of individual member states.

To preserve or gain influence as a single member state in EU negotiations will become more difficult. Bigger member states are in general better equipped for this task than smaller member states. They have more power and more means at their disposal. (In addition, the bigger states also try to compensate for their relatively weaker position in an enlarged Union with more smaller states by boosting the importance of European Councils and by organizing more meetings among themselves.) Smaller member states tend to focus on the most important issues for them, operating as "single-issue states," and there is no clear-cut recipe for improving their position. (To date, attempts to organize themselves have not been very successful.) This picture becomes more complicated when the existence of complex federal structures is taken into account. Such structures do undermine the effectiveness of member states (whether large or small) in EU negotiations.

Within the context of regulated negotiations, I would like to stress the growing importance of the negotiator (as an individual). I have tried to emphasize that member states that allow their negotiators to be active participants in quickly evolving negotiations with a flexible enough mandate do have an added value in comparison with member states that have a more rigid structure. The speed and the complexity of negotiations demand a flexible approach. Moreover, frequent, intense meetings create a social dimension to negotiations, from which states can draw benefit. In a growing European Union, where there are a greater number of interests at stake and where the outcome of negotiations is becoming less predictable, investing in EU negotiation capabilities should be at the forefront of member states' concerns.

Notes

1. These impressions are based on experiences from 1996 to 2004 with negotiations in the first pillar, in particular within Council working groups on shipping, aviation, inland transport, intermodal and horizontal questions, COREPER I, and the Transport Council. All opinions expressed are solely those of the author and do not represent official positions of the government of the Netherlands or the European Maritime Safety Agency.
2. A few meetings are held in Luxembourg. The EU Council of Ministers meets in Luxembourg in April, June, and October, all other months in Brussels. All meetings of the working group and COREPER take place in Brussels.

Chapter 9

The European Council under Construction: EU Top-Level Decision Making at the Beginning of a New Century[1]

Peter van Grinsven

Introduction

"We cannot go on working like this." These words of the British Prime Minister, Tony Blair, at the end of a chaotic European Council meeting in Nice in December 2000, say it all. This European Council summit ended late at night on the third day instead of early in the evening on the second day as planned. The European leaders had struggled on the so-called Amsterdam leftovers, the necessary institutional reforms for an enlarged European Community (EU) upon which no agreement could be reached over three long days at the Amsterdam summit in 1997. During the Nice negotiations emotions rose high at times and eventually a meager package deal of several compromises was agreed upon.

In retrospect the Nice summit seems to be a good example for providing insights into the decision making of the highest political body of the European Union: the European Council. The poor result and the public fights between some of the European leaders in the aftermath of the Nice summit made it painfully clear that the European Council, if it wanted to retain its important role within the European framework, needed to be restructured and, preferably, reformed.

The processes of deepening (expansion of policy areas) and widening (enlargement) of European integration have forced the European Council to tackle some tough challenges. The threat of a possible crisis in top-level European decision making underlines the necessity of reforming the European Council—especially after 1 May 2004, when no fewer than ten new members acceded. If the current generation of political leaders is not able to reach agreement on necessary reforms, future decision making in the European Council could eventually turn out to be a "mission impossible."

Thus, despite a successful record the European Council at the end of the 1990s and the beginning of the new century seemed to have lost its grip on the integration process. Adaptations of the decision-making process, still based on a negotiation structure that has remained unchanged since its creation in the 1970s, are needed if the European Council wants to continue its important and guiding role in European integration.

Since Tony Blair showed his frustration at the internal proceedings of the European Council much has happened. Two parallel processes of European Council reform were initiated or intensified and were set to be finalized before actual enlargement of the European Union took place. The first process dealt with the operational settings of the European Council summits. These reforms were initiated at the Helsinki summit in December 1999 and agreed upon at the Seville summit in June 2002. The second process dealt with the institutional structure and the balance of power among the EU institutions. These reforms will most probably be finalized at the end of the 2003–2004 Intergovernmental Conference (IGC) leading to a completely renewed constitutional EU treaty, in which the position of the European Council will be strengthened once again.

The main purpose of this chapter is twofold. The first goal is to present some information on the historical evolution and current functioning of the European Council. Although this top-level decision-making body has been very influential on the progress of European integration, paradoxically not much research has been done on its true record. The summits are still surrounded by a great deal of secrecy and informal decision making. This chapter will try to give an outsider's view of the true decision-making processes of this very powerful body with particular reference to the last few years.

Second, an overview will be presented on the current reform processes needed to prepare the European Council for effective decision making in an enlarged EU25. It is argued that the European Council, in line with current developments in international relations, has accurately overcome many of its problems and critics by ensuring a stronger institutional position in the future EU. The European Council will be in the driving seat more than ever before!

Historical Evolution[2]

The creation of what would later become European Council meetings within the rather "supranational" Community framework came into existence in the 1960s after strong insistence, if not compulsion, by the most influential European politician of that era: the president of the French Republic, Charles de Gaulle. It was de Gaulle's resentment of supranational dominance in international or European relations that made him instigate the first two summits in Paris in February 1961 and that in Bonn in July 1961. The European Council actually became a success, however, through the efforts of political leaders from the respective member states in the post–de Gaulle era who brought European integration much further than the former French president would ever have expected or hoped for.

The first influential summit was not held until 1969 in The Hague. This summit was successful in two ways: first, agreement was reached on British accession and second, the idea of foreign political cooperation, so-called European political cooperation, was formally initiated, thereby extending the rather economic focus of the integration process. The positive European spirit even made the French president, Pompidou, speak of "complètement, approndissement et élargissement" (completion, deepening, and enlargement).

This Euro-optimism was soon to change into "Eurosclerosis." After two lackluster summits in Paris (1972) and Copenhagen (1973), the European political leaders decided during the Paris summit in 1974 to hold regular meetings of what was formally called the "European Council." This institutionalization of the epitome of intergovernmentalism was needed for three reasons: the international economic crises had forced the member states to refocus their international economic policies; the Community method had almost completely stagnated especially since the "Empty Chair Crisis" in Luxembourg in 1965 which was in practice a blocking majority vote; and the ministers of foreign affairs were finding it difficult to coordinate the activities of a growing number of Council formations, especially with regard to the European Political Community.[3] A strong intergovernmental input was needed to bring European integration further: the European Council changed from an ad hoc informal gathering into a formal arena and was used by the political leaders for European negotiations. Paradoxically, the emergence of the European Council coincided with a gradual strengthening of supranationalism.

The two founders of the current setting of European Council meetings, French president, Valéry Giscard d'Estaing, and German chancellor, Helmut Schmidt, also continued to have regular bilateral meetings that were opposed to this supranational tendency. Wishing to regain as much political power as possible, they decided to initiate the high-level meetings of the European Council. They preferred to keep these meeting as informal as possible. The participation of high officials during these meetings was not appreciated. "But the other member states insisted, in 1974, upon their limited participation" (Werts 1992, 98).

From the Dublin summit in 1975 onwards, these meetings have been held at least twice a year. Dinan (1994) rightly argues that "many meetings of the European Council stand out as turning points in the EU's history." The most important and successful European Councils were:

- The Hague (1969), foreign political cooperation and first wave of enlargement;
- Paris (1974), "creation" of the European Council;
- Milan (1985), convoking the Intergovernmental Conference that led to the Single European Act (SEA);
- Maastricht (1991), agreement on the creation of the European Union, eventually leading to the Treaty on European Union (TEU);
- Amsterdam (1997), conclusion of the Treaty of Amsterdam;
- Brussels (1998), selection of member states to join Stage III of the European Monetary Union (EMU);
- Tampere (1999), third-pillar issues and institutional reforms;
- Lisbon (2000), Information and Communication Technologies (ICT), and economic development; and
- Copenhagen (2002), EU enlargement with Central and Eastern European countries (CEECs), Cyprus, and Malta.

This short list shows the enormous influence and impact the outcomes of the European Council negotiations have had on the European integration process.

Still, the status of the European Council and its decisions have been the object of many academic debates. According to de Schoutheete (2002, 30): "Part of this problem stems from the fact that for the first twelve years of its existence (1974–1986), the European Council met, and exercised significant power, without any legal basis in the Treaties."

The European Council was given a constitutional and legal basis only in 1987 in the Single European Act which stated in its Article 2:

> The European Council shall bring together the Heads of State or of Government of the Member States and the President of the Commission of the European Communities [EC]. They shall be assisted by the Ministers of Foreign Affairs and by a Member of the Commission.
>
> The European Council shall meet at least twice year.

However, no tasks, functions, or competencies were laid down in the Single European Act. These continued to evolve informally during the European Council meetings in the aftermath of the SEA. In the Treaty on European Union that was agreed upon during the Maastricht European Council in 1991 the composition of membership and the frequency of meetings were restated and the treaty went even further by laying down in its Title I, Article D, that "the European Council shall provide the Union with the necessary impetus for its development and shall define the general political guidelines thereof." This formulation is a clear example of the intergovernmental primacy in the integration dynamics that dominated the 1990s and in fact gained even more momentum in the first years of the current decade. For the Treaty on European Union can be seen as the final phase of the formal institutionalization of the intergovernmental European Council. In the Treaty of Amsterdam the above-mentioned article was renumbered Article 4 TEU. Here the article was reformulated:

> The European Council shall provide the Union with the necessary impetus for its development and shall define the general political guidelines thereof.
>
> The European Council shall bring together the Heads of State or Government of the Member States and the President of the Commission. They shall be assisted by the Ministers for Foreign Affairs of the Member States and by a Member of the Commission.
>
> The European Council shall meet at least twice a year, under the chairmanship of the Head of State or Government of the Member State, which holds the Presidency of the Council.
>
> The European Council shall submit to the European Parliament a report after each of its meetings and a yearly written report on the progress achieved by the Union.

Unlike the European Parliament, the Council, the Commission, the Court of Justice, and the Court of Auditors, however, the European Council is not legally an institution of the European Community. Nevertheless it does play a vital role in all European Union fields of activity either by giving impetus to the Union or defining general political guidelines, or by coordinating, arbitrating, or disentangling difficult questions.[4]

From 2004 onwards it is very likely that a new chapter will be added to the evolution of the European Council. In June 2003 the so-called Convention on the Future of Europe presented its proposal for a new constitutional EU treaty, including reforms concerning the (institutional) position of the European Council. The ratification of this treaty will have direct consequences for the position of the European

Council, as will be argued at the end of this chapter. Before going into detail on the future position of the European Council, however, an overview will be presented of the current functioning and proceedings of this top-level EU decision-making body.

The Current Functioning of the European Council

Since the beginning of the 1990s, as in the 1970s, the European Council has received an ever-increasing amount of attention and media coverage. Most of the attention is concerned with the European Council having supposedly become the most powerful EU institution. Indeed, the European Council is at the heart of the European balance of power. This top-level decision-making body is often described as the "motor" of European integration. The European Council has evolved from being an informal gathering of the political leaders of the EC/European Economic Community (EEC)/EU member states in the 1970s into what seems to be an influential and guiding institution of the European Union of today. A semipermanent, top-level decision-making arena has come into existence. Compared to top-level decision-making institutions of international organizations such as the United Nations, the Association of South East Asian Nations (ASEAN), G7/G8, and Mercosur, the European Council has a rather unique if not ambiguous position. On the outside the European Council seems to comply with all the essential criteria of a top-level, decision-making institution within an international organization: executive participation, diplomacy at the highest political level, long-term agenda setting, brokering of interests, media exposure, and more. At second glance, however, the European Council is undoubtedly distinct in several ways: the institutional structure in which it needs to operate; its range of tasks and competencies; and its working methods and decision-making procedures (de Schoutheete 2002).

The European Council increasingly acts as the real broker for the most fiercely contended stalemate issues and usually solves them through package deals.[5] In issuing manifold declarations and memoranda, it has become a major EU agenda builder giving the green light to the Commission which usually acts quite responsively (van Schendelen 2002, 75). The highest authorities in the EU political system are the "summits" of the EU heads of state or government. European Council meetings are the place where final agreements and compromises are reached on treaty reforms. The European Council takes a central political leadership role, guiding the work of the lower meetings of the Council and the Commission, and setting the long- and medium-term objectives of the EU (Hix 1999, 28–30). In a way the European Council seems to be perceived as some kind of "circus" that is solely responsible for the current direction of European affairs.

How then does this "circus" deal with all its tasks? How is it able to get to consensual decision making in a dynamic environment like the European Union? In other words, how does it operate? The following section will provide an overview at an operational level of the working methods of the European Council.

Working methods:[6] a general overview[7]

The meetings of the European Council usually take place over two days, although some European Council meetings, such as that in Nice in December 2000, lasted four days. These two days provide a striking contrast between the privacy of the meetings and the enormous activity outside the room which nobody can enter without showing their credentials (a red pass). There is a contrast, too, between the informal, flexible character of the meeting and the boundless ingenuity which the Presidency and the Secretariat must show in order to provide translations, security arrangements, secretarial assistance, and information for the national delegations sitting in adjacent rooms and for upwards of two thousand journalists covering the event (de Schoutheete 2002, 33–39).

As de Schoutheete (2002, 22) rightly argues, "this is the essence of the European Council: a limited number of political figures, headed by the chief executives of all member states, meeting in a closed room with no assistants."

The restricted composition of the European Council gives it a rather informal character. Some even compare it to a traditional chat around the fireside. Though this is definitely not the case, some of the working methods used do, in fact, stem from an era that seems to have passed with the introduction of computers and the Internet. Though there is no formal set of agreed and legal binding rules of procedure as exists for the Council of Ministers (Werts 1992, 77), the composition, setting, and proceedings are usually as follows.

Composition

The formal composition of the European Council (Article 4 TEU) has already been mentioned earlier in this chapter: two delegates per member state (the head of state or government and the minister of foreign affairs), the president of the Commission and a member of the Commission. In practice, however, more people are directly involved in the European Council negotiations. Added to these thirty-two negotiators, a growing but still-limited number of officials has also been allowed into the conference room over the years. This increase in the number of EU officials is a direct consequence of the growing influence of the European Council on the process of European integration, as described in the first section of this chapter. These officials are from the Presidency, the Commission, and the Council Secretariat.

Since the merger of the functions of Secretary-General of the European Council and the High Representative, this function has gained importance in the European decision-making structure, especially in the context of the European Council. The Secretary-General, currently the former Spanish foreign minister, Javier Solana, has become a (semi)political function. He is closely involved in the preparation of the meetings and his Secretariat is responsible, among other things, for the drafting of the conclusions. This evolution of the Council Secretariat can also be witnessed physically at the negotiation table, as both the Secretary-General and his deputy have been assigned chairs next to the president of the European Council.

Furthermore, two delegates per member state are allowed to enter the conference room to pass notes or messages. They are explicitly not allowed to join the negotiations nor to stay in the room permanently.

Some additional remarks must also be made. Sometimes an absent foreign minister is replaced by another minister (or state secretary) or, in their absence, by the permanent representative of the country. Furthermore, the French president is sometimes replaced or assisted by the French prime minister. This is most often the case during a period of "cohabitation," when the two politicians are from different political backgrounds, as during the Chirac/Jospin era.

Setting

The main meeting room, to which access is limited, is isolated from the outside world. If a member of the European Council wishes to call upon one of his/her close assistants or on a permanent representative for clarification or advice about a dossier, he/she presses a button sending a signal to the adjacent room to the so-called Antici Group.[8] The members of this group are diplomats and close assistants of the permanent representatives who stay close to the main meeting room at all times and pass messages to their respective national delegations which are accommodated further away. It is their function to convey requests and keep delegations informed as to how the discussions are progressing. Proceedings are relayed to the outside world by a system of note takers. An official from the Council Secretariat is present during the discussions and takes notes for about fifteen minutes after which another Council official replaces him/her. The official, after having left the room, briefs the Antici Group orally in their separate room. Philippe de Schoutheete, a former Belgian permanent representative to the EU, rightly argues that "this indirect dissemination of informal information guarantees that national delegations know something of the proceedings inside, but with a considerable delay and in a way which makes direct attribution of specific words to any participants nearly impossible. Such an extraordinary system would not have survived if heads of government were not happy with the result, namely, that they operate at some distance, both in space and time, from the views and comments of their own civil servants" (de Schoutheete 2002, 26–27).

As all delegations are allowed to speak in their own language there are also many translators present. They are situated to one side of the plenary room in a row of boxes. Their simultaneous translations can be accessed only by the negotiators at the table. The national delegates in the adjacent rooms have no access to these direct translations and have to wait for the oral briefings by the civil servants of the Council Secretariat and the Antici Group.

Furthermore, in the corners of the meeting room several seats are reserved for five different kinds of professionals: officials from the Presidency, officials from the Council Secretariat, the Secretary-General of the Commission, the note takers mentioned earlier and, finally, some technical staff. This all leads to the following overview of the meeting room itself as shown in *Figure 9.1*.[9]

Proceedings

It has been the practice since 1987 to begin the proceedings with a speech by the president of the European Parliament. Before the European Council's work officially begins, the president informs the European Council of the Parliament's position on the main issues at stake, and after a short discussion, leaves the room. The heads of state or government of the applicant member states are usually also invited to join this first-day opening session. The first day of work, sometimes called the "plenary session," is devoted to an exchange of views on the current concerns of the European Union.

At the end of the day, the proceedings are suspended for dinner. The heads of state or government and the president of the European Commission continue to discuss on their own the issues they have decided to address. The foreign ministers dine in another room, and add final touches to certain dossiers. The heads of state or government and the president of the Commission then adjourn for the least formal part of the proceedings, the fireside chats, where they can broach whatever subjects they wish in strictest confidence. Meanwhile, in the light of the day's discussions, the Presidency and the Council Secretariat tidy up the conclusions which will be made public the following day, and the foreign ministers discuss current issues and where necessary, prepare declarations on common foreign and security policy (CFSP) matters.

The next half-day's work is preceded by a working breakfast for each delegation, during which informal bilateral contacts can be made where appropriate. Once the traditional "family photo" has been taken, the last plenary session is devoted to finalization of the conclusions. The drafting of this text sometimes involves prolonging discussions into the afternoon or simply omitting lunch, with consequent last-minute changes to the departure time of the delegations.

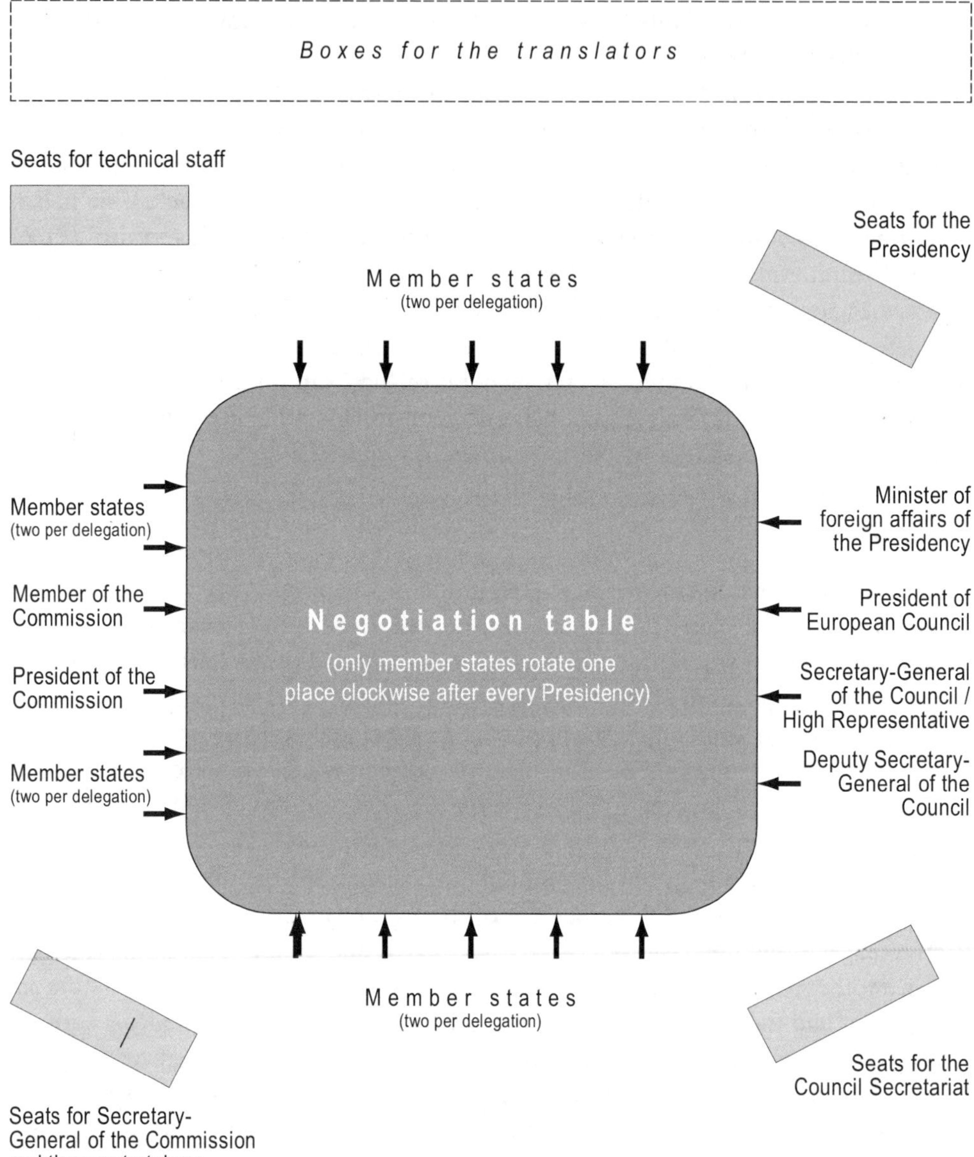

Figure 9.1. The plenary negotiation room—a schematic overview

The final part of the proceedings is the system of press conferences. After the final discussions of every European Council all parties involved (Presidency, all member states, Commission, and Secretary-General of the Council) give separate press conferences in which they put forward their positions, their "successes," and perhaps most importantly their interpretation of the discussions. This circus of media attention is first and foremost a public-relations offensive used by the political leaders to communicate with their peoples and legitimize their actions. An interesting aspect of these press conferences stems from the sometimes-different explanations of some politicians. These differences are due to no formal notes having been taken during the European Council meetings which gives room for different interpretations of the substance. This example of "public diplomacy" par excellence is the final piece of the negotiating puzzle of the European Council proceedings.

The Presidency

The "among-equals" character of the European Council does not apply to the position of the Presidency. The member state holding the Presidency is clearly more equal than others. The main advantage is that the Presidency is allowed to have two kinds of (national) negotiators at the conference table: the technical chair of the meeting (the head of state or government) and the actual negotiator (minister of foreign affairs) who will defend the national positions. The history of negotiations in the European Council has made it clear that one cannot really speak of a "technical" or a "neutral" chair. Two essential characteristics, therefore, need to be mentioned for a complete overview of the proceedings: "agenda setting" and the (drafting of) the conclusions of the Presidency.

The setting of the agenda is, in all negotiations, an important tool by which the chair can influence the proceedings and the outcomes. The sequence and number of the respective points on the agenda make or break the negotiations. The sequence in the case of the European Council is determined by the Presidency. The chair, thereby, is able to directly influence the contents of the negotiations. One of the main criticisms of the current system of the rotating Presidency is the "natural" reflex of most member states to (mis)use their term in office as EU Presidency to put on the agenda or even push through their own national interests. The agenda of the European Council changes slightly, as a consequence, every six months. As in all negotiations, it is easier to get an issue on to the agenda than to remove it. This process of broadening the agenda is one of the main dilemmas in the current crisis.

Another source of influence is the tight time schedule. The Presidency has a fair amount of autonomy when it comes to filling in the actual negotiating time left. It is the Presidency that decides the percentage of time to be spent on certain issues and when and with whom to arrange the "confessionals."

Clearly, a complex, unique, and informal set of proceedings and working methods has come into existence. It is questionable, however, if these practices will be applicable to an enlarged EU with at least twenty-five member states.

A Potential Crisis in European Top-Level Negotiating? The Need for Reforms

Since the second half of the 1990s a mounting number of critics, both from within the European Council itself and from other EU institutions, have been heard on the functioning of the European Council. The main criticisms have been the decreasing sense of direction being given to European integration, an overload of low-level decision making, an ever-growing gap between European Council guidelines and the actual policy making by the other institutions and, finally, increasing difficulties in getting to consensual decision making.

Currently the ever-changing political agenda of the European Union is largely dominated by two different but immense challenges: the unique enlargement with the countries of Central and Eastern Europe on one hand and the constitutional debate on the future institutional settings of the European Union on the other. Both challenges require decision making at the level of the European Council. Ever since the Maastricht treaty (1992) European leaders have tried to reach agreement on both topics. So far, they have been unable to do so, and they are running out of time.

Thus, despite its rather unique and potentially powerful position, the European Council currently has to deal with these tough challenges. European top-level decision making seems to be in heavy weather. In fact, at the end of the 1990s it seemed as if the European Council had partly lost its control of the integration process. If it wants keep up its image as the most important source of European leadership, it needs to reform (van Grinsven and Melissen 2002, LVI, 421–26). So far, the European Council has been struggling to come up with a satisfying response to the increasing number of criticisms both from national politicians and European citizens. Things are, however, changing for the better: the likely consensus on the provisional constitutional treaty could turn out to be the ideal solution to this dilemma.

The sources for this potential crisis in European top-level decision making are twofold. On an operational level the negotiation procedures and methods seem to have reached their limits. The current proceedings of the European Council meetings, as described earlier in this chapter, are hardly even applicable to an EU15, let alone a European Union with twenty-five or more member states. In other words, the negotiation methods used during the European Council meetings need to be reformed now more than ever before.

There is, however, another practical source for the current discussion on the functioning of the European Council. This deals with the malfunctioning of the Council of Ministers, in particular the General Affairs and External Relations Council (GAERC). As argued earlier the European Council meetings are part of a larger cyclical negotiation process in which other institutions also play an important role. One of the most important links in the EU negotiation chain is the preparation of the European Council meetings by the Council of Ministers. The latter is supposed to take most of its decisions along Community lines. If it fulfills its task properly, the European Council can focus primarily on its own main task: giving impetus to the European Union and taking political decisions on issues of "high politics." The last couple of years, however, the Council of Ministers (and GAERC in particular) has been increasingly unable to fulfill its function properly. Decision making in the Council has thus stagnated more and more: on a large number of negotiation dossiers the Council has been unable to reach agreement. As a direct consequence these undecided dossiers have been passed on to the European Council, transforming the European Council into some sort of final court of appeal. It is increasingly asked to "spend time on laborious low-level drafting work, which adversely affects normal Community procedures" (Council of the European Union 2002, 2). In other words, the European Council has been sidetracked from its original and most important purposes.

These two dilemmas, the old-fashioned methods and proceedings on the one hand and the malfunctioning of GAERC on the other, are clearly linked, as has been recognized by both the European Council and the Secretary-General of the Council of Ministers, Javier Solana. At the Helsinki summit in December 1999 they jointly started a process of operational reforms of both the European Council and the Council of Ministers, and this was completed in June 2002 during the Seville summit (see later in the chapter).

The second source of potential crisis stems from the ongoing debate in the EU on institutional reforms. Since the creation of the European Union, as agreed upon during the Maastricht summit in 1991, a (semi)permanent discussion on its institutional structure has been taking place. This year we will witness the third Intergovernmental Conference (IGC) in less than ten years dealing with the question of the "balance of power" between the institutions (and the member states). Since the beginning of the 1990s a semipermanent round of negotiations on the institutional structure has been taking place both within and outside the setting of the so-called IGCs. Ever since the creation of the European Union by the 1992 Treaty of Maastricht (which was also preceded by an IGC) two IGCs have already been finalized and a third took place before actual EU enlargement in 2004: IGC 1996–1997, IGC 2000, and IGC 2003–2004, not to mention the extrainstitutional Convention on the Future of Europe in 2002–2003. The main goal of the convention, created in December 2001 at the Laeken summit in Belgium after the European Council recognized that it was unable to solve these dilemmas itself, was to smooth the way for the European Council to reach agreement before actual enlargement took place in May 2004. At the end of the 2003-2004 IGC the European Council is expected to reach agreement on the third treaty revision in those same ten years.

This institutional process deals primarily with the (re)distribution of the balance of power among the EU institutions. Undoubtedly the European Council has played an important role in this process. In fact, as will be argued later on in this chapter, the European Council has used this institutional process to strengthen its position in the EU negotiation process. This year, it will most probably decide on a complete overhaul of its own structure, the Presidency in particular. The consequences of these reforms will be crucial for future European Council negotiations. Before presenting an assessment of both reform processes, the above-mentioned sources of conflict will be presented at length.

The outdated working methods and proceedings: a "numbers game"

The working methods currently used are still based mainly on the initial European Council meetings of the six founding member states in the 1970s. As described above, since then the European Council has gradually evolved from these informal, ad hoc "chats around the fireside" into the powerful institution of the European Union with hundreds of politicians, civil servants, and diplomats directly involved in its work, not to mention the hundreds of journalists covering the multimedia events.

An excellent example of the European Council's outdated working methods and proceedings was its discussion of the reopening of the Gotthard Tunnel; this came in for twofold criticism by Gerhard Schröder: first, that the issue was on the agenda of the European Council at all and second, the length of time needed to discuss it—it took over an hour for the fifteen political leaders to reach agreement on this issue of rather "low politics." The often-used *tour de table* (in which every delegation is given the opportunity to have its say on a topic) will, after the enlargement, be *quadrupled* in terms of time spent. Even if only two to three minutes are given per delegation, this would lead to a *tour de table* of over one hour on each topic, not to mention the discussions afterwards. The same line of argumentation can be applied to the so-called confessionals.

The enlargement of the EU has led to an increase in the number of official languages. Currently the EU has twenty official languages. As every negotiator is allowed to speak in his/her own language, an enlarged European Council will demand more translators and more trapped translations[10] with an implied increased margin for error and misunderstanding. This will slow down the negotiations and create a potential source of irritation. Fortunately some reforms have already been instituted to prevent this tower-of-Babel scenario.

The numbers game can also be witnessed in the size of the delegations. Currently the European Council meetings involve hundreds of national diplomats and civil servants who play their role in facilitating and coordinating the processes from a national perspective. The European Council has evolved from an informal "chat around the fireside" into an extravaganza of national delegations of sometimes over thirty civil servants and diplomats per member state. The media often makes the comparison with a traveling circus.

These hundreds of national delegates all have something of a role to play in the multilayered and complex proceedings surrounding the actual negotiations by the political leaders. This implies a complex and nontransparent web of coordination, deliberation, and consultation structures (national delegations, COREPER, Council Secretariat) in the margin of the European Council meeting. The direct consequences of the ever-expanding number of indirect participants are visible in the current problems of the drafting of (Presidency) conclusions and in the process of coordinating national positions during the negotiations in the European Council: the political leaders have to wait too long for answers on their direct questions; too many diplomats have to study the drafts of the Presidency conclusions; more delegates imply more differing opinions to discuss; and so on. In other words, to increase the efficiency and effectiveness of the total process of European Council negotiations, a limitation on the number of delegates is needed.

The expansion of tasks and competencies has led to an increase in so-called third-party meetings: meetings with important political institutions or persons during the European Council summit, such as the political leaders of the applicant member states and political figures from outside the EU. This mounting number of meetings is squeezed into the already-tight time schedule of what is normally a two-day meeting. These time-consuming activities leave less time for actual negotiating. Finally, from the perspective of the "numbers game," the obstacles to any (potential) outcomes are also being increased by the broadening of the agenda.

The increased influence of the European Council on the successful process of postwar European integration has led to a growing number of competencies in a growing number of (national) policy areas. Nowadays, the European Union has an impact on almost all policy areas, including foreign and defense policies: the Europeanization of the national policy agenda is under way. This expansion of EU influence on national decision making has broadened the European negotiation agenda, and the increased number of negotiating points combined with the limited time available has complicated the negotiation process. The malfunctioning of GAERC mentioned earlier has broadened the negotiation agenda still further. The European Council should be reformed to refocus on its core business: strategic and political decision making instead of concrete policy dossiers.

The malfunctioning of the General Affairs and External Relations Council (GAERC)

One of the most important functions of GAERC is to coordinate EU policies and dossiers in preparation for the European Council meetings. For the last couple of years, however, GAERC has been increasingly unable to fulfill this function properly. In fact, it seems that GAERC has used the European Council as a kind of final court of arbitration. As a consequence the European Council has lost its most important function as the "motor" of integration through guiding the process and determining the political direction of the European Union. More and more, the European Council has replaced GAERC primarily by taking decisions on tough and specific policy dossiers.

An interesting example is the speech of Gerhard Schröder at the Den Uyl-lezing in Amsterdam in the aftermath of the Barcelona European Council in 2002. The German chancellor publicly showed his frustration at the proceedings of the Barcelona European Council where the leaders of the fifteen member states had had a round-table discussion on the reopening of the Gotthard Tunnel. Schröder cynically stated that such an issue "could not be the task of the European political leaders."

This sign of frustration on the part of the German chancellor seems to be the tip of the iceberg of general concerns about the negotiating process in the Council of Ministers. The widening gap between the political statements of the European Council and the decreasing decision making in the Council of Ministers has forced the European political leaders to negotiate on an ever-expanding agenda within an unchanging, two-day time schedule.

The consequence of this process has been a shift in the actual decision making on policy dossiers from GAERC to the European Council. The European Council should cease working out the details of policies at this level and focus on its main strategic tasks. One could argue that in a way the European Council has taken over one of the important tasks of the Council, which takes up too much of its valuable time. In the case of policy decisions the European Council should function only as the institution of final resort.

In international-relations literature the decision-making process is often described as a six-stage ongoing cyclical development: preparatory phase, agenda setting, negotiation of formula, bargaining on details, agreement, and implementation/postnegotiation, as shown below.

This cyclical process is perfectly applicable to the European Council. It is clear that in the case of a malfunctioning Council of Ministers in the preparatory phase, the entire chain of European Council decision making starts to stagnate. The European Council's dependency on the functioning of other EU institutions has made it institutionally vulnerable.

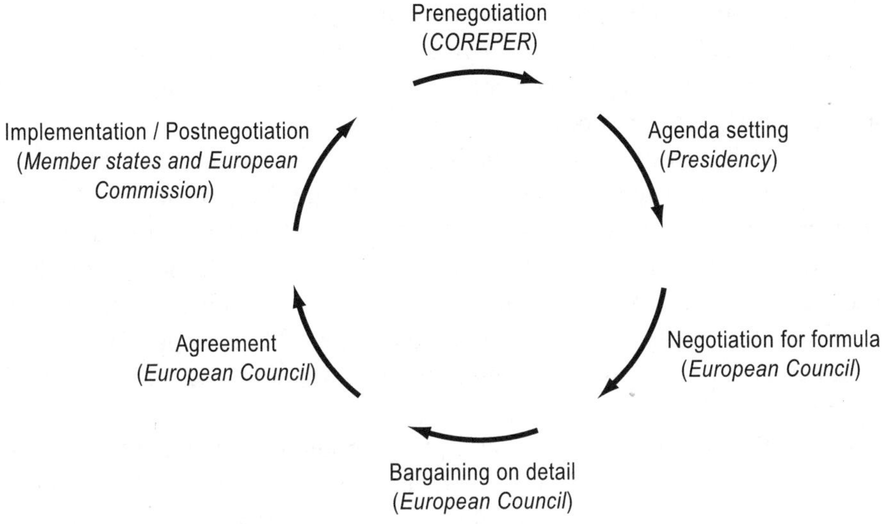

Figure 9.2. Process of international decision making in a multilateral context applied to the European Council

This vulnerability has led to what is called here a "delivery deficit." The European Council has persistently shown a high level of ambition in its decisions and presidency conclusions. In fulfilling its function of giving impetus to the integration process the European Council has launched several ambitious plans over the last couple of years in different policy areas. As the Council of Ministers has not been able to live up to these initiatives, however, a widening gap can be witnessed between top-level decisions and the actual implementation of EU policies. In other words, the EU cannot practice what it preaches.

Safeguarding the European Council: Processes of Reforms

To avoid the threat of stagnation mentioned earlier, the European Council, the most high-level decision-making body of the EU, is, for the first time since its creation in 1974, itself the subject of reform. Based on the analysis described above, the European Council needs to tackle the following five dilemmas:

1. The main task of the European Council is to provide the EU with the necessary impetus for its development and to define the general political guidelines thereof (Article 4 TEU). The implication of this task is that the European Council will primarily focus on European "high politics." The term, high politics, implies a high sensitivity surrounding the issues. In other words, the European

Council has to decide upon policy areas in which the member states are very hesitant to hand over power and sovereignty to the EU (e.g., defense, taxes, social policy, and voting power in the institutions). Therefore, it is difficult to produce satisfying outcomes on a regular basis.

2. The bulk of European decision making takes place within the so-called Community structure of the Commission, Council, and Parliament. The European Council almost never interferes with this process. In other words, a large part of European decision and policy making takes place outside the direct influence of the European Council. Therefore, it is not possible to look at the European Council as the sole leading institution at the center of European politics. In fact, the other EU institutions, the Commission in particular, also play an important role here.

3. Closely linked to these first two remarks, it should be noted that the European Council has no direct influence or power over the implementation and control of its own decisions. The implementation and control of EU policies are autonomous competencies of the other EU institutions (Commission, Council, Parliament, *and Court*).

4. One of the main problems seems to be the malfunctioning of the Council of Ministers, GAERC in particular. This Council is increasingly unable to reach consensus on actual policy decision making. Over the last couple of years, GAERC has increasingly used the European Council as a final court of appeal, with all policy dossiers that could not be decided upon within the Community structure being put on the agenda of the European Council meetings. This overload of work has led to such an extended agenda that European Council decision making is in real danger of stagnation. The European Council itself has realized this potential threat and has already launched an internal reform, based on two reports of its Secretary-General.

5. The main internal dilemma stems from the old-fashioned working methods, the unchanged structure of negotiating, and the ever-increasing number of participants. The summit meetings of the European Council seem disruptive, resulting in insufficient decision making. Reforms are needed before actual enlargement takes place. The twenty-five member states, after 1 May 2004, will have to find a new mode of cooperation.

The European Council has initiated two different but closely linked processes of internal reform: an operational one, focusing on the day-to-day functioning of the European Council, and an institutional one, focusing on the future power position. Both processes will be discussed now at length.

The operational process: Helsinki (1999) to Seville (2002)

The European Council at its Helsinki summit from 10 to 11 December 1999 already recognized the potential dark clouds of the upcoming enlargement. In its conclusions the European Council put two important issues high on the agenda: effective institutions and transparency. In its Presidency conclusions it stated that "the scale of the coming enlargements coupled with the wider scope of the Union's actions could well slow the Council down, and ultimately paralyze it. That risk is already perceptible now and represents a threat to the smooth operation of the Union, given the Council's central role in Union decision-making" (Helsinki European Council 1999).

The Götenborg European Council (December 2001) revisited these problems. The Secretary-General was mandated to present suggestions on how to improve the way the European Council (and the Council of Ministers) operates.

In his report of 11 March 2002, Secretary-General Javier Solana presented a clear analysis of the current problems of the EU negotiating process (Council of the European Union 2002). His analysis and recommendations formed the basis of the reforms regarding the future constellation of the European Council proposed at the Barcelona and Seville European Council meetings in 2002 that have effectively been in practice since 1 January 2003.

According to the Secretary-General the main problem is the following: "The European Union is the Union's supreme political authority. It possesses a legitimate power of decision. It represents the unity between the Union, on the one hand, and its member states, on the other, in its closest form. Its task is 'to provide the Union with the necessary impetus for its development and define general political guidelines'. That presupposes clarity of objectives, transparency of decisions, and continuity of action. For some years now, the European Council has been sidetracked from its original purpose. Owing to the malfunctioning of the Council, it is increasingly asked to spend time on laborious low-level drafting work, which adversely affects normal community procedures. The drift in the working of the Presidency has reduced its meetings to report-approval sessions or inappropriate exercises in self-congratulation by the institutions" (Council of the European Union 2002).

The European Council meeting in Barcelona (15 and 16 March 2002), however, once again turned out to be a clear example of the internal difficulties between the heads of government preventing them from reaching agreement on the reform of their negotiating processes. Even with the help of two reports by the Secretary-General of the Council, Javier Solana, the European Council was not able to take its first cautious steps along the path of internal reform. Eventually, partly based on the mounting pressure of the proceedings in the convention, "the European Council instructed the Presidency, in close cooperation with the Council Secretary-General, to make all appropriate contacts [...] with a view to submitting a report at the Seville meeting proposing specific measures for adoption."[11] In other words, the point of no return seemed to have been reached.

The Seville summit, a couple of months later, turned out to be more successful. For the first time in its history the European Council was able to reach agreement on some initial internal reforms of working methods and proceedings. The Spanish Presidency, in cooperation with the Secretary-General/High Representative, Javier Solana, argued in its report of 13 June 2002, "the view is widely held that, following the next enlargement, the European Council will have increasing difficulty in fulfilling its task with the authority and efficiency expected of the highest political authority of the Union. It is also generally admitted that one way of improving the functioning of the European Council, by refocusing it on its essential tasks, would be set precise and binding rules for the *preparation, conduct* and *conclusions* of its proceedings" (Council of the European Union 2002). The most important changes are:[12]

- The European Council shall in principle meet four times a year. Only in exceptional circumstances may it convene an extraordinary meeting.
- The meetings shall be prepared by the newly formed General Affairs and External Relations Council (GAERC) which shall coordinate all the preparatory work and draw up the agenda (draft agendas, brief outlines).
- The proceedings shall last for one full day, preceded (the day before) by a meeting restricted to heads of state or government and the president of the Commission.
- Meetings in the margins with representatives of third states or organizations may be held in exceptional circumstances only. They must be approved in advance by the agenda-setting General Affairs and External Relations Council.
- The Presidency is given more tools and competencies (e.g., order of contributors) to influence the agenda and to streamline the discussions. Furthermore, a new timetable will come into effect during the sessions (limiting speak time).
- Delegations shall receive summary briefings on the outcome and substance of the discussions on each item as proceedings continue in such a way that confidentiality is safeguarded.
- Each delegation shall have two seats in the meeting room. The total size of delegations shall be limited to twenty(!) persons for each member state and for the Commission. That number shall not include technical personnel assigned to specific security or logistic support tasks.
- The Presidency conclusions will set out only policy guidelines and decisions, placing them in their context and indicating the stages of the procedures.

- An outline of the conclusions shall be distributed on the day of the meeting before the start of the proceedings with a distinction being made between those parts that have been approved and those parts that need to be discussed.

Most of these changes have been put into practice by the Danish Presidency from the first half of 2003 onwards.

The institutional process: (post-)Nice (2000) to IGC 2003–2004[13]

As mentioned earlier the institutional implications of the enlargement of the European Union have been high on the political agenda for over ten years. Ever since the creation of the European Union (1992), agreement on which was reached at the Maastricht summit in 1991, the member states have tried to reach agreement on their future position of power in an enlarged Europe. The institutional balance of power and the division of power between the member states on the one hand and the EU institutions on the other have dominated the political agenda ever since. At the Amsterdam summit in 1997, the European political leaders were not able to construct a satisfactory new balance of power for an enlarged European Union. Though a new EU treaty was established, no agreement was reached on what later became known as the "Amsterdam leftovers": the future national weights in European decision making (inter alia, size of the Commission, voting weight in the Council of Ministers, seats in Parliament).

These "Amsterdam leftovers" were the main issues during IGC 2000 that concluded with the Nice summit in December 2000. At this summit some consensus was agreed upon regarding the institutional leftovers, which resulted in the Nice treaty. That same European Council recognized, however, that the Nice treaty would not sufficiently prepare the EU decision-making process for enlargement.

Eventually, therefore, it was the European Council itself that set up the unique Convention on the Future of Europe at the Laeken summit in December 2001. The convention, consisting of one hundred five members[14] and presided over by the former French president and cofounder of the European Council, Valéry Giscard d'Estaing, was an extrainstitutional EU body that was requested to deal with one very specific task: preparing a new constitutional EU treaty for an enlarged European Union.[15] One of the fundamental reasons behind the decision to convene such a constituent, extrainstitutional assembly was "the realization that previous intergovernmental conferences had failed to produce reforms bold enough to prepare the EU adequately" (Michalksi 2003, 3). Another reason stemmed from the criticism "leveled against the EU that treaty reforms had hitherto been closed shops where political and bureaucratic elites decided on Europe's future without involving the European public or their parliamentary representatives" (Michalski 2003, 3).

On the European Council the provisional EU treaty contains the following articles that will most probably be approved and ratified without any changes:

Article 20: The European Council

1. The European Council shall provide the Union with the necessary impetus for its development, and shall define its general political directions and priorities. It does not exercise legislative functions.
2. The European Council shall consist of the Heads of State or Government of the Member States, together with its President and the President of the Commission. The Union Minister for Foreign Affairs shall take part in its work.
3. The European Council shall meet quarterly, convened by its President. When the agenda so requires, its members may decide to be assisted by a minister and, in the case of the President of the Commission, a European Commissioner. When the situation so requires, the President shall convene a special meeting of the European Council.
4. Except where the Constitution provides otherwise, decisions of the European Council shall be taken by consensus.

Article 21: The European Council Chair

1. The European Council shall elect its President, by qualified majority, for a term of two and a half years, renewable once. In the event of an impediment or serious misconduct, the European Council can end his or her mandate according to the same procedure.
2. The President of the European Council:

    - shall chair it and drive forward its work,
    - shall ensure its proper preparation and continuity in cooperation with the President of the Commission, and on the basis of the work of the General Affairs Council,
    - shall endeavour to facilitate cohesion and consensus within the European Council,
    - shall present a report to the European Parliament after each of its meetings.

    The President of the European Council shall at his or her level and in that capacity ensure the external representation of the Union on issues concerning its common foreign and security policy, without prejudice to the responsibilities of the Union Minister for Foreign Affairs.

3. The President of the European Council may not hold a national mandate.

How then to assess both these processes with their respective reform proposals? What will be the consequences for the functioning of the European Council? Will the proposals prove to be sufficient? Has the European Council been able to turn around the threat of stagnation in EU decision making or has it even improved its position?

The Future of the European Council: Leading the Way in Europe

The operational process has already been put into practice. The Danish Presidency applied most of the reform proposals during the first half of 2003. This has so far led to shortened meetings (limited in time), more concentrated Presidency conclusions, and a renewed functioning of the General Affairs and External Affairs Council. One could argue that the operational reforms have been quite successful. Still, it is questionable whether the reforms are sufficient for the proper functioning of a European Council of twenty-five member states. The limitation to a maximum of twenty delegates per member state would still lead to *five hundred* persons surrounding the European Council summits. Furthermore, EU history shows that difficult issues cannot be solved within the setting of a single summit. So, what will happen, if the European Council has to decide on politically sensitive issues?

The Convention on the Future of Europe appears to have found the solution to this question by presenting some *additional* reforms in combination with other operational reforms that have also made it into the provisional constitutional treaty of the convention. The summits will be held quarterly and will eventually all take place in Brussels. The General Affairs and External Relations Council will be split up and given clearer guidelines. In fact GAERC will be presided over by a newly created function—a European minister of foreign affairs.

In judging the reform proposals,[16] it is argued that the European Council has been able to tackle three of the five dilemmas defined earlier: the working methods have been modernized, the procedures and tasks of GAERC will be changed, and the European Council will be more strongly embedded in the institutional EU structures.

What remains are the interdependency of the functioning (and especially implementation) of the other EU institutions and the question of high politics, two dilemmas that are inherent to the current system of EU top-level decision making. The "new" European Council will have to deal with these dilemmas and continue to guide European integration.

It seems, therefore, that the European Council reforms, especially those from the convention, fit perfectly into some of the current global developments in top-level decision making. These changing international relations, especially in the post–Cold War era, have had a clear impact on the system of international decision making. The process of globalization, leading to a growing interdependence between nation states and the rise of international organizations and regional cooperation, has made the European Council "grow in number, become more complex technically and politically, and acquire new dimensions, such as being an alternative to coercive solutions of disputed problems" (Kremenyuk 2002, 22–23).

The scope of issues on the agenda has also increased immensely. Some international organizations tend to deal with almost all policy areas, as is the case with the European Union. An increasing number of dossiers and negotiations in the respective international organizations are becoming interlinked, leading to a growing complexity in decision making as a direct consequence. On the other hand, this expanding scope lowers the threshold of (total) package deals and intensifies the contacts between the parties involved, which in itself facilitates the possibility of the necessary creation of consensual decision making.

Finally, one could argue that international *top-level* decision making is becoming more and more institutionalized. Decisions are no longer just a means of reaching the ultimate goal of getting to an agreement but have become an autonomous part of the decision-making process. Many international summits have permanent meeting places and are prepared by an in-house secretariat.

The European Council is an excellent example underlining these latest developments in international decision making. First, one has witnessed a significant increase in the *number* of European Council summits over the last years. The average number of meetings per year has doubled from two summits in the first half of the 1990s to four summits at the beginning of the new century.[17] Furthermore, over the years, several kinds of European Council summits have come into existence. The Presidency conclusions speak of *normal* and *extraordinary* meetings, as happened in case of the September 11 attacks (2001) and the war in Iraq (2003). De Schoutheete rightly mentions a third kind of meeting: *informal* meetings of which no official notes, conclusions, or decisions are published, such as the first informal European Council summit in September 1995 on the ongoing proceedings of the IGC (de Schoutheete 2002).

These different kinds of meetings coincide with the ever-expanding agenda of the European Council. As mentioned in the historical overview, the European Council has been involved in an *ever-expanding number of policy areas*. In fact, the European Council is currently considered as the guiding EU body in almost all EU policies, especially in foreign policy, institutional developments, justice and home affairs, and external representation. In this sense the European Council's *expanding agenda* reflects the ongoing process of European integration, characterized by a high level of interdependency and complexity.

Finally, some remarks on the institutionalization of the European Council. Ever since its creation in 1974 the European Council has become more and more embedded in EU structures. It is very likely that with the new constitutional treaty the European Council will take the final step toward becoming a formal, powerful EU institution with a permanent president and its own staff and secretariat. In fact, it already decided on some preliminary steps at its Nice summit in December 2000. In the "Declarations adopted by the Conference," Article 22 laid down: *"Declaration on the venue for European Councils: As from 2002, one European Council meeting per Presidency will be held in Brussels. When the Union comprises 18 members, all European Council meetings will be held in Brussels."*[18]

This means that the European Council will be given a *permanent seat* with every opportunity of building up its own secretariat and diplomatic staff.

In other words, the European Council has been able to bend a potential threat to its decision-making process into a strengthened position within the European Union. As soon as the new treaty is ratified the European Council will have an indirectly elected President, and will be able to start building a secretariat and to enjoy a stronger institutional position than ever before. One could argue that Giscard d'Estaing, as leader, has been able to fulfill almost personally the final phase of his political intentions of the seventies: to create a strong, powerful, formal, intergovernmental, top-level institution that can counterbalance the overly supranational influence of the European Commission and Parliament.

One particular international-relations reflex should not be forgotten, however. Changes in procedures and methods always lead to unexpected new problems and dilemmas. No one can tell how the European Council will actually operate now twenty-five member states are represented. Undoubtedly, new reforms will be needed in future to keep the European Council in the EU driving seat. Much will depend on the *person* who will become the first President of the European Council. Will he or she show real leadership or just fall into line behind the European political leaders? Time will tell.

Notes

1. The author would like to thank his Clingendael colleagues, Jan Melissen and Paul W. Meerts, Gunnar Sjöstedt of the Swedish Institute of International Affairs and the University of Stockholm, and William Zartman of the Nitze School of Advanced International Studies (SAIS) of the Johns Hopkins University, Washington D.C. for their comments on earlier drafts.
2. This section is taken from van Grinsven 2002.
3. An interesting link with the present dilemmas can be witnessed here. One of the main reasons for the current crisis in the European Council stems from the malfunctioning

of the Council of Ministers, in particular the General Affairs and External Relations Council (GAERC) which is discussed at length later in this contribution.

4. It should be noted that the Treaty on European Union stipulates that the "Council, meeting in the composition of the Heads of State or Government" exercises several functions: determining by unanimity the existence of a serious and persistent breach by a member state of certain principles, such as the respect for human rights and fundamental freedoms; deciding to move to the third phase of economic and monetary union and determining which member states meet the conditions for joining the single currency; and allowing "enhanced cooperation" in the Community field. The "Council, meeting in the composition of the Heads of State or Government" does not mean the "European Council": the president of the Commission is not, for example, a member of the former although he/she is a member of the European Council, and the decision-making rules are not the same. Similarly, a distinction should be made between the powers of the "Governments of the Member States at the level of Heads of State or of Government" (which intervene for example in the appointment of the president, vice-president and other members of the executive board of the European Central Bank) and the term "European Council." See <http://ue.eu.int/en/info/eurocouncil/sommet.htm>.

5. For an excellent analysis of the European Council up to the Maastricht treaty, see Werts (1992).

6. The author has gratefully used the official website of the Secretary-General for information to provide insight into the working methods of the European Council.

7. Other parts of this chapter are based on interviews with mostly Dutch diplomats who have attended European Council summits.

8. This group was named after its Italian originator (1975) and was created to alleviate the workload of COREPER.

9. This picture is primarily based on the press photos on the website of the European Council. See <http://ue.eu.int/en/Info/eurocouncil/index.htm>.

10. Translating from the original language into one of the three working languages of the EU (German, French, and English), then translating again into the language of the receiver. For example, a contribution in Greek being translated into German, then translated from the German into Czech.

11. *Presidency Conclusions*—Barcelona, 15 and 16 March 2002, page 23.

12. *Presidency Conclusions*—Seville, 21 and 22 June 2002, Annex I, pages 19–21.

13. It is important to stress that at the moment of writing of this chapter no agreement had yet been agreed upon by the twenty-five (future) member states in the IGC.

14. For additional information on the convention, see <http://www.europa.eu.int/futurum/index_en.htm>.

15. The topics the convention had to deal with were defined at the Laeken summit and laid down in the Annex IV of conclusions of this summit.

16. Once again it is important to stress that at the moment of writing of this chapter no agreement had yet been agreed upon by the twenty-five (future) member states in the IGC.

17. For a complete overview of all European Council meetings, see <http://europa.eu.int/european_council/conclusions/index_en.htm>.

18. For the Treaty of Nice, see <http://europa.eu.int/eur-lex/en/treaties/dat/nice_treaty
    _en.pdf>.

Chapter 10

Cookbook of the Presidency of the European Union

Alain Guggenbühl

In the European Union (EU) time has incrementally shaped the role and functions of the authority that is in charge of convening, conducting, and concluding the negotiations between its member states. In negotiation matters the EU has, in fact, moved from improvisation to a set of customary requirements and official logistical rules that have been imposed on every member state under the format of a "Presidency"[1] of the European Union lasting six months. The Presidency, at its birth in the first European Community, was intellectually, politically, and logistically restricted to an administrative function that consisted mainly of convening meetings and following a formal agenda. Later, the Presidency started to guide discussions among the member states of the European Union, and finally it faced the challenge of conducting negotiations among them. No detailed provisions, code, or guidelines have, however, been elaborated or enacted by the European Union to formalize the precise substance of the strategic and tactical tools of its Presidency in the context of managing European negotiations. Member states have basically been obliged to create their own approach and to do the job intuitively.

Indeed, the Presidency of the European Union resembles a collection of culinary recipes that have been handed down through the generations without anybody actually having bothered to refer back to the official version or to one particularly established way of doing things. When following a recipe, many people rely on habit, instinct, and trial and error. For example, almost everybody in the EU would have his/her own method, individual technique, or family recipe for preparing a dish of spaghetti. However, we have all seen our culinary preparations fail where, in the apparent absence of precise rules, we have relied predominantly on tradition and improvisation. As a matter of fact, even a simple spaghetti dish can fail under such circumstances, with the ingredients being wasted, the money lost, and gourmet satisfaction ruined. For if one looks at the problem more closely, one can see that an actual technique is needed to prepare this recipe successfully. For example, durum wheat should be used to make the pasta; the pasta should be cooked in a very large amount of water to retain its firm texture; salt should be put into the water to speed up the cooking; there is a precise, optimum moment to remove the pan from the heat which the cook senses by watching how the pasta is behaving; and finally, adding a little oil after a certain cooling-down period will add to the overall taste. Similarly, the success of European negotiations will depend on how the Presidency handles factors such as preparation and timing, whether it allows delegations sufficient room for maneuver, its listening capacity, its ability to provide face-saving opportunities, if it can add enough "oil" or supply other compensatory measures to win over the last resisting delegation, and its efficient management of the cooling-off periods, such as recesses or confessionals.

This chapter offers an analysis of those factors and, more precisely, of what is needed to prepare and execute the particular recipe of the Presidency of the Council of the EU. The chapter will follow the format generally established by cookbooks which usually present in sequence the origin of the recipe, the reasons for choosing it, the ingredients and preparatory tasks required, and finally a "method" advising how the ingredients should be mixed together for a successful result. The chapter will present, in four sections, the origin of the Presidency function, the benefits a member state might derive from holding the Presidency, the tasks of the Presidency, the required ingredients for a presidential strategy, and finally some specific techniques for managing the negotiation process and national interests both inside and outside the meeting room.

The Origin and History of the Recipe

The history of the recipe of the Presidency of the European Union is characterized more by a long maturation process than by a precise date of birth. We have witnessed the evolution of a function rather than the appearance of an institution as such (Ruiz Tartas 1995). In other words, the Presidency has benefited from development by default rather than by design (Kirchner 1992). Today the debates surrounding the Presidency focus on transforming the status of the function: on making it more akin to an institution—personifying it through the appointment of a President of the European Council for a duration of two and a half years.[2] The evolution that has brought us to the point of considering a quasi-institution as the future "President" of the European Union has been fueled by a series of factors of a historical, political, and administrative nature.[3]

Historically, the gradual empowerment of a function serving an institution that represents the member states was triggered by the disappearance of some of the founding fathers or leading figures of the early days of European integration. The identifiable and charismatic leaders of the Community have vanished and, with them, the inspiration and political impetus that had always inspired not only the founding fathers of European integration but the other visionary leaders who contributed to extending or accelerating the deepening of European integration. In this context, mention should be made of visionary leaders such as Walter Hallstein, Jacques Delors, Valéry Giscard d'Estaing, and Helmut Schmidt. In the absence of "father figures" and personal visions for the European integration process, holding the Presidency is the opportunity for a country to associate itself with a grand political scheme and historical landmark events: to be, itself, remembered by history. When treaties are signed or intergovernmental conferences (IGCs) are launched, the interests of the country holding the chair can be served through that country's association with these historic events, rather than some foreign, albeit charismatic, leader monopolizing all the success and fame. In other words the Presidency has become a symbol among all the other symbols that constitute Europe: a tree in a forest of trees. Indeed, the EU mix of regulative, normative and cognitive pillars is wrapped up in symbols (Laffan 2001), and, in its substitutive move, the Presidency has turned into one of them.

Of course, the symbolic role of the Presidency can serve the cause of European integration in that it can act not only to counterbalance the dominant role of national leaders who may be pushing integration in the "wrong" direction but also effectively to resist such influence. In the absence of resistance by charismatic figures such as Hallstein or Delors to attempts by de Gaulle or Thatcher respectively to personify the resistance of national identity to European integration, a well-fledged Presidency might take on the role of safeguarding the prospects of further European integration. One could argue conversely that the Presidency function could also be viewed as a mere "pushover" by charismatic adversaries of further progress in European integration; moreover, the harm that could be caused by such adversaries might be heightened when their own country is holding the Presidency.

A second historical factor with obvious political seeds may further explain the growth of the Presidency function. After five years of European summits, the European Council was created in 1974; in 1983 by the Solemn Declaration of Stuttgart it was charged with giving impetus to the development of the Community, with the Presidency thus being offered a more obvious seat as the driver of general Community business.[4] De Schoutheete (1988, 74) argues that the very concept of having a European Council to represent member states in high politics can be compared to the raison d'être of the Presidency in that both Council and Presidency reflect an institutional style, if not fashion, based on the Fifth French Republic created by de Gaulle.

Turning to political factors, a determining element with considerable administrative implications lies in the boom in daily EU business and the ever-growing agenda of the Council over time. The increasing number of meetings in Brussels is merely a material and logistical illustration of the combined effect of the deepening and widening of European integration. The Presidency has witnessed and has gradually managed the soaring number of items on the Council agenda, which is a direct consequence of the overlap in EC jurisdiction, EU competences, and policy areas, as well as of the successive enlargements of the European Union. On average, each Presidency will need to manage at the various levels of the Council—across the three pillars and even outside the European Union for certain aspects of external relations—between two thousand and two thousand five hundred meetings that aim to coordinate the external policies of member states and manage certain aspects of EC external relations. The progressive erosion of the power and efficiency of the Commission as an independent executive actor is another political factor with institutional implications (Wallace 1985, 12) that is directly linked to the increase in Council activity and the deepening of integration in intergovernmental fields.

Finally, the Presidency function has grown in importance because of demands in the media for political counterparts at European Union level and increasing media attention in general. At the time of popular principles such as subsidiarity, accountability, and transparency, the Presidency quickly appeared as a beacon, concentrating all the necessary means and channels of communication into bridging the gap between European citizens and the European governance system.

In fact, the Presidency has been "invented" over the years as a means of improving the merging of high- and low-level institutional management (Rittberger 2001) where pursuance of the high political goal of cooperation is coupled with the necessary management of growing policy areas and competencies. All in all, the Presidency has been conceived gradually in order to bring coherence within the European multilevel bargaining and negotiation system.

The Motives and Hidden Agenda of the Cook

Generally, when choosing a particular recipe, one has in mind specific targets and is driven by precise intentions. These motives can, for example, be epicurean—to satisfy a definite longing or taste, to leave a good impression, to seduce, to contribute to a positive atmosphere, or simply to socialize. When embarking on the culinary route of the Presidency a member state will similarly follow certain objectives; hence it will dedicate particular methods, means, and resources to achieving self-defined priorities and objectives and to balancing its individual and collective gain by combining national payoffs with the collective EU interest. The following section will consider the "dividends" a member state can anticipate after "investing" in the Presidency; in other words, why it actually pays to run the EU Presidency for six months and what is the typical motivation behind the national plans presented by member states on the eve of their Presidency.

No member state holding the Presidency is totally free to do whatever it wants. Every member state will actually need to put in place a program of action to ensure continuity with the preceding Presidency, thereby subjecting itself to the so-called rolling agenda where the policy areas, actions, and decisions of the European Union are viewed as part of a wider and longer spectrum than just the six-month program of each Presidency. Basically, it means that the job of managing the EU agenda must be carried out, and that the product must be wrapped up or made ready for further manufacturing by the Presidency that will take over next. Each Presidency program inherits a "rolling" element consisting either of planned long-term EU action or simply unfinished business or leftovers from the previous Presidency. In fact, the program of every Presidency will largely depend upon how much the previous Presidency's program accomplished, in other words, on the performance of the predecessor. When presenting the Austrian program, the minister of foreign affairs metaphorically and vociferously expressed these two dimensions of the Presidency process: *"Presidencies succeed each other, and it is every Presidency's obligations to keep the ship on course and to hand it over unharmed to the next helmsman six months later. We Austrians are fortunate to have the United Kingdom as our predecessor...."*[5] Denmark did not express similar satisfaction when it received twenty leftover dossiers from the Spanish Presidency in the field of environment alone (Dosenrode 2002). In this respect, one observer noted that a chairperson is nothing more than a pawn within a continuum of policy- and decision-making processes (Rood 1997, 130).

Despite the rolling agenda of commitments for the EU which fuels every member state's Presidency program, the Presidency needs to be ready to face unexpected events and therefore to plan some flexibility into its program. The most striking example of how a country holding the Presidency might be called upon to change its initial program and action planning to manage a crisis occurred during the Belgian Presidency in the second semester of 2001. In the aftermath of 11 September, and in order to reinforce solidarity and cooperation with the United States, the Belgian Presidency on 21 September 2001 urgently convened, inter alia, an extraordinary European Council which adopted an action plan to fight terrorism and to upgrade the international role of the European Union. The Presidency suddenly had to manage numerous meetings, convene experts and directors-general, draft texts on definitions and lists of terrorists for the European mandate, and speed up the adoption of European legislation dealing with Eurojust in terms of money laundering and the freezing of criminal assets. The greatest diversion from the initial program undoubtedly came from the extensive travel arrangements and missions of Belgian ministers and high diplomats. The troika traveled notably to Egypt, Iran, Pakistan, Saudi Arabia, and Syria.

A crucial objective present in the strategy of every member state embarking on the Presidency is to enhance its reputation, sometimes even to gain prestige. There is clearly a benchmarking process at work in Brussels. As far as member states are concerned, for example, a new member state taking up the Presidency will strive to perform as well as another new member state that entered the EU at the same time as it did and has already run a Presidency. Similarly, the first new member state taking on the Presidency will undoubtedly strive to set the benchmark high and earn a reputation for being the first among the other newly entered member states to set that benchmark. Furthermore, the race for excellence commits a member state to performance excellence not only compared to other new member states but also to states with comparable leverage in the EU. For example, it is hard to believe that a large member state would decide to prepare its "recipe" badly and thus take the risk of jeopardizing the power it usually derives from its size. It is also in the interests of a smaller or medium-sized member state to invest in the Presidency with a view to outperforming others within its category so that it will come to be associated with the larger member states that have sufficient resources to be able to perform well. For new member states a good performance in the Presidency actually contributes to offsetting, if not combating, stereotypes about certain member states' ability to truly join the club and run a Presidency according to the club's standards. By investing in the Presidency, new member states basically become part of the "politically correct" in the EU. The benchmarking process occurs over time for every member state. A member state, because of a prior performance, may have a positive or less-than-positive reputation and thus an interest either in sustaining or redeeming that reputation.

For a long time the importance of reputation has motivated Belgium to invest in the Presidency to serve the Community's interests. Evidence of the success of this strategy can be found in the words of Jacques Delors when he eulogized the expertise and reputation of Belgium in an assessment of its 2001 Presidency. Belgium had, Delors said, "a quasi-institutionalized identification with the European project, difficult internal experiences with the construction of a form of 'co-operative federalism' that respects particularly difficult and uncompromising identities, and an incontestable know-how in the art of compromise and soft governance" (cited in de Winter and Türsan 2001). At the end of the previous Belgian Presidency, the

President of the European Commission had already expressed not only the *rare happiness* the European Commission had experienced in working with the previous Belgian Presidency in 1993 but also how, in that time, he had enjoyed some of his most exceptional moments in his nine years in office (Frank and de Wilde d'Estmael 1994, 53). In 2001, it was thus in Belgium's interest to preserve the image of being a servant of European integration that it had acquired during its previous presidencies and to demonstrate once again its experience in bridge building thanks to the domestic practice it had in this matter. The Belgian "capital" of reputation stems notably from the good performance of Belgian presidencies in handling the difficult economic situations of 1973 and 1977, the budgetary crisis in 1982, the Delors package for economic and social cohesion in 1987, and the entry into force of the Treaty of Maastricht in 1993.

Holding the Presidency is also the opportunity for a country to undertake public relations activities aimed at better managing domestic issues and national policies. The Presidency can be used either to divert domestic opinion from a crisis affecting the country's interests or to help it recover from such a crisis. In 2001 Belgium took over the Presidency while its government was making strong efforts to recover from the dioxin scare. Sweden embarked on its Presidency with a similar double-edged domestic objective—the Swedish government decided to couple a national campaign against the widespread euroskepticism prevalent among Swedish citizens who were disappointed at the concrete benefits of full membership to a Presidency program clearly designed to deliver tangible results of EU membership and thus make Swedes more EU-friendly (Miles 2002, 193). The three Es—Enlargement, Employment, and Environment—chosen as the priorities of the Swedish Presidency were definitely not a coincidence. Environment, for example, constituted not only a policy issue with which the Swedish government sought to persuade a largely euroskeptic domestic audience of the merits of deeper integration; it was also selected as a lever to push for the adoption of transnational policy measures close to the heart of the Swedish public (Wurzel 2002).

Further illustrations as to how a Presidency can use public relations to garner domestic support, restore reputation, and divert attention away from domestic issues are frequent in British presidencies. The last British Presidency, the first under the "New Labour" leadership, clearly had the objective of restoring the British government's shattered image and reputation as a member of the European group, or club (Henderson 1999; Ludlow 1998). This public-relations objective was quite obvious from the words of the British minister for Europe at a conference in Bonn: "We see Europe as our natural home. We know that our future lies with Europe. We see Europe as an opportunity, not a threat, and as a strength, not a weakness. We are determined to play a leading role in the European Union and we want to help shape its future" (Henderson 1998, 3). Reading between the lines one gets the signal that the British government simply wanted to move away from the Conservative years and start projecting an image of being fully involved rather than an "à la carte" consumer of European integration benefits. Put more bluntly, the Presidency offered an opportunity for the government to break with Britain's reputation of being an awkward partner (George and Sowemimo 1998, 20).

The Austrian Presidency presented a program that encapsulated most of these public-relations endeavors, both outside and inside the country: "Externally the six months' Presidency offers Austria an opportunity to enhance its European credentials and diplomatic visibility. Internally, Austria's governing parties presumably hope that the sight of their leaders presiding over EU business will help assuage popular concerns regarding aspects of European integration and might possibly even enhance their prospects at the general election due in the autumn of 1999" (Luther 1998, 3). There are two main underlying reasons for undertaking such a public-relations strategy in Austria, and these were obviously common to Finland and Sweden when they took over their first Presidency (Luther 1998). First, Austrian popular support for EU membership is not, and never has been, unconditional. Second, where citizens may be more skeptical of the abstract benefits of membership, they can be "persuaded" if tangible benefits from membership can be identified, possibly with the help of their own Presidency program.

Turning to exclusively domestic and internal motivation, the Presidency can help cement or hold together a crumbling government coalition (Dinan 2000a, 245). In the case of Belgium the Presidency program appeared to be quite lengthy and ambitious. This, one should note, was the direct result of an internal negotiation process where each partner of the government had basically made a shopping list of its own interests. In fact, the political tendencies of all the partners were clearly represented in the political choices for the Presidency program which set out priorities for the EU in the fields of jobs, social standards, citizenship, and environment. Beyond this consensual program, holding the Presidency had several benefits for the stability of the Belgian government. First, being able to defend Belgian interests at EU level during the 1999 dioxin crisis speeded up the process of forming a new national government in spite of Belgium's multilevel domestic bargaining process involving eight political parties. Second, the promotion of the Belgian prime minister as a key European player came at a welcome moment for the government ruling coalition which had not managed thus far to make any breakthroughs in many of its core policies because of opposition between two coalition partners on the one hand and a third partner on the other. "Thus, in spite of these profound antagonisms, there is a clear consensus that the government cannot afford a major crisis before the end of the presidency, for the sake of its national and international image and its ministers' responsibility for running the Councils" (de Winter and Türsan 2001, 39).

Similarly, the program of a Presidency and the way it is run by a member state may also reflect domestic issues directly associated with that country's internal constitutional, political, and administrative organization. During the French Presidency, notably, it was possible to witness the tension of "cohabitation" between the directly elected right-wing national president and the government which was the product of a general election that had brought to power a coalition of left-wing parties and a socialist prime minister. The French presidential elections, due only a few months after the French Presidency of the EU, and for which both the president and prime minister were expected to run, noticeably downgraded the internal consistency of the French EU Presidency because the latter actually offered national politicians the chance to promote themselves when speaking on behalf of the EU Presidency. The tone was set on 29 June 2000 when the French secretary of state for European affairs declared on behalf of his government that the speech recently given by President Jacques Chirac to the German *Bundestag* was not at all the position of the French authorities. In that speech, Chirac had expressed his wish to deepen European integration through the action of a group of "pioneering states" (Costa 2000, 394). In the case of Belgium an ambitious program, relatively hastily conceived, clearly aimed to distract the attention of the media from the internal dissent of the ruling coalition regarding the details of any constitutional reform (de Winter and Türsan, 2001).

At this stage of the investigation of the motives for investing in the Presidency, the question must be: what happens to the Presidency if the cook decides to adapt the recipes to his/her own taste and actually takes a few liberties with the "method" laid down in the recipe book when establishing the six-month program? The real question therefore to address is: how neutral is the country holding the Presidency and how much of its national interests or local tastes may it pursue during its term of office? Does it actually happen that member states holding the Presidency concentrate on domestic interests and strive for national payoffs when presenting and implementing their Presidency program?

Even though there is no definitive or affirmative answer to that question, a study of the history of the Presidency shows that, to a certain degree, elements of national agendas, domestic preferences, or historic principles are often reflected, even if they are not solidly present, in the program of the country holding the Presidency.

Broadly speaking, national preferences that might show up in Presidency programs always reflect the values, and quite often the cultural features, that characterize and hence differentiate member states inside the European Union. The Finnish program, for example, set as priorities a number of principles and policy orientations very commonly associated with the country's national interests and way of life; the Finnish priorities were transparency, ecology, information, and technology. Finland even took commercial and marketing advantage of being renowned for its efficient ways of "connecting people." As for Sweden, it too took advantage of the potential of the Presidency to focus on regional external relations of importance to itself, making sure, however, that these would be phrased and presented as being in the interest of the EU generally (Bengtsson 2002). Still in the northern EU, even though Denmark complained about the twenty dossiers left over by the Spanish Presidency in the environment field, this policy area has traditionally been of paramount importance to the country and its citizens. It was therefore very easy and legitimate for the Danish Presidency to add in other objectives to reflect well-established national principles such as transparency and good governance.

By the same token, the size and power of a member state of the European Union may become one of those characteristics that a country would aim to protect, if not assert, when holding the Presidency. Hence, during its 1993 Presidency, Belgium showed reluctance to open the agenda of the Presidency to a substantial institutional debate that might have jeopardized the prerogatives of small member states (Frank and de Wilde d'Estmael 1994, 37). Three years later, just before the Irish Presidency, the foreign affairs ministry of Ireland issued instructions to the entire administration, literally urging officials to protect Ireland's *acquis* and prestige as a small but active member state (Humphreys 1997).

Being in the driving seat of the Presidency thus allows specific preferences, sometimes obsessions, to be dealt with, as well as profound interests, which can famously place a particular member state in opposition to some, if not all, the other member states. This explains why Luxembourg was so active in dealing with the dossier on banking secrecy during its 1997 Presidency, and why Sweden so enthusiastically took the military question on board in its Presidency program rather than dodging it. Luxembourg simply wanted to control the possible ramifications of a European compromise by restricting damaging commitments rather than one day finding itself trapped in a corner and politically (or institutionally because of a new voting procedure) not being in a position to resist an solution that might be intolerable to it.[6] Sweden invested all its efforts in the civil aspects of crisis management inside the second-pillar agenda, an approach that applied notably to the administration of the regional crisis, particularly in former Yugoslavia. This led to the unexpected outcome of a Presidency run by a neutral state managing to contribute to the establishment of a European military identity. As Walch (2001) puts it, whatever the political and military profile of a member state, its six-month presidential term allows it to lay its own stone to the building while recognizing its identity in the collective end product.

During the 1996 IGC negotiations a number of correlations between national preferences and the presidential agenda became more apparent. At the time, the Austrian minister for foreign affairs called such national preferences *the hobby-horses* of member states holding the Presidency. The Dutch government was obviously interested in pushing for the integration of Schengen; the Spanish Government pressed ahead with the discussion of fundamental rights and freedoms; the Italian government emphasized flexibility; and Ireland focused on nuclear safety (Svensson 2000). In the Dutch case it has become obvious that the importance the government attached to cooperation in the field of justice and home affairs derived not only from a political interest in dealing with its bitter dispute with France over their respective drugs policies but also from the recent adoption of a fairly restrictive policy toward asylum and immigration directly influenced by conservative activism inside the Dutch government (Kwast-van Duursen 1996, 9).

An even more obvious connection appeared in April 2002 when Spain exerted considerable pressure and lobbying to delay the reform of the common fisheries policy while it was holding the Presidency. It even went as far as trying to get the head of the European Commission official in charge of the dossier served up on a plate.

More evidence of national preferences being defended by a country during its Presidency occurred in 1998 during the British Presidency where one particular dossier under negotiation concerned ornamental plants. At first sight one cannot detect any specific national interest in this field. A closer look into the way the agenda was approached, however, actually sheds light on British preferences of a broader magnitude. Linked to this dossier were, in fact, a series of other issues of decisive importance for the United Kingdom relating to the degree of regulation, the type of methodology or approach, and the comitology procedure to be used for more efficient and simplified European legislation relating to the internal market. The dossier on ornamental plants thus fit into a larger British stake in the internal market and the subsidiarity principle. Furthermore, during the same Presidency, it was obvious that by reaching agreement on an EU code of conduct for the arms trade, Britain would manage to control one of its main competitors in the market even if it failed to actually compete with it. Finally, during the latest British Presidency, Robin Cook, the then British foreign secretary, agreed more or less to deal with the issue of employment but only if simultaneous progress were seen in the field of the single market—a quasi-permanent "squatter" on the UK's shopping list in Brussels. By trading on the issue of jobs, the British government was pursuing its interest in extending the single market to energy, financial services, and aviation (George and Sowemimo 1998, 19).

Another overlap between national preferences and a Presidency program appeared during the last Dutch Presidency when the Netherlands was able to deal with the leghold trap issue in a way that satisfied national goals and needs, both from a member state's perspective and as President. When the Netherlands inherited this dossier from the rolling agenda, it was in fact the only member state complying with the provisions of the regulation and it was waiting for international endorsement in the form of negotiations between the Commission and third countries as regards imports of fur (Harrems 1998). The Netherlands almost had a legal obligation to fill this legal vacuum though relevant Council action and finally managed to put the leghold trap dossier on the agenda of the February 1997 General Affairs Council for appropriate political consideration.

One can easily imagine the negative impact for a Presidency of being caught "with its hand in the till" in the defense of national interests. This happened during the German Presidency with the negotiations on the *End-of-life Vehicles Directive*, when Germany was caught chasing national interests (in fact payoffs for the Volkswagen Audi Group). Wurzel (2000) reports that it created a poisonous atmosphere and ill feelings among member states as well as exacerbating already negative attitudes around the table which, in turn, failed to contribute to a positive outcome for the negotiations.

A conclusive remark on the type of national preferences at stake during a Presidency may be drawn from the last Belgian Presidency's priorities reported by de Winter and Türsan (2001). The priorities of the 2001 Belgian Presidency actually emerged from four of the motives mentioned in this section:

- Matters that are already part of the European agenda and need to be followed up during the Belgian Presidency.
- Recurrent international problems such as those related to Russia, the Middle East, and the Balkans.
- Matters to which the six partners of the government coalition, ministers, and public opinion attach particular importance and are announced in the government agreement, such as employment creation, common social standards, environment, fiscal harmonization, liberalization of public enterprises and services, institutional reforms and citizenship.
- Long-term concerns stemming from the Belgian policy paradigm regarding European integration.

The Tasks of the Presidency or the Cook's To-Do List

The missions and duties of the Presidency of the European Union have evolved with such magnitude and diversity that the need recently arose to create categories in which to group the different tasks associated with this six-month job. The first attempt to categorize and group the tasks of the Presidency was by Kirchner (1992), according to whom, the Presidency undertakes four broad tasks:

- Tasks of an administrative nature, notably when organizing meetings, the minutes or the six-month work plan;

- Tasks of initiative, notably by offering a work program or agendas;
- Tasks of EU representation during negotiations with third countries, or in codecision with the European Parliament; and
- Tasks or functions relating to coordination, notably of EU activities in the three pillars but also coordination over time when taking over from a previous Presidency.

In their categorization of the functions of the Presidency, Hayes-Renshaw and Wallace (1997)[7] list duties specifically linked to negotiations inside the Council. According to those authors, the Presidency is also the broker of European compromises and package deals among national delegations. Schout (1998) puts these challenging missions into perspective by noting that, when trying to fulfill them, each Presidency will need simultaneously to juggle neutrality and political leadership as well as some of the national interests analyzed above. A final encompassing categorization has been offered by Svensson (2000) who pictures four categories of functions. The managing role consists of organizing meetings, setting up timetables, writing minutes, and making sure the negotiations can take place. The Presidency is also the agenda setter and can thus influence the conditions under which a policy area or item is discussed and negotiated. Finally, the Presidency also builds consensus through a mediation and brokerage role.

Rather than using another functional categorization to describe the tasks of the Presidency, we will look at these from a chronological perspective and describe the succession of duties and efforts required to run the Presidency. In this section, we will look into the phase of preparing the recipe, in particular the cook's to-do list (i.e., before any eggs actually get broken), and managing the meeting. There are two broad sets of tasks in the cook's list; the first relates to the preparation of the kitchen, or the logistics and politics, and the other to the preparation of the ingredients, or the strategic conditions for the negotiation.

Preparing the Kitchen: Logistical and Political Planning

The Presidency is required to prepare a series of actions of a logistical nature that have political ramifications or implications. These range from booking the negotiation rooms to negotiating on behalf of the Council.

The first logistical operation the Presidency needs to undertake involves Council meetings and the agenda. First of all a timetable of all Council meetings should be drawn up and made available to the Council Secretariat seven months before the start of the Presidency. Meetings of the Council include meetings of working groups or working parties, COREPER, and special committees such as the special committee on agriculture and the political and security committee.[8] Ministers can meet within the nine formations of the Council decided at the June 2002 European Council in Seville and immediately implemented by the Danish Presidency that followed.

Meetings of the Council take place at its official headquarters. The Council of Ministers meets in Luxembourg, however, during the months of April, June and October.[9] Member states also convene abroad for coordination purposes, notably during negotiations with third countries. The negotiation process will be conducted either by the European Commission or the Presidency or both, depending on the division of powers between the EU and its member states provided for the policy area at issue. For exceptional reasons, the Council or COREPER may also decide that the Council is to be held elsewhere.[10]

The meetings of working parties are convened by a communication sent out by the Secretariat, in principle one week before the meeting. If less than a week's notice is given, permanent representations are also advised by phone. The decision to convene working party meetings depends greatly on the availability of meeting rooms and interpreting facilities. It is generally agreed that notification of meetings of the Council should be given with one month's notice.[11] The Presidency should send out the agenda for every Council meeting at least fourteen days before the beginning of the meeting.[12] A safety net is even provided by Article 3.5 of the Council rules of procedure (CRP) for legislative decisions to be taken by the Council: "If, by the end of the week preceding the week prior to a Council meeting, COREPER has not completed its examination of legislative items (. . .), the Presidency shall (. . .), remove them from the provisional agenda." This period thus includes an "appearance" at COREPER and, of course, the necessary translation within the Secretariat. Consequently, the Secretariat will generally advise the future Presidency to schedule group meetings at intervals of at least fourteen days, with its work finishing at least three weeks before the Council session. If a dossier is not ready for the scheduled COREPER meeting, the Presidency can always postpone to a subsequent COREPER meeting any legislative item on which a committee or working party has not completed its discussions at least five working days prior to the COREPER meeting.[13]

In parallel with the required planning of the meetings, CRP Article 1.2 obliges the Presidency to provide, obviously before the start of its six-month term of office, a detailed work program to allow for efficient management of content and to set out a time frame. The work program should set out an indicative agenda for each Council meeting.

The second logistical duty of the Presidency with political implications is to represent the Council in its relations with the European Parliament.[14] At the various stages of the codecision procedure, during which the Presidency establishes contacts and conducts negotiations with the European Parliament on behalf of the

Council, the Presidency follows a precise sequence of actions. First, the chair of COREPER makes all the necessary preliminary contacts with the chairs of the relevant parliamentary committees and the rapporteur both to discuss the Parliament's approach and flexibility, and to jointly establish a method of dealing with priority matters and set a time frame. Informal meetings are subsequently convened between the three trilogue actors during the first and second readings, the Council delegation being headed by the Presidency (i.e., either the chair of COREPER or the chair of the working party) for informal trilogues or technical meetings, respectively. In the event of a conciliation between the Council and Parliament, the Presidency decides upon the dates for convening the conciliation committee and the frequency of the informal trilogues. During trilogues the Presidency is the exclusive voice and spokesperson of the Council. During the conciliation phase the Council is represented by a minister of the member state holding the Presidency. The existence of the conciliation secretariat in the European Parliament is of exceptionally valuable help to the Presidency in organizing these logistics.

The tasks of the Presidency in representing the Council before the European Parliament are complemented by three other procedures involving the European Parliament. First, according to Article 21 of the Treaty on European Union (TEU), the Presidency has the task of consulting Parliament on the main aspects and basic choices of the common foreign and security policy (CFSP); the purpose of this consultation is to "ensure that the views of the European Parliament are truly taken into consideration." Second, in the field of external relations, the Presidency may be asked by the European Parliament under the "Luns" and "Westerterp" procedures to inform the relevant parliamentary committees orally on the negotiations of respectively association and trade agreements with third countries. The Presidency can in particular be requested to inform the Parliament on the substance of the mandate of negotiation issued by the Council to the Commission under Article 300 of the Treaty Establishing the European Community (TEC), and then on the substance of the agreement itself once it is ready for a decision. Third, Article 39.2 TEU provides that the Presidency should keep the Parliament informed on matters relating to cooperation in the field of justice and home affairs.

This third duty of the Presidency yet again involves the functions of representation and negotiation on behalf of member states or the Council, this time in certain external-relations activities of the European Union. The conditions under which the Presidency is required to represent the Union greatly depends upon the policy area, the actions, and the external partner. The bottom line is that where the conclusion and/or implementation of international agreements constitute the external dimension of an internal Community policy or activity, the Presidency must ensure the necessary horizontal consistency between all these activities. A more direct and visible role is dedicated to the Presidency as the spokesperson of the

Community's position in the framework of mixed agreements.[15] In this case, the role of single spokesperson for the Community and the member states is assigned to the Presidency in so far as the institutional protocol in the considered agreement establishes meetings at ministerial level for negotiation, political dialogue, and implementation of the agreement. As regards representing the Community in international organizations and conferences, the Community may be represented by the Presidency if the scope of the organization in question coincides with Community competences and the jurisdiction of member states that are also full members of this organization. In practice there is a shared representation between the Presidency and the Commission here, with either one or the other representing the Community depending on the circumstances and the topic at hand. This is the case notably in the World Trade Organization, the United Nations Conference on Trade and Development, the United Nations General Assembly, the Food and Agriculture Organization, and the United Nations Economic and Social Council. The widest power of representation has been given to the Presidency in matters falling within the CFSP, including implementing decisions and expressing the Union's position in international organizations and international conferences (Article 18 TEU). Under Article 24 TEU the Presidency may be authorized by the Council to negotiate international agreements. Regarding implementation of the CFSP, Article 12.4 of the Council rules of procedure provides that the Presidency can in particular trigger a simplified written procedure, called *Correspondance Européenne* (COREU), by which a proposal shall be deemed to have been adopted by the Council at the end of a period laid down by the Presidency. This procedure clearly applies to urgent matters and only under consensus, that is, if no single member state objects to the use of this procedure.

Finally the Presidency also has the logistical and political task of contributing to the obligations of openness and transparency imposed on the Council's deliberations. Articles 5 and 6 of the CRP provide that Council meetings are not held in public and that the deliberations of the Council are covered by the obligation of professional secrecy. Among the exceptions to this rule, however, are two specifically involving the Presidency. First, Article 8.1(a) CRP empowers the Presidency to recommend that the presentation by the Commission of its most important legislative proposals, and the ensuing debate in the Council, be made open to the public. Furthermore, the Presidency can propose issues or specific subjects for public debate by the Council. Article 8.3 provides that such debates be transmitted to the public. The practice today in this field is a broadcast on the channel *Europe by Satellite* which is also permanently on air in the buildings of some of the European Union institutions. It is customary for every Presidency to broadcast a dozen events during its six-month term. Such events may be the very early if not preliminary examination by the Council of a new Community program of action that will not entail any negotiation as such. In fact, the public is merely offered a succession of political statements from the delegations. The Greek Presidency of the first semester of 2003, for example, planned public debates on the western Balkans, the midterm review of the common agricultural policy, competitiveness and entrepreneurship, the directive on the quality of bathing water, the future of the European employment strategy, and the wider Europe.

A normal logistical preparation phase such as that described here has been seen to start twenty-six months before the program of the Presidency is actually ready (Humphreys 1997, 22).

Preparing the Ingredients: The Strategic Preparation of the Presidency

Generally speaking, having a strategy improves negotiation performance, and this is also true of negotiations run by the Presidency. This section will deal with the strategic preparation that should pertain for the Presidency when it is handling individual cases or dossiers from its six-month program. Just as culinary ingredients need to be sorted, weighed, peeled, cleaned, and sliced, so the conditions and parameters of the negotiation process need to be geared up for a Presidency to have successful outcomes. There is a strong element of Taylorism in the preparation required both for a recipe and for the Presidency, in the sense that results will depend on the level of scientific organization and preparation of the work involved.

The first strategic investment for a new Presidency is to ensure a smooth transition from the previous Presidency. For this purpose, the Council General Secretariat advises every Presidency to consider the following courses of action to keep the Council cruising at an efficient speed (Council Guide: Presidency Handbook 2001):

- All dossiers should be examined in the six-month period should be updated.
- The timetables for the procedures to take place within each institution should be cross-checked; in the case of the European Parliament, it is vital to know the timetable for plenary sessions and committee meetings.
- All dossiers should be sorted according to the level and type of decision-making procedures (consultation, cooperation, codecision, or assent).
- The Presidency should assess the importance of each dossier, notably its political and technical elements because they affect the course of the procedure to be followed by the Council.

The second ingredient that is indispensable to Presidency strategy is a clearly identified objective. Since the report of the Three Wise Men in 1979 on the functioning of the EC institutions, it has been widely acknowledged that the simple objective of any Presidency should be to "get results."[16] This implies a series of preparatory acts. At the outset, when sorting the dossiers according to the set procedure, the Presidency should, for example, separate out those dossiers that, realistically, might be ripe for adoption at first reading of the codecision procedure from those expected to go to a second reading and, those likely to go beyond even that stage—to conciliation. The Presidency can subsequently allocate its resources more strategically and devote the necessary political clout and public relations initiatives where they are most needed. Since the Swedish Presidency, we know that sending Ministers to the battle front as early as possible in difficult cases considerably eases the tensions between Parliament and the Council and consequently dispels the prospect of there not being an agreement between these two institutions.

When suggesting an agenda, the Presidency should also look at its overall goal—to get a result—by considering the most appropriate method of approaching negotiations. The Presidency might choose to go for the most easy point in the dossier in order to establish a positive working atmosphere on the basis that the actors will naturally be motivated by progress early on. It might also choose to start off the discussion on the central or core provision of the dossier in order to create a domino effect regarding other more minor or directly related items or provisions. If looked at too early, such secondary provisions could be used by some delegations as an excuse to be overly resistant or even tactically prepare for later trade-offs by pretending they have a vital interest in these items. In other situations, the most appropriate method will be an article-by-article discussion because the dossier under negotiation is built as a logical succession of definitions, objectives, and commitments; starting with the final article would not make real sense and would considerably complicate the understanding of the dossier.

Information is the third ingredient needed to assist understanding of a dossier and to politically prepare the ground for the negotiation. Information is on the cook's shopping list and should be "shopped for" through the widest possible channels and means.

The best way for the Presidency to collect information to aid comprehension of the dossier is first domestically, from national experts: not only from administrative entities but also from the academic world. Contacts with the Commission officials in charge of the dossier will also help in mastering the technicalities of the policy area and the particular dossier in question. The quality of internal coordination within a member state will in turn determine the quantity, quality, and cost-efficiency of the information needed by those Presidency actors exposed to or in charge of the planned negotiations.[17] Evidence of how this equation can actually produce "poor trading results" came to light during the Belgian Presidency. The regional governments within the Belgian federal state had previously decided which dossiers and meetings of the Council each of them would be in charge of. This decision was merely founded on the principle of alternation vis-à-vis the arrangement of earlier Belgian presidencies. It led some governments to preside over dossiers that they had not in fact looked into or defended at the European level, not to mention dossiers that they had no appropriate human resources or knowledge to deal with. The sharing of the pie between the intermediate-level governments to determine who would be in charge of what during the Belgian Presidency had once again been a highly political game; thus the sharing of information and internal coordination were frequently used as battlefields either for one government to take political advantage of another or where a government could assert its "sovereignty." For example, one government inherited jurisdiction during the Presidency over maritime transport without having any direct access to the sea and without *a fortiori* having sent anyone to represent Belgium in the competent Council working group. Another decided on a matter of principle that it would not request any information pertaining to the dossier on genetically modified organisms from another regional government but instead pay 1,200 euros a day to a private law firm in the region to provide the required information.

Political moves and gestures are also critical to channeling information, either to or from the Presidency. Ministers in particular should both gather and transmit information to establish appropriate conditions for confidence building and agenda setting. Let us mention in particular contacts between the competent minister and the Presidency to ensure smooth transition and takeover of dossiers ready for adoption; the necessary talks with the European Commission by national officials and moreover by the competent minister; the *tours de capitales* by the minister; the contacts between Presidency officials and national delegation officials, and finally the contacts with the officials of the Council Secretariat.

This networking or intelligence management requires national delegations to be used strategically by the Presidency. The national representatives of the country holding the Presidency can be mandated by the Presidency to collect information, either by approaching other delegations or by participating with them in informal meetings or coalition building. In such a position, the national delegation can also test the water and assess how strong the chances of success might be of a Presidency compromise proposal. The Presidency can, in this respect, use its national delegation as a sparring partner.[18]

One general rule to observe when managing information with national delegations is to act equitably (i.e., to approach all delegations and not just a few, in order to create the necessary legitimacy and confidence regarding the Presidency's intentions). Moving even one step away from this rule may yield collateral damage and force delegations to refuse to negotiate at a later stage merely because they feel they have been treated unfairly. Consequently, if the plan of the Presidency, to the detriment of some delegations, is to go for a decision adopted by qualified majority, then all delegations should nevertheless be involved in the early stages of the process to secure the widest possible majority.

General negotiation theory, since the introduction of Fisher and Ury's win/win concept, has widely tried to demonstrate that, regardless of apparent initial disagreement or conflict between interlocutors, the more a negotiation process moves away from the positions of the negotiation actors and focuses on their interests and needs, the more likely it is to succeed (Fisher *et al.* 1997; Lewicki 2003; Susskind *et al.* 1999). This pattern also tends to hold true for multilateral negotiations among member states chaired by a rotating Presidency. Finding ways of moving away from the national positions will therefore be the fourth task needing attention by the Presidency when preparing its strategy. When trying to get a result the Presidency will need to try to understand the real concerns of the delegations regarding the matter under negotiation. Holding a formal plenary meeting with a succession of positions expressed by all the delegations will yield not much more than a heavy workload for the interpreters and the Council Secretariat. The Presidency should thus be tasked with intelligence work to discover what interests and needs lie behind the official positions of the delegations.

For example, while a delegation may set an ultimatum at the outset of the negotiations, insist on a proposal being drafted in a precise manner, or ask for a definition to be worded in a particular way, it would only very rarely express what outcome it would like to see or might consider satisfactory. Very often these initial positions or claims will be used as bargaining chips by member states when revealing their true commitments or efforts in other provisions of the legal act under negotiation. The genuine payoffs for the delegations can usually be found in subsequent provisions of the proposed course of action, and definitely not in the positions they claimed early on. In recent times, a European Commission official chairing the meeting of a comitology committee was very perplexed to witness two delegations strongly opposed to any progress in the discussion. The representatives of the delegations would systematically obstruct any alternative proposals, any suggestion of alteration or amendment put on the table. The two delegates had actually begun an intimate relationship which they could best enjoy in Brussels when convened to meetings of the committee.

The most common scenario witnessed by European negotiators would involve one or two delegations either insisting on the legal document having the narrowest possible scope of application possible or making their support dependent on the acceptance of one or two precise provisions. Their positions would be dropped, or more precisely conceded, in return for sufficient European support or compensation later. These early claims would merely be bargaining chips aiming at securing the negotiators' true interests and needs, usually of an economic nature.

From these examples it is obvious that the salvation of the Presidency lies in having access to the more authentic and genuine interests of member states regarding issues so as to be able to come up with alternatives capable of meeting the widest possible interests of the delegations. The life expectancy of a Presidency compromise put forward to bridge the gaps between the delegations and force an agreement will largely depend on the number of alternatives that the Presidency has been able to gather. It will also depend on the distance the Presidency has managed to put between these alternative solutions and the first positions officially expressed by the delegations.

Consequently the Presidency should, as much as possible, anticipate the technical and political alternatives to the first text, most probably a European Commission proposal serving as a compromise solution and conveying, if not actually including, the interests and needs of the delegations. These alternative avenues, which are the fifth ingredient of the Presidential strategy, should be put together in conjunction with the European Commission and the Council Secretariat. Both these institutions not only have the technical expertise to work out legally and technically correct provisions but also, as the "long-stayers" in the business of European compromises beyond the term of any Presidency, they possess the political experience to decide what typical tools or instruments would work in stalled situations. Some technical and political alternatives are particularly useful and deserve to be mentioned. First, compromise in the EU can be reached by changing the scope of the proposed piece of European action to avoid any decision impacting on a product, part of an industry, or even a region of a member state. The alternative might reside in enlarging the scope of the legal act with wider definitions or a larger product-based implication. Alternatives might further envisage geographic differentiation or derogations for some parts of the European Union. Differentiation over time is another way of looking for a common denominator, with the commitments of member states spread over time or some provision applying only after certain conditions are met. Finally, the European compromise is very often based on solidarity and compensation. The EU has at its disposal a variety of economic and social cohesion instruments, as well as numerous programs with either a geographical basis or research and development resources which are used to compensate, either financially or technologically, one or several member states for adhering to a proposed compromise. As the guardian of the EC treaty and manager of EU funds the European Commission will naturally be the first institution the Presidency will confer with when building up these alternative avenues and actually assessing their technical, legal, and financial viability.

The sixth stage in strategic presidential preparation should be to research the logistic conditions and requirements surrounding the items planned for negotiation. One way for the chair to fish for information and craft compromises—as well as to establish a positive atmosphere that may induce a good working environment and dynamics during the negotiation—is to consider approaching national delegates on an individual basis for lunch or coffee. The person initiating any such strategic socialization should be part of the group in which this will operate. A delegate will therefore need to spend time inside a group before being active as a president in it. Each group has a routine when it comes to informal contacts, ranging from the language spoken to the place and time to meet; the future president will need to learn about this routine and adopt it. This is where some linguistic knowledge of both French and English will prove to be an asset. With regard to languages, interpretation and translation will play a crucial logistical role before, during, and after the negotiation. Seventeen rooms with full interpretation facilities are available in the Council building. There are currently only thirteen full interpretation teams available to provide simultaneous interpretation in all the official languages. This is why some working groups have reduced their working languages to three or at most eight languages. As for translation, the Presidency should realize that at Council working-group level, the negotiation documents are increasingly circulated in English only, even though, occasionally, they are still translated into French. Official versions of the texts will, however, need to be tabled in all official languages for formal adoption by the Council. Article 14.1 of the CRP provides indeed that, "except as otherwise decided unanimously by the Council on grounds of urgency, the Council shall deliberate and take decision only on the basis of documents and drafts drawn up in the languages specified in the rules in force governing the languages." Paragraph 2 even provides the usual safety net should the preceding provision be ignored: "any member of the Council may oppose discussion if the texts of any proposed amendments are not drawn up in such of the languages referred to in Paragraph 1 as he or she may specify." This does not, however, prevent a text which is not available in all official languages being the object of a "political agreement" on its substance.

Logistical preparation further requires the role and configuration of "informals" to be planned for (i.e., meetings, discussions, confessionals and negotiations held outside the plenary sessions of the Council). At the ministerial and working-group level, the number of informal meetings provided for in the EU budget has been limited to five for each Presidency (Council Guide 2001, 45). All other informal ministerial gatherings are simply called "ministerial meetings." The Presidency should keep track of any informal gatherings and invest heavily in sufficient new ones notably via corridor diplomacy: ministerial lunches, socialization between the members of a group, but also the briefing session with the Council Secretariat and the Commission the day before the meeting is due.

As far as chronology is concerned the last ingredient of a logistical nature to be considered by the Presidency in its strategy is the time factor. Before deciding to use time as a means of pressure during the negotiation, the Presidency should be aware of the reaction of the delegations to the dossier under negotiation. Some might be quite vulnerable and indeed feel pressurized by time to agree; some might not. Thus the Presidency should always consider and plan intermediary targets within the dossier under negotiation so that the different time resources available to all delegations can be safely accommodated.

Mixing the Ingredients: Managing the Negotiations and National Interests

Just as the cook will need savoir faire and various techniques to successfully mix the ingredients at the right speed and in the correct sequence, the Presidency will also need to deploy management, communication, and negotiation techniques to craft compromise proposals and get results in the meeting room.

It is important for the President to be available before the plenary meeting starts and after it is over. Before the plenary, the President should consider using all modern communication devices to approach the individual members of the group, and even envisage coffee or lunch meetings if the matter at issue requires deeper informal discussions or prior socialization. The day before the meeting itself, the President will be briefed in the Council Secretariat on the basis of a report it has prepared either for the upcoming meeting itself or for a discussion within COREPER. The Secretariat will also prepare a note for the chair of COREPER containing the detailed positions of delegations on particularly sensitive issues, the very issues that are handed over to COREPER through the so-called lift between the levels inside the Council; unlike the Secretariat report issued after the meeting and containing the minutes, this note is not a document that will be circulated widely to all negotiation actors. One can infer from this that the chair of COREPER is a strategic well of information, able to envisage alternative avenues and compromise solutions from a political point of view. As he/she is a central actor, decisions to link dossiers will be in his/her hands alone. Let us not also forget that it is up to the COREPER chair to decide whether the dossier is ripe for discussion in COREPER or whether it still needs refining at the working-group level.

The technical, financial, and legal angles of the compromise, for their part, are the expertise of the European Commission, which consequently will need to be consulted almost before anybody else. The Presidency should not, however, in the final analysis rely on the Commission's briefing but should also seek the opinion of the Secretariat and its legal service, especially where matters are subject to interpretation. Even though the Presidency should rely on the Secretariat to prepare the meeting, to envisage alternatives and draft compromise texts, even papers or non-papers, it should not blindly transfer all its tasks to that body. There have indeed been some rare cases where the Secretariat simply went its own way and worked out compromise solutions with the Commission well away from the path initially laid down by the Presidency. Article 23.3 of the CRP clearly provides for leadership by the Presidency: "under the responsibility and guidance of the Presidency, (the CGS) shall assist (the Presidency) in seeking solutions."

If the Presidency, primed with creative ideas and strategic information, approaches the individual delegations during the half hour preceding the meeting, this apparent effort at socializing with colleagues will transform its efforts into a strategic mission to prepare negotiations informally. After the meeting the President should devote another half an hour to bilateral contacts with the delegations that have expressed flexibility, reservations, or any difficulties that would prevent them from coming to an agreement before the next round of negotiation. The Presidency's task will be to diminish as many reservations as possible before the next plenary meeting using the same communication devices as before.

These methods particularly suit multilateral discussion and negotiations in a European Union of twenty-five members where *tours de table* will be restricted to the inaugural session and the speaking time for each delegate considerably limited. Basically, the Presidency will need to monitor, follow, guide, and influence the negotiation outside the plenary meeting. For this purpose, the Presidency could sometimes consider using questionnaires and national position papers to replace the *tours de table*, as well as planning and making efficient use of recesses or interruptions during the plenary sessions. Provided the Presidency respects some fundamental rules, playing the ball outside the official field provides valuable tools for clearing up impasses in negotiations. To illustrate this, let us look at the classical situation where some delegations have fought hard and resisted long on a particular issue under negotiation. Over time, the force driving the delegates' resistance to a compromise proposal might well have simply become a matter of keeping up appearances. Allowing those delegates to leave the room and come back in at the plenary session announcing that they have managed to convince their "capital" of the advantages of adhering to the compromise is a precious tool that can help them save face vis-à-vis the group as a whole. There is evidence to show that only very rarely do delegates in such a position actually contact any higher authority to obtain the supposed green light for agreement.

It should be noted that whenever a recess is scheduled, the Presidency should always announce how long it will last and the reason for the interruption. If the objective of the recess is to allow time for consulting delegations and for drafting a compromise text, the Presidency should announce this and ensure that all delegations are, in effect, approached. Maintaining equity between all delegations is an essential ingredient of the Presidency's legitimacy, hence the room for maneuver it has been accorded.

Another useful face-saving device at the disposal of the Presidency is its power to transform an item informally agreed at working-group or COREPER level into a "fake" B point on the agenda of the next meeting of the Council of Ministers. "B" agenda items are those subject to discussion by ministers whereas "A" items are adopted in bulk without further attention. This trick would allow a member state to keep some face domestically by pretending it is still planning to forcefully defend its national position.

A member state might also be inclined to adhere to a Presidency compromise proposal by doing so half-heartedly. In the TEC, whenever unanimous voting is required, the decision of a member state to abstain will not prevent a unanimous decision. The Presidency should therefore investigate the conditions under which a delegation might be interested in not blocking the agreement while still being able to advertise some kind of opposition.

Managing support by the delegations and planning the appropriate voting conditions are indeed quite vital challenges for the Presidency. Even though formal voting rarely ever takes place, and if it does so, it is at ministerial level, Article 11 of the CRP provides that the Council shall vote on the initiative of its President. However, the President shall be required to open a voting procedure on the initiative of a member state or the Commission, provided that a majority of member states agrees on this procedure. In the final stage of the negotiation, in all instances, the Presidency should be able to collect indicative voting or be aware of whether or not the delegations intend to support its compromise; it should use time pressure and possibly tactics to influence the sequence of acquaintance. In this respect, when planning to table a compromise proposal after a recess the Presidency could approach delegations expected to support its text and request them to ask for the floor as soon as the meeting resumes so that they can express that support. This technique is somehow more subtle, or at least less obvious, than planning for early support to be shown by the national delegation of the country holding the Presidency. These days one should also avoid another blatant technique whereby the Presidency tries to build its legitimacy and an image of neutrality inside the group by outrageously rebuffing its own national delegation's supposed opposition to the compromise proposal.

At all stages it remains important for the Presidency to constantly liaise with the Commission, not only to implement the prepared alternatives or make sure the Commission will agree to table a revised proposal on the basis of the compromise, but also to short-circuit opposition of delegations requesting more data or information before being in a position to agree. One quite powerful technique is for a Presidency to prepare with the Commission, prior to the Council meeting, a list of the reports, assessments, or other information that might prove useful at the meeting. Such "cards" would be kept hidden by the Commission and made available in a timely fashion in the course of the meeting as and when delegations express their willingness to agree on condition that they can access such information.

Conclusion

In despair, political scientists often use the label *sui generis* to explain the originality of the European integration process and to describe the identity of the European governance system. As an integral part both of this historical evolution and the "home-made" political system, the Presidency of the Council of Ministers of the European Union is definitely of the *sui generis* variety. The home-made European recipe for the Presidency of an international institution appears to have six specific and intertwined features that are worth inventorying. First, it is a dynamic recipe that evolves with time and with the incremental deepening and widening of European integration, grabbing more competences and jurisdictions, gradually being empowered with new duties and becoming ever more accompanied by the procedural rules of the Council. Second, the Presidency of the EU is nevertheless a little-regulated function more governed by customary *dos* and *don'ts*, and principles and precepts, such as reputation or precedents, than by overwhelming rules of procedure. Third, the Presidency is indeed concerned with individuals who have embarked upon a human adventure where socialization and the degree of proximity between the negotiators inside a particular Council body will play a determining role. Fourth, the EU Presidency will harvest more crops outside the meeting room by deploying corridor diplomacy to achieve its essential objective: to get results. Fifth, the Presidency depends on a structured network of information, data, knowledge, and intelligence, centered around the European Commission and the Council Secretariat's scientific assistance before, during, and after the meeting. Finally, the Presidency offers an opportunity for the member state holding it for six months to influence EU business with integrity and use the rolling European agenda as a Trojan horse to defend or assert certain localized national preferences or hobby horses.

Notes

1. The appropriate and official reference should be "Presidency of the Council of Ministers." This chapter will invariably refer to the generic and more broadly used terms of "Presidency," "EU Presidency," or "Presidency of the EU." Similarly, the term "president" will refer to the chair or chairperson of a meeting.

2. I refer here to the draft text produced in February 2003 by the Convention on the Future of Europe which delivered its final proposals to the member states at the Thessalonica European Council in June 2003. This chapter does not deal with the institutional debate about the future format and functioning of the Council of the EU or the European Council.

3. This inventory of factors for evolution is based on de Schouteete (1988); Edwards and Pijpers (1996); Kirchner (1992); O Nuallain and Hoscheit (1985); Wallace and Edwards (1976); Westlake (1995).

4. European Council in Stuttgart, 17–19 June 1983, *The Stuttgart Solemn Declaration*, Bulletin of the European Communities No. 6, 1983.

5. Speech of Wolfgang Schüssel on the occasion of the conference on *Austria and the European Union Presidency*, London, 3 June 1998.

6. I am indebted to Peter Goldschmidt for this comment.

7. Five categories of functions are identified: business management, promotion of initiatives, European political cooperation management, package brokerage, and liaison and collective representation.

8. Council rules of procedure (CRP), Article 1(1). Council Decision (2002/682/EC, Euratom) of 22 July 2002 adopting the Council's rules of procedure OJEC L 230, page 7 of 28 August 2002.

9. Article 1.2, CRP.

10. Article 1.3, CRP.

11. This one-month deadline also applies to the agenda due for the meeting of the European Council. Article 2.3(a) of the CRP provides that the General Affairs and External Relations Council should draw up an annotated draft agenda on the proposal of the Presidency at least four weeks before the meeting of the European Council.

12. Article 3.2, CRP.

13. Article 21, CRP.

14. Article 26, CRP.

15. A mixed agreement is signed by both the Community and its member states because both Community and national competences or jurisdictions are covered by the scope of the agreement, as opposed to an agreement applying to a policy area or activity where the Community has the exclusive competence or jurisdiction to act on behalf of the member states.

16. Three Wise Men, 1979, Report on the European Institutions by the Committee of the Three to the European Council (Report of the Three Wise Men), Luxembourg: Office for Official Publications of the European Communities.

17. For a discussion of the general challenges of national coordination at the time of a Presidency, see Schout and Vanhoonacker (2002).

18. I am indebted to Peter Goldschmidt for this analysis of the role of the national delegation.

Chapter 11

Negotiating the Enlargement

Alice Landau

Enlargement has been on the European Communities' (EC) agenda almost since their inception. Indeed, for virtually its entire existence the European Union (EU) has reacted to applications to join by negotiating accession with prospective members and absorbing them, normally after a period of transition. For the EC, unlike the other institutions, enlargement is not so much a discrete issue as an ongoing process. As a result the EU has considerable experience in enlargement, and the process of enlarging has a degree of normality and acceptability about it. The EU had more than doubled in size by 1995, from six to fifteen members; the new members have been quite diverse: in terms of wealth/per capita gross national product, they range from Denmark and the United Kingdom (UK) on the one hand to Greece and Portugal on the other; in terms of size, from Spain and the UK down to Ireland; and in terms of political outlook, Austria, Finland, Ireland, Portugal, Spain, and Sweden being relatively in tune with the aspirations of the original six members, and Denmark and the UK rather less so.

The British application triggered those of Denmark, Ireland, and Norway. The decisions of these countries to seek EU membership also arguably stemmed from economic self-interest and especially their close links with the UK, rather than from the pursuit of any vision of an integrated Europe. Political factors were much to the fore in the second Mediterranean round of enlargement. Greece, Portugal, and Spain applied to join the EU in 1978, having emerged as democratic states following a long period of authoritarian rule. Acceptance of the membership bids resulted largely from the EU's desire to support and help their economic weaknesses, although the protection by the French and Italians of their farm interests delayed Iberian accession for several years.

The 1993–1994 accession negotiations with the European Free Trade Association (EFTA) represented the first enlargement effort since the ratification of the Treaty on European Union (TEU) and the first occasion on which the new Union acted collectively (Avery 1995). A parallel can be drawn between this northern enlargement and the applications of the Central and Eastern European countries (CEECs). When Austria asked for membership in 1989, many members were quite reluctant to agree. It was decided to give preference to achieving the internal market before 1993 as the first step toward and economic and monetary union and to strengthening the EC's foreign policy and security role. This negatively affected EC policies toward Central and Eastern Europe. When the CEECs knocked at Europe's door, German unification, monetary union, and the implementation of the Maastricht treaty were all on the EU agenda.

Enlargement of the EC has always taken place in groups with more than one new member at a time, with only one case of accession by a single country (Greece, in 1981). Accession has also always been conducted separately with each applicant, but in parallel with other applicants. This has sometimes allowed the Union to obtain concessions from one candidate which the others were then under pressure to agree to.[1]

The "divide-and-rule" aspects of separate negotiations with the Union have been counteracted by an effort on the part of the candidates to unite in a common front, which was the case with the 1993–1994 enlargement that brought in the EFTA countries and with Portugal and Spain. None of the applicant countries wanted to be left behind in the race for membership, and those that were more economically advanced were worried that the less well-off might delay them. A perfect example is the recent enlargement taking in the CEECs (see *Tables 11.1* and *11.2*. The enlargement process demonstrates that the negotiations can also take on a life of their own. After spending a considerable time at the negotiating table, actors develop an independent interest in actually bringing the negotiations to an end (Friis 1998, 99). The cost of no agreement becomes more painful as the negotiations gain ground.

Nevertheless, the literature on how the EU actually negotiates accession deals is limited (Friis 1998, 82). Little is understood about how the enlargement deals are hammered out in practice, and little has been done to conceptualize this process. Although enlargement negotiations share a number of similarities with other negotiating activities with nonmembers, they are qualitatively different in form and content. As Graham Avery (1995) has summed up, "accession is about how a non-member is to join the Union, and apply the rules of the Union. It is not aimed at

Table 11.1. Timetable of the EU enlargement

Countries	Request for accession	Commission's opinion	Opening of accession negotiations	Accession Treaty	Full membership	Total
United Kingdom	10.05.67	29.09.67	30.06.70	22.01.72	01.01.73	5 years
Denmark	11.05.67	29.06.97	30.06.70	22.01.72	01.01.73	5 years
Ireland	11.05.67	29.06.67	30.06.70	22.01.72	01.01.73	5 years
Norway	21.07.67	29.06.67	30.06.70	22.01.72	01.01.73	
Greece	12.06.75	29.01.76	27.07.76	28.05.79	01.01.81	5 years
Portugal	28.03.77	19.05.78	17.10.78		01.01.86	8 years
Spain	28.07.77	29.11.78	05.02.79		01.01.86	8 years
Turkey	14.04.87	14.12.89	–	–	–	
Austria	17.07.89	01.08.91	01.02.93	24.06.94	01.01.95	5 years
Cyprus	04.07.90	30.06.93	–	–	01.05.04	
Malta	16.07.90	30.06.93	–	–	01.05.04	
Sweden	01.07.91	31.07.92	01.02.93	24.06.94	01.01.95	3 years
Finland	18.03.92	04.11.93	01.02.93	24.06.94	01.01.95	2 years
Switzerland	26.05.92	–	–	–	–	
Norway	25.11.92	24.03.93	05.04.93	24.06.94	–	
Hungary	31.03.94	15 July 1997	1998	16.04.03	01.05.04	7 years
Poland	05.05.94	15 July 1997	1997	16.04.03	01.05.04	7 years
Romania	22.06.95	15 July 1997	1997	16.04.03	01.05.04	7 years
Slovakia	22.06.95	15 July 1997	1997	16.04.03	01.05.04	7 years
Estonia	21.11.95	15 July 1997	1997	16.04.03	01.05.04	7 years
Latvia	13.10.95	15 July 1997	1997	16.04.03	01.05.04	7 years
Lithuania	08.12.95	15 July 1997	1997	16.04.03	01.05.04	7 years
Bulgaria	14.12.95	15 July 1997	1997	16.04.03	01.05.04	7 years
Czech Republic	17.01.96	15 July 1997	1997	16.04.03	01.05.04	7 years
Slovenia	10.06.96	15 July 1997	1997	16.04.03	01.05.04	7 years

Source: Granell, Francisco 1995. The European Union's Enlargement Negotiations.

an agreement between the Union on the one hand and an external partner on the other, as is the normal case in international negotiations, but with the way in which an applicant country will function as a member. The negotiations are not about future relations between "us and them," but rather about relations between the "future us." Enlargement is concerned with "external" becoming "internal." It follows that accession negotiations are not at all the traditional fare of external negotiations.

In this chapter we intend to look at how the EU negotiates and what factors determine the outcome of enlargement negotiations. It is the institutions, more than member states' preferences and power, that impact on the negotiations. The study of the process provides an opportunity to take into account the multiplayer game between member states and the Community institutions. Complexity characterizes

Table 11.2. Timetable of the enlargement process

Copenhagen December 1993	Achievement of stability and security through the construction of common European institutions. Candidate countries have to achieve: stability of institutions (guaranteeing democracy, the rule of law, human rights, and respect for protection of minorities), a functioning market economy, and the capacity to cope with competitive pressures and market forces within the Union. The candidates also have to be able to adhere to the aims of political, economic, and monetary union.
Corfu June 1994	The Commission is invited to make specific proposals for the further implementation of the Europe Agreements and on the strategy to be followed with a view to preparing for accession. The proper functioning of the Union has to be created at the 1996 Intergovernmental Conference, which would therefore need to take place before accession negotiations began.
Amsterdam June 1997	The Commission states its intention to present by mid-July its opinions on the accession applications as well as a comprehensive communication ("Agenda 2000") covering the development of Union policies including the agricultural and structural policies. The European Council points out that all states will join the European Union on the basis of the same criteria and that they will participate in the accession process on an equal footing. The accession process will be launched on 30 March 1998 by a meeting of the ministers of foreign affairs of the fifteen member states of the European Union, the ten Central and Eastern European applicant states, and Cyprus. A single framework for these applicant countries will be established.
Cardiff June 1998	Strategy of preaccession with priorities for agriculture and the environment and transport established in the accession partnerships. Effective coordination between these instruments and Phare, as well as with operations funded by the European Investment Bank (EIB), the European Bank for Reconstruction and Development (EBRD), and other international financial institutions will be essential. The European Council notes that the screening exercises for seven chapters of the *acquis* have been completed
Helsinki December 1999	The European Council stresses the principle of peaceful settlement of disputes in accordance with the United Nations Charter and urges candidate states to make every effort to resolve any outstanding border disputes and other related issues. Failing this they should, within a reasonable time, bring the dispute to the International Court of Justice. The European Council will review the situation relating to any outstanding disputes, in particular concerning the repercussions on the accession process and in order to promote their settlement through the International Court of Justice, by the end of 2004 at the latest.

Compiled by the author

the EC negotiating process, as evidenced by the number of agents involved in the process and the multiple levels of interaction, as well as by the large number of parallel negotiations taking place inside the EU negotiation system.

The accession policy provides a good example of this complexity. In the EU there is interplay between and among the various actors and institutions, and each individual actor and institution has its own set of strategies for its own set of interests. Different institutions or actors compete with each other to identify themselves, resulting in innovative or radical solutions being found. Actors find themselves in constant negotiations on rules and procedures. There is an ongoing process of bargaining between and among institutions and actors.

No fewer than five Directorates-General (DGs) were involved in the enlargement process, each having its own vested interests and striving to defend them, and fifteen other Directorates-General were consulted (Torreblanca 2001, 99). The distribution of formal competencies among several DGs and the Commission and the Council, and between the EU institutions and the member states, has become an increasingly critical issue (Schneider *et al.* 1994, 489). Various DGs may "play solo" vis-à-vis one another, although their ability to do so will depend on how well they "play together" as a team (Matlary 1993, 131). Formally, each of them fulfills differentiated functions but they are interrelated and there is an overlapping of functions between them. The preferences of the member states are also shaped by the Community context, and the Commission can set the agenda. Supranational institutions and national governments are, so to speak, competitors in agenda setting (Friis 1998).

The Allison Model

In this perspective, the work of Graham Allison may provide some useful insights into the complexity of the EU negotiating process. In his study of the Cuban missile crisis (Allison and Zelikow 1999) he argues that different models of public decision making have significant consequences for the outcome of the analysis. In other words, the assumption and hypothesis will be reflected in the conclusions. There is a serious danger tht the chosen model will determine the final findings. In the first model, the *rational actor model* the government is assumed to be a rational actor which calculates its choice within specified constraints. The second frame of reference emphasizes factors that limit rationality in decision making. In the *organizational model* power is splintered into a conglomerate of organizations, each with existing goals and programs. Organizations avoid uncertainty by establishing a negotiated environment that regularizes the reactions of other actors and by coordinating their positions. But organizations also generate parochialism, rigidities, and pathologies.

Organizational norms and memories, prior policy commitments, inertia, routines, and established procedures distort the structuring of problems and the dissemination of information necessary to calculate maximal gains. Organizations develop a tendency to find a course of action that will satisfy the most minimal goals instead of seeking the course of action with the best consequences. Decision making within organizations is "dominated by bargaining for resources, roles and missions, compromise rather than analysis" (Hosli 1995, 49).

According to the *bureaucratic politics model*, decisions are the outcomes of various overlapping and hierarchically arranged bargaining games among individual players. Cognitive aspects, as well as the orientation of the organization to which they belong, determine their actions. Their power stems from their bargaining advantages (drawn from formal authority and obligations, institutional backing, constituents' expertise, and status), their skill, and other players' perceptions of the first two ingredients. Each player picks the issue where he/she can play with a reasonable probability of success, but no player's power is sufficient to guarantee satisfactory outcomes.

Both the organizational and the bureaucratic models focus on the dynamism of the policy-making process—driven by the interaction of conflicting interests—and on its constraints, such as inertia, prior policy commitments, and the long process of bargaining. Each actor has conflicting perceptions, values, and interests that may arise from parochial self-interest and different perceptions of issues arising ineluctably from a division of labor. In organizations and bureaucracies, the game consists of making compromises that keep the players entering the bargaining reasonably satisfied, or at least not dissatisfied enough to obstruct decision making, instead of looking for the course of action with the best consequences.

Although the models are based on the United States administration, they provide some insights into the EU decision-making process and could explain some of the characteristics that were most salient in the enlargement process: parochial interests, a lengthy bargaining process, and the use of expertise coupled with difficulties in disseminating information. The outcomes more or less satisfied each of the players, even if the players did have to minimize their goals.

The Commission: A Multifaceted Actor

The Commission has a paradoxical role in the enlargement negotiations which are, in effect, an intergovernmental exercise (Interview, DG Enlargement, March 2002). The Presidency of the Council presents the so-called common position. However, the Commission is well placed to speak of the *acquis communautaire* (the body of laws and rules that have been developed over the years without significant change) which is at the core of the enlargement negotiation process and which has been divided into thirty-one sectoral chapters. The applicant countries formulate their requests in the form of position papers. The Commission evaluates each request and issues a draft common position which is passed on to the Enlargement group[2] and subsequently to the Committee of Permanent Representatives (COREPER) and the Council of Ministers before becoming a European Union common position (EUCP). The EUCP is then transferred to the Enlargement Intergovernmental Conference which can either accept it or request supplementary information from the candidate countries, in which case the whole process repeats itself.

The negotiation of the association agreements came under the responsibility of the DG for Eastern Europe (DG I-E) of the Directorate-General for External Relations. The authority of this unit, however, was very limited. Having been subject to scrutiny not only by the Council's Group of Eastern Europe and COREPER but also by other commissioners and Directorates-General in the Commission, the unit was transformed, when the accession negotiations began, into the Enlargement Directorate-General with three hundred officials and incorporating what became the Enlargement task force and officials from different DGs. This was a political decision, which made this enlargement process qualitatively different from the others.

The Commission has a pivotal role to play in the process. As the Commission cannot act unless it gains support of the member states, it consults national representatives prior to making policy proposals as the shadow of a possible veto in the Council of Ministers will eventually decide the fate of the proposals. Thus, the Commission has to frame proposals which must obtain the approval of the member states. It has to consider what the member states will be prepared to agree among themselves. The Commission often makes preliminary contacts with national administrative and political elites in order to ensure the adoption of its proposals in the Council (Nielsen 1971, 546).

Pursuing its Own Strategy

The Commission also pursues its own strategy, using issues as an opportunity to capture more power and thus gain more involvement in a policy area (Matlary 1993, 11). It is well equipped to do so: the Commission is a cohesive group benefiting from its members' expertise and sense of loyalty to what is a truly communitarian organization. Its ability to perform the task successfully is influenced by its internal structure.

Fragmentation and complexity are the most salient features of the Commission. There are multiple networks of negotiations and sometimes conflicts of influence within the Commission, among directors-general negotiating in their personal capacity with their foreign counterparts or among commissioners who consider their appointment as a political opportunity with a bearing on their future career prospects; hence there is a complex pattern of responsibilities. The DGs have rival policy conceptualizations but complementary interests in promoting the organization (Peters 1994, 14–16). These interlocking relationships hinder the Commission's decision-making and autonomous policy-implementation powers and thus make building coalitions within the Commission, as well as across institutional boundaries, an imperative.

The process of interservice consultation was essential to enable DG I-E to draw on the expertise of the other Commission services, as well as to safeguard the overall coherence of Community policies. The fact that fifteen Directorates-General were consulted in the course of the enlargement process gives a good idea of the complexity of the policy package. For instance, the Directorates-General for Enterprise, Health and Consumer Protection, Environment, and Agriculture were all involved in the circulation of goods chapter.

The task of DG Enlargement is to explore the positions of other Commission services and commissioners and, through informal talks and the presentation of nonpapers, take the pulse of member-state positions and their relative strengths in order to anticipate how much support they might expect from the Council in the future.

Commission services naturally have to defend the policies and interests of their portfolios. Each DG has its own terms of reference and technical interpretation. The Commission services tend to downplay the frictions between them. Yet, according to the member states, conflicts of interest are positive, otherwise, the Commission would lack credibility (Interview, Swedish delegation, March 2002). All interests must be balanced. This is similar to the situation within member states where each minister bargains for resources, jealous of his/her own portfolio, and perhaps unwilling to make concessions.

Enlargement comes under the aegis of the ministry of foreign affairs of a member state, but other ministries (finance, trade, or agriculture) or even a head of state could exert influence and try to alter the position of the minister involved. In some countries, the interests of such ministers could ultimately prevail either because there is no adequate mechanism for interministerial coordination or because of domestic political conditions or political games. In some member states like France a coordinating mechanism (the *Secrétariat général de coordination interministérielle*) was established to harmonize the French position on enlargement. But even here, finance or trade ministers have had different positions and defended them.

The tight web of contacts between cabinets, Directorates-General, and units aimed at facilitating both vertical and horizontal coordination can do little to reconcile conflicting rationales (Torreblanca 1998, 140). From time to time DGs refuse to make concessions; the issue is deadlocked at the Commission level and has to be settled by the Commissioners. Such was the case for the taxation of cigarettes.[3] The Commission hesitated to make concessions to the CEECs lest these trigger parallel demands from industries vis-à-vis the Commission which, in turn, would weaken the EC's negotiating position.

Some DGs prepared quite early for enlargement in order to have a solid basis for adopting positions; others, for example, the DG for Health and Consumer Protection, started quite late so were under time pressure to catch up with the process; thus they did not have a complete understanding of the problems.

The foreign ministers sitting in the Council of General Affairs were likely to show greater sympathy for the approach defended by DG III (Industry) than for the foreign-policy approach embodied in the proposals of DG I (External Relations). The fear that political pressures might lead to further trade concessions to Central and Eastern Europe turned the European Confederation of Iron and Steel Industries (Eurofer) into an active polity entrepreneur. The EC steel industry started to deal directly with Eastern European companies, offering them technical assistance in return for production cuts and seeking to strengthen the antidumping and state-aids provisions of the association agreements. Collusion also occurs between DGs and member states against other Commission services. The German and Spanish governments maintained the exemption of their coal sectors from the EU's single market and competition rules; and this immediately mobilized the United Kingdom, DG IV (Competition), and DG XVII (Energy).

In negotiations, maintaining uncertainty about concessions is crucial. The negotiations are devoted to lowering expectations to the minimum acceptable deal for each of the players (Fisher and Ury 1978, 42), hence the problems with the negotiating ability of the EU. As quoted in Wallace (1989, 194), "for the negotiator faced with a tough and tight range of options and other players with similarly circumscribed room for maneuver, the best may well be the enemy of the 'could'." Even if the ministers agree on the final outcome, the best ways and means of achieving it are for the member countries to withhold as much control as possible and to delay the decision as long as possible until the costs of the decision outweigh the benefits. The more consistent the preference, the less flexible the position. The less intense the preference, the greater the bargaining power (Moravcsik 1993, 300; Spector 1994, 78), hence a situation of status quo, which is difficult to overcome. Budget, agriculture, and regional policy are the last issues for negotiation.

As the EU is an ongoing negotiation process it is always engaged in a number of negotiations, and each negotiation is bound to touch upon historical package deals, parallel ongoing games, and the prospect of future negotiation. It has difficulty in producing swift decisions. Indeed, a policy of postponement emerges as the dominant tendency. The sense of crisis brought about by blocking a decision has a potentially heavy political cost. Member countries thus avoid being isolated. Axelrod (1984, 234) argues that institutions embody and affect actors' expectations. They can alter the extent to which governments treat defection not as an isolated case but as one in a series of interrelated actions. An ongoing process without an exit in which pressures to attain some kind of agreement are powerful enhances the bargaining logic in which "logrolling," "package deals," and "side payments" solve conflicts (Moravcsik 1993, 303–4). Coalition building and interstate bargaining also take place at the core of the Council of Ministers (Wallace 1989, 194), but they result in an even more unwieldy process.

Member states have unequal weight. Coalitions that do not include major players—France, Germany, the United Kingdom—are unlikely to be formed. Some are short-lived, such as that between Belgium and France; others are enduring, such as that between France and Germany; and others are tactical, such as that between France and the "Med" countries. Others are more fundamental: the opposition of the free traders, such as Germany, the Netherlands, and the UK; and the protectionists, such as France, Greece, and Italy. Coalitions are always part of the enlargement negotiating process. The net payers, such as France, Germany, the Netherlands, and the United Kingdom, have a say in designing regional policy and agriculture.

Network of Special Relationships

The attitudes of the member states can be critical. There was apparent agreement on the enlargement issue as far as member countries were concerned. The issue reflected the network of special relations that had grown up between the existing and future member states, in some cases almost as a patron-client relationship (Avery and Cameron 1998, 127). Member states saw the enlargement through the prism of their national interests and history (Interview DG Enlargement, March 2002). They were ready to make concessions that were agreed on in previous enlargements.

As argued by Kitzinger (1973, 79) the bulk of the formal negotiation on how to meet the formal requirements of the applicants is in a sense carried on not so much between each candidate and the member states but among the member states themselves. Member states spend far more of the formal sessions talking to each other than talking to the applicant states. As one Commission official said, "We spend 90 percent of our time in discussions with member states and 10 percent with the candidate countries."

EU relations with Central and Eastern Europe illustrate the difficulty of constructing a consistent policy when the spheres of interest of the members differ so greatly (Mayhew 1998, 106). The interests of member states in applicant countries were generally determined by geographic proximity coupled with the historic links to which geography has given rise. For example, Austria tended to be interested in the accession of its immediate neighbors, the Czech Republic, Hungary, Slovakia and Slovenia. Italy had close links with its neighbor, Slovenia, and was one of the countries that might have played a larger role in leading the EC's new *ostpolitik*. Italy, like Germany, viewed the association agreements with the East as a means of expanding its political and economic opportunities.

The Italian government wanted to be a key player in the resurrection of *Mitteleuropa*. Greece was interested in the accession of Cyprus, but also of Bulgaria and Romania because of its role in the Balkan region. The three Nordic states (Denmark, Finland, and Sweden) were interested in the accession of their Baltic neighbors (Estonia, Latvia, and Lithuania). Belgium was more reluctant to enlarge, and had long been prominent in asking for institutional reform before enlargement took place (Phinnemore 1999, 75).

The position of the EC leaders varied considerably both in attitudes and content. According to Article 237 of the EC treaty, any European country can apply for membership. Reservations on the part of those in favor of a wait-and-see attitude were first raised by France, Italy, the Netherlands, and Spain who maintained that there was insufficient political and economic stability in the region to engage in a policy of association. Internal consensus was thus going to be very difficult to achieve. Countries more sympathetic included Portugal and Spain which showed a natural sense of solidarity with the democratization processes in Central and Eastern Europe. Yet Spain as a net-receiver country was not in a hurry to see enlargement as it would absorb large amounts of the cohesion and structural funds. The United Kingdom seemed to be victim of its own preferences in terms of the European integration process. The British vision of a looser EU had naturally turned into firm support for enlarging the European Union with new member states. However, the enlargement both represented and required a strengthening of both the EC and the European Commission, which was not easy for the British to digest. Relations with the CEECs also revealed fault lines in the EU between those countries with a liberal approach to economic policy such as the Netherlands and the United Kingdom, and those such as France and Spain with a more protectionist stance in which the state is given a larger role. These differences have been obvious in the retention by the EU of an extremely high level of protectionism in agriculture. No country is likely to enter the EU if it does not have a champion among the existing members. Champions do exist. The Czech Republic, Hungary, and Poland relied on Germany's support; Estonia counted on Finland and Sweden; and Slovenia was supported by Austria and Italy (Phinnemore 1999, 81).

Taking up All of the *Acquis*

There is a classical method of enlargement that is best portrayed by Preston (1995). According to this the first principle of enlargement is the full implementation of the *acquis*, which entails more problems for member states as it involves packaging the compromises underpinning the CAP and the structural funds. The second component represents the problems created by economic diversity which is addressed by establishing new policy instruments that overlay existing ones. For the three enlargements, the EU established structural funds and then expanded their size to lessen the impact of integration on peripheral agricultural and declining industrial sectors. The right of access to the structural funds is now part of the Community's bargaining process. Even the Scandinavians have received funds despite being net contributors to the EU budget on account of their above-average EU levels of GDP (Preston 1995, 400). The third principle of enlargement is based on limited institutional adaptation. The fourth principle is the EU preference for negotiating with closely linked groups; for example, the linkage between the EFTAns facilitated the accession process. Although the Union prefers groupings that raise similar policy issues, it does have limited scope for constructing the ideal accession "convoy." Finally, and most importantly, the classical enlargement method concerns the practicalities of the applicants taking on the *acquis*.

Though each enlargement is different, and different topics can be debated, they have one thing in common: the obligation to take up all of the *acquis* or take up nothing. The EU has always insisted on the applicant country accepting the *acquis* but at the very beginning the *acquis* was not particularly extensive. That did not mean, however, that its extension and interpretation could not be envisioned in the future.

The situation became more complex with the advent of the internal market in 1992, two of the pillars of the Maastricht treaty (the common foreign and security policy and the justice and home affairs policy), and the introduction of the euro. The first two enlargements were relatively easy. The internal market did not exist. Even the EFTA enlargement was eased because of the European Economic Area (EEA) which more or less concluded the negotiations on the internal market. In other words, negotiations did not have to start all over again. The CEEC enlargement was difficult because the candidate countries came from different political and economic systems. Thus, before accession could take place the implementation of the *acquis* had to be verified by a screening exercise and annual report, which is something new.

What could be negotiated were the transitional arrangements. The United Kingdom wanted the common agricultural policy (CAP) to be introduced gradually by stages and for safeguards to be included to prevent any problems occurring. Two other topics were on the agenda: the sugar protocol (allowing imports of cane sugar to the United Kingdom from the Commonwealth countries to be maintained)[4] and the financial contribution of the United Kingdom, which became part of the enlargement debate. This was clearly a case of interconnected policy games, as depicted by Torreblanca (1998). The British side assessed their financial contribution at 2.6 percent to 3 percent, and the French at over 20 percent (Kitzinger 1973, 100–101). The UK wanted to retain the Commonwealth preferences and the external trade regime with its former EFTA partners as long as possible (Preston 1995, 452).

The logjam was resolved through the usual method of package deals, by the coupling of different issues. The negotiations with Portugal and Spain were held up by the dominance of domestic issues implicit in the enlargement process (Mayhew 2000). The Commission asked the Spanish government to put its steel sector into shape and to end state aid to steel industries. The Greek government demanded a compensation mechanism for agreeing to another Mediterranean country joining the EU.

In the EFTA enlargement the *acquis communautaire* constituted the legal basis of the agreement, and the EFTA countries agreed to adopt the relevant EC legislation with some justified exceptions and time-limited transitional periods, setting target dates for the dismantling of tariffs and quotas and ensuring legal harmonization and policy alignment. It could in no way involve amendments to the Community rules. The EFTA enlargement was the fastest, as the European Economic Area paved the way for the accession negotiations. Accession could have been prevented by a genuine joint decision-making mechanism in substance and in form being instated. Economically, the EEA constituted a far-reaching agreement but remained a political dwarf. The Commission retained the exclusive right to initiate, whereas the EFTA countries could obtain only a *droit d'évocation* (Miles 1996, 59). The objective of EFTA accession negotiations was the establishment of transitional periods and the authorization of certain derogations.

The Scandinavian states were interested in five areas (Miles 1996, 68): maintaining the nature and levels of Nordic support to agriculture and the component regions; conserving their stringent environmental policies and standards and the principles of sustainable development; conserving their generous national social policies and welfare provisions; guaranteeing that EU membership would not dilute Nordic liberal democracies and traditions; and developing a stronger EU international role in the Baltic region. The applicant countries were allowed to maintain their more far-reaching environmental and health and safety rules and standards for a period of four years during which EU legislation would be reviewed. The common agricultural policy needed some adjustments: Sweden maintained equivalent or lower prices than those obtained in the EU while the other applicants gained higher levels of prices and protection for their agriculture. The Commission devised a "lump-sum" payment as compensation toward the cost of adjusting to agricultural prices as well as the adjustment effort already undertaken by Sweden (Avery 1995). For a transitional period digressive aids to farmers were authorized, and every candidate received an agrobudgetary package. Austria did not insist on a permanent exception to the acquisition of land by foreigners, and it received a five-year transitional period. There was also an example of creative adaptation (Preston 1995, 453) in that the objective six regions utilized population density rather than average GDP eligibility criteria to support Arctic regions. Negotiations on access to water and resources and market access for fish were difficult, and compromise between the Norwegian and Spanish positions was uneasy.

The EU was permitted to fish an extra three thousand tons of cod, and Norwegian sovereign rights to manage fisheries resources were to be gradually taken over by the EU by 1998. Finland, Norway, and Sweden were allowed to continue herring fishing for the production of fish oil and fish meat for a transitional period of three years. The Scandinavians received some return from the structural funds despite being net contributors to the EU budget. Austria maintained its right to restrict transalpine transit of heavy vehicles (ecopoints) for nine years. The institutional dispute over future voting rights within the Council was embarrassing for the Union, and became a problem within the twelve. On the one hand, both Spain and the UK insisted that the blocking minority for the Council's qualified-majority-voting criteria should remain unchanged at twenty-three; on the other hand, most of the member states and the European Parliament argued that it should be raised to twenty-seven in order to maintain the roughly one-third "blocking minority" needed to stop EU legislation (Miles 1996, 77). The agreement on the common foreign and security policy was useful and symbolic for it cleared the way for the question of "neutrality" after the TEU came into force, and it defused what might have become a troublesome subject for some of the applicant countries (Avery 1995).

Ambivalence about the Eastern Enlargement

The EU has often seemed ambivalent and unenthusiastic about the whole concept of the CEEC enlargement and took rather a long time to respond to the Central and Eastern European countries' hopes of joining the EU. The Commission did not want to commit to membership because it did not know if transition in the CEECs would last (Interview, Directorate-General Enlargement, March 2002). In 1989 the EU was finding it difficult to cope with the pace of events. Internal consensus was difficult to achieve, and the positions of leaders differed considerably. At the beginning the question was only that of upgrading relations and providing Hungary and Poland with better terms of association. When the question of membership appeared on the agenda at the Lisbon European Council in June 1992, the EU could not refuse to consider such a possibility without undermining the positions of reformers in Eastern Europe (Torreblanca 2001, 51). First, the EU envisaged that the Eastern countries could be incorporated in the EEA, together with the EFTA countries, forming an outer circle to the Community and having the status of associated membership.

Thus the Commission designed an association framework based on a political dialogue, a free-trade area, and financial and technical assistance for market reforms, but without including any guarantee of membership. The EU distinction between association and membership was maintained. The benefits of trade liberalization were openly weighted in favor of the Community, as nonspecific quantitative restrictions, safeguard clauses, and equivalent effect measures were applied on products from the Eastern countries. Agriculture was excluded from the agreement. In January 1993, the reshuffled Commission was invited to make proposals for the Community's relations with Eastern Europe.

President Delors had consistently rejected the inclusion of a membership perspective in the agreements. DG VI (Agriculture) and DG III were openly trying to water down the proposals of the commissioner responsible for DG I, Frans Andriessen, and DG I itself, which they thought were being too generous with Central and Eastern European countries and too weak in the defense of the EC's sectoral interests. Andriessen was preparing an association framework that would ultimately lead to membership. He was sympathetic toward the idea of including the prospect of membership in the agenda because such a perspective would play a crucial role in strengthening EC member states' commitment to the economic content of the association agreements.

The twelve member states had to negotiate among themselves as to how far they were willing to let the Commission go. DG I, and more particularly Andriessen, formed part of the of EC foreign-policy inner circle. The Commissioners and Commission services and the member states themselves saw DG I only as their "spokesperson" vis-à-vis third countries. This was evident in the dense network of controls that limited DG I's capacity for leadership and policy entrepreneurship (Torreblanca 2001). The main difference between Andriessen's plan and the EC's traditional approach to enlargement was his proposal to break the principle of the indivisibility of the *acquis communautaire*. Accepting the whole *acquis* without exception was the standard procedure for assuring that newcomers would neither weaken the Community nor attempt to obtain à la carte membership. DG III opposed the principle of asymmetry and made five counterproposals to DG I's draft.

At decisive moments, it was easier to find allies within the Council than among fellow Commissioners. The weak and not very cohesive coalition formed by DG I and the EU foreign ministers found it very difficult to resist the pressures from these coalitions: the Commission, its DGs, ministries of member states, and interest groups. The interservice consultation procedure usually worked against the interest of DG I but the positive side of the process was that it assured a degree of cohesion and control over the negotiations, which was beneficial to the Commission. DG III, DG IV, and DG VI succumbed to the temptation dangled before them and turned the negotiations at expert level into separate negotiations whose content and path they unilaterally determined.

Czechoslovakia and Hungary continued to put pressure on the Community to come up with wider and deeper contents and a faster timetable for the association agreements. The Community remained adamant that no guarantee of membership would be included in the association agreements.

The Copenhagen European Council was a watershed in the EU policy for the CEECs. Although no timetable was given the statement marked a major shift in EU policy. The prospect of membership, however, was offered as a "carrot" to support the reform process in the CEECs. The Council stated that membership required that the candidate countries should achieve institutional stability (thus guaranteeing democracy, the rule of law, human rights, and respect for the protection of minorities), the existence of a functioning market economy, and the capacity to cope with competitive pressures and market forces within the Union. The candidates would also have to be able to adhere to the aims of political economic and monetary union. The Commission was invited to draw up a preaccession strategy to be identified as the Europe Agreements. Thus the Council raised the expectation that these agreements would be a first step toward full membership.

As well as the Europe Agreements the Commission was also invited to institute PHARE, a program of Community aid for the CEECs, and to proceed to the full development of a structured relationship between the EU institutions and the associated countries. It was also asked to prepare a White Paper on integration into the internal market. In July 1997, the Commission published a set of key documents on enlargement and the future of the Union itself, entitled Agenda 2000. This contained a detailed assessment by the Commission of a whole range of issues concerning enlargement, the reform of the CAP and structural policies, and the new financial framework for 2000–2006, as well as the Commission's *avis* on the ten applications from the CEECs prepared on the basis of the replies to detailed questionnaires sent to all the applicant countries in April 1996 (Gower 1999, 7–15). The enlargement introduced one new element: the verification of the implementation of the Community *acquis* before accession took place. In previous enlargements verification by the Commission or by member states did not take place. The accession treaties were signed on the understanding that the *acquis* would be implemented by the candidate country as agreed in the treaty.

The Commission advocated opening negotiations with five CEECs—the Czech Republic, Estonia, Hungary, Poland, and Slovenia, which began in December 1997, and delaying negotiations with the other applicants until they were in a better position to assume the burdens of membership. Reforms were necessary for enlargement. Extending the CAP and the structural fund would prove prohibitively expensive. As far as the structural funds were concerned it was estimated that admitting the Visegrad Four (the Czech Republic, Hungary, Poland, and Slovakia) would cost 26 billion euros, thus requiring almost a doubling of expenditure and exhausting projected structural expenditure. A further 30 to 40 billion euros per annum would be required to meet the extra cost of extending the CAP and the Cohesion Fund to the CEECs. In the Commission proposals issued in January 2002 newcomers would qualify for only 25 percent of the level of subsidy given to Western farmers in stages over the following ten years. The EU suggested quotas for production.[5] Moreover, member countries have already reckoned up what the situation will be after 2006, and are no longer willing to accept any more subsidies after that date (Interview, DG Enlargement, March 2002). All other chapters regarding the enlargement are problematical: the environmental chapter because of the financial implications; the free movement of capital with the liberalization of short-term capital movements; and the agricultural chapter as regards the purchase of agricultural lands and forestry areas by citizens of nonmember countries of the EU.[6]

Faced with resistance or opposition at home to the admission of the CEECs, national ministers could pander more to domestic lobbies and adopt less-flexible negotiating positions (Phinnemore 1999, 77).

Conclusion

The latest enlargement has been more complex than anything that the EU has had to deal with for a long time. It provides evidence of the ongoing bargaining process within the EU, the multilayered shape of the EU with its cluster of actors—Community institutions and member states, not to mention pressure groups—and the interplay of bargaining games among and within them. Institutions, be they intergovernmental or communitarian, are not always a single actor with a collective personality but sometimes institutions where different actors pursue their own interests and have their own strategies. It is because the EU is conditioned by political issues and plagued by so many vested interests and habits of power play that the actors are compelled to compete.

This picture offers some validation of the models provided by Allison. Negotiating the enlargement has entailed the interrelation of actors all of whom were involved in a power struggle. The decision to enlarge was a combination of the outcomes of various interwoven bargaining games among players trying not to maximize their interests but to satisfy their expectations as best they could and gain reasonable advantages.

The interwoven bargaining games within the Community institutions and with the member states entail a risk. There is a search for increased power within the bureaucratic structure of the Commission, which again corroborates Allison's models. All the Directorates-General—with their shared interest in protecting the organization and their differing policy conceptualization—want to retain power. Finally, the institution itself is looking for increased power vis-à-vis member states that wish to maintain their overwhelming control over the institution. The Commission is a skillful player and a multifaceted actor. It acts as a policy promoter in forging full reform and in selecting innovative and viable proposals; thus it is able to act as an agenda setter and as a moderator between member states. It can create a sense of crisis in order to achieve its goals and advance its interests. A thorny process, enlargement has been a difficult decision to digest; but as usual, the EU overcame its problems, and enlargement took place successfully on 1 May 2004.

Notes

1. The outstanding example was the decision by Finland finally to accept the immediate alignment of its agricultural prices, which was followed by identical concessions from Austria and Norway. Applicants are also allowed to refuse something that another candidate previously conceded: an example was in the field of environmental standards and the single market where Austria originally accepted the Union's proposal that it keep its own standards for a period of three years, only for Sweden to obtain a four-year concession shortly thereafter.
2. The Enlargement group is composed of all the member states.
3. Poland increased its transition period by a one-year extension. Germany blocked this, and refused the concession. The decision was settled by the Commissioners.
4. The French wanted the quantities of Commonwealth sugar sold on the United Kingdom market to be drastically reduced over the transition period. This was settled by the renegotiation of the Yaoundé Convention (which governed the association of seventeen African states and Madagascar with the Community).
5. The Economist, 9 February 2002.
6. Poland obtained a seven-year transition period to limit the purchase of land by foreigners—longer than any other candidate countries (The Economist March 2002).

Chapter 12

European Union Negotiation

Paul W. Meerts

Lessons

As we have seen in the preceding chapters, the European Union (EU) can be characterized as a sustained negotiation process with distinctive features that underline its uniqueness among world negotiation processes. Negotiations are a vital instrument for integrating Europe. "Negotiations are central to the functioning and dynamic development of the European Union. Negotiation is seen as the predominant policy mode and the main source of the EU's successful functioning" (Pfetsch 1998, 293). In this, the concluding chapter, we will summarize the contributions of the authors to discern how far European Union negotiation processes are indeed different from other bargaining processes. We will then ask what lessons can be learned to make EU negotiations more effective as well as the extent to which those lessons can be applied to non-EU processes. We will do this with a particular eye to future developments in peaceful interstate interactions concerning give-and-take processes.

The European Union as a process of international negotiation can survive only if a certain quantity and quality of outcomes is reached. In other words, unless effective outcomes to the negotiation process are assured, the "building" will collapse. While in other international negotiation processes, open-endedness is—though not preferable—often unavoidable and, for a certain length of time, acceptable, this is much less the case in European Union negotiations. There being no increase in the number of decisions to be taken means an actual "decrease" in

"

the Union. Without progress in the integration process the EU will slide into disintegration. The negotiation process in the Union is therefore of relatively greater importance than negotiation processes in other international bodies. Though not of the same importance and intensity as national negotiation processes, the EU negotiation process is of more general value than negotiation processes among states. It can thus be characterized as having an in-between position.

Because of the supranational character of vital segments of the European Union, the EU negotiation process can be positioned halfway between national and international negotiation. It contains more assured outcomes than international bargaining processes but fewer than national bargaining processes. It is more centralized and controlled than other international negotiation processes, one reason being the existence of the European Commission. But at the same time it cannot (yet?) match the consistency of the internal negotiation processes of the well-functioning national state. As we will see, however, such national negotiation processes are often of an extremely complex nature, and the coordination of internal priorities is one of the main problems the member states of the Union face in shaping their own EU negotiation processes. It should be noted that the supranational character of the Union does indeed have a clear impact on the nature of the EU process, but it should not be forgotten that major parts of the EU negotiation processes are still of an intergovernmental nature. This intergovernmental dimension, however, is of a more integrated nature than in other international organizations. Because of the very close cooperation among the EU member states and the existence inside the Union of supranational actors who also exert a great deal of influence on the intergovernmental negotiation process, even this part of the process can be seen as unique in the world. Both the supranational and intergovernmental facets of the EU provide for a negotiation process where outcomes are more secure than in other international forums.

The democratic dimension of the Union is mentioned in this book as another aspect that helps distinguish EU negotiation processes from others. Indeed, in "regular" international negotiation processes the people play only an indirect role through governmental and nongovernmental institutions. In the European Union democratic actors are directly involved in the negotiation process at the European level, though there are enormous differences in the role they play depending on the level of the negotiations and the dossiers at hand. The impact of the representative organs of the Union on the processes of negotiation generally has the effect of complicating matters. However necessary from an ideological, democratic point of view—as all EU member states are democracies—this political dimension does not always help to further effective processes and assured outcomes. On the contrary, many perceived assured outcomes have not been achieved because of interventions by politicians—interventions that were often motivated by national interests that worked against the common European good. In that sense it is possible to see the EU process as more puzzling than the "normal" international negotiation processes.

While international negotiation processes are defined here as interstate processes (i.e., between sovereign actors), the peculiarity of the EU process is its mixed character. Sovereign actors play a role that is even more important than that of EU bodies like the Commission and the Parliament. But there is a distinct interplay between these two kinds of international actors: the states and the EU institutions. It is not easy to find an example of such a dense negotiation process between states and supranational or international institutions anywhere in the world, for it is a unique process of negotiation in which the states have lost most of their power monopoly. Through this "enhanced interaction" member states and European institutions negotiate their deals in a multitude of forums in ways that are characteristic of EU processes.

The classical Westphalian situation with sovereign actors negotiating on a voluntary basis has largely disappeared in a European Union where a substantial part of sovereignty is vested in the EU institutions. States cannot act at will—except in the intergovernmental conferences (IGCs)—as they have lost most of their "freedom to decide" in negotiating certain issues. In other words "best alternatives to negotiated agreements" (BATNAs) are often absent: if matters are on the agenda, then the alternative of nonnegotiation is no longer present. Here "classic" theories do not hold, and only active prenegotiation can provide states with something like a BATNA instrument. But even this is hardly true anymore. Essentially speaking the fact that the EU and member states share sovereignty in the core areas brushes the BATNA issue aside and enhances the possibility of assured outcomes—or should one say "unavoidable outcomes." A major exception here are the negotiations on common foreign and security policy (CFSP), an arena in which the negotiations are essentially classic international interactions where BATNAs do play their classic role. It should come as no surprise that in the CFSP area the EU hardly exists, as has been observed over and over again in recent years. Even if there is concerted action, this can easily wither away again. Here we are in the EU area of "unassured outcomes."

The negotiations arena of the EU is a rich resource of negotiation options and opportunities for coalition building. On the one hand this provides negotiators with a multitude of options and alternatives that enhance their power positions; on the other, it obscures their opportunities because of its ambiguity. In the end much of the negotiation process in the EU is about the creation of legislation as a consequence of political prioritization. To set clear priorities, however, negotiators have to clarify their strategies, and to be successful in implementing those strategies, they have to master the complexity of the process. As processes are more complex within EU negotiation than in other international bargaining processes, highly professional negotiators are needed.

For that reason countries are creating a new layer of negotiators between diplomats and national civil servants, and between generalists and specialists. This new type of negotiator, a specialist in *Public-Affairs Management* (PAM), in other words, an archetypal EU negotiator, is needed to manage the complexity of the European negotiation process. As PAM negotiators have roles specifically linked to the very nature of EU negotiation, their operations will facilitate European integration through negotiation. Thus, the growth of European unity is not only shaping a new institution on the world stage, it is also creating a new kind of international negotiator and—as we will see—a new kind of international negotiation process.

What happens at home is vital for understanding the EU negotiation process. It all starts with insight into the negotiation processes within the member states of the Union—the coordination of negotiation processes at the domestic level. The EU bargaining system is characterized by extraordinary procedural complexity on a heterogeneous playing field suffering from increasing politicization. There is procedural clarity at the negotiation table but not between the different levels of negotiation processes. This is because of the unclear separation of powers within the Union. Though the EU, as such, is a complex of institutions that should support negotiation processes, the connection between these processes is ambiguous because of the unclear linkages between the platforms on which the negotiations take place. A horizontal overview is therefore difficult, obscuring opportunities for coming up with effective package deals between different policy areas.

Vertical insights are also hard to obtain, as the tempi of the dossiers vary enormously. While some dossiers will make it to the highest levels of EU negotiation platforms, the vast majority will be settled at midlevel platforms, reducing the opportunities for remaining dossiers to be included in package deals. Package deals are therefore more dependent on the availability of still-negotiable dossiers than on the most effective linkages. While this unclarity is an obstacle to the creation of clear-cut national strategies for effective negotiations in Europe, it can also be seen as an opportunity for negotiators. It would be extremely difficult for negotiators to be effective if they had to follow strict procedures laid down by the home front, as there are so many unpredictabilities in the EU negotiation process. They would lose too much flexibility. As it is impossible, therefore, for the ministries back home to construct rigid mandates, the EU negotiator obtains the flexibility he/she needs to cope with the surprises in the process he/she is going into.

Meanwhile more and more players from different institutional levels are entering the arena—not only through enlargement of the Union, whereby EU 2004 has twenty-five state actors, but also through the participation of a growing number of regional governmental, nongovernmental, public-, and private-sector organizations. Confronted with the problem of a fuzzy level playing field in Brussels and problematic prioritization at home, the member states are clinging to negotiation procedures concerning their own coordination practices that can no longer cope with the complexity of the EU negotiation process. The ministries of foreign affairs, traditionally the coordinators of national EU policies, are overwhelmed by the multitude of actors and issues in the EU negotiation processes. Here we have a clear distinction between EU and other international negotiation processes: a quantitative difference with qualitative effects on the bargaining among negotiators together with the growing importance of national civil servants on a terrain that is the traditional domain of the international civil servant (i.e., the diplomat). Another differentiating factor between "regular" international negotiations and EU negotiations is the impact of politics. As most EU issues are of an internal rather than an international nature, parliamentarians and other politicians tend to mix in with the processes run by the professional negotiators which, though positive from a democratic point of view, obscures the transparency of the negotiation processes at hand. While diplomats are trained to look for compromises and collaboration, politicians are often striving for polarization and competition. Therefore, in many cases, political intervention creates obstacles to the integrative negotiation needed to obtain the desired outcomes of these processes.

The role of the member states in the EU negotiation process may be less prominent than non-EU negotiators often postulate. As EU negotiators are aware, there are only limited opportunities to influence EU negotiation, and states have to operate within strict legal limits in these areas. Strategic planning is therefore of paramount importance. This brings up the point of qualified-majority voting (QMV) as a tool in making progress in EU negotiations. Without this instrument the Union would not have been as successful in decision making as it is today. However, the fact that countries can be outvoted puts a great deal of pressure on their negotiators. Coalition building is one of the answers in this context, as is a change in attitude. Negotiators will have to show an increased willingness to accept compromises, something not too common among the actors entering the EU negotiation scene after the enlargement of the Union by ten new member states.

Actors in the EU negotiating process are bargaining not only on their needs but also on their common and opposing values. It should be noted that values do play an important role in EU negotiations. The bargaining process can be described as an exchange of commodities, but the underlying values should not be overlooked. These values are the objects of the trading process, as well as influencing it. Within Europe a modest clash of EU civilizations is one of the characteristics of the EU negotiation processes, for example, the cultural differences between the northern and southern member states and the new members from Central and Eastern Europe. These differences express themselves in the languages used by the negotiators. In many plenary sessions of EU Council working groups the countries north of the River Rhine speak in the Germanic language we call English, while those from within the former Roman Empire use the Latin language we call French. Moreover, what may be seen as ethical in the eyes of a Swede may be unethical in the perception of a Greek.

Different negotiation styles, the "software" of negotiations, can be observed. These are not so much a consequence of differences in national cultures as a result of national political and bureaucratic structures. For example, the French structure produces effective coordination combined with a reasonable amount of negotiation freedom for its well-educated and skilled negotiators. The German system makes life quite difficult for its negotiators. The federal mode obstructs efficient and coherent decision making at the national level, which leads to constraints on German negotiators in their deadlines in Brussels. The British are—in general—well placed for negotiation. They combine a pragmatic and flexible attitude in the negotiation process with a tough defense of their interests. Spanish negotiators seem to be more effective than their Italian colleagues, which has to do with the strength of their bureaucratic organization. The larger member states have in common a potential for dealing with the whole range of EU issues in a balanced way, while the smaller member countries—because of the relative smallness of their governmental apparatus—are forced to follow more of a single-issue strategy.

Most EU governments have relatively limited options for influencing EU negotiation processes, the large ones being a notable exception. As far as the future is concerned, this room for individual needs will further diminish because of the growing importance of the EU institutions and the rising number of member states due to the enlargement process of the Union. Strategic planning and the effective use of tactics are therefore important in pushing for the needs and values the individual states want to fulfill. As has been said, coalition building is one of the major options here but this will, in turn, water down the position of the individual actor. This is a strange paradox: a particular position can be successful only if it is compromised upon before the actual bargaining process starts. From the perspective of the common good this is a wonderful instrument for forcing partners into a given frame, but for those who want to uphold the priorities set by their governments, this dynamic is problematic to say the least. Prioritizing is important, however, as it will help the individual country to get its act together. How can it concede, if it does not prioritize? On the other hand, in an intense process such as that of the EU, where negotiators get to know each other and sit around the table together for years on end, the negotiators are forced to acknowledge the specific needs of their counterparts if they want their opponents to respect their own specific interests. In other words, though there is an ongoing give-and-take process, certain very specific interests are respected and will not be outvoted as this would damage the very integrity of the countries involved. Negotiators can be open to a smooth process of conceding and obtaining only if they feel safe. And they will feel safe only if they can put trust in the ability and willingness of their colleagues to take their core interests and values into account.

EU institutions and IGC negotiations play their own intricate game. Supranational EU institutions have gained significant influence on the outcomes of intergovernmental conferences. How negotiations were structured and conducted has mattered in terms of the ability of supranational actors to gain influence in IGCs. The member states have often needed the supranational bodies as facilitators in order to reach agreements. The Council Secretariat—though a nonsupranational body—has been especially influential in this respect; this has to do with its expertise and with the fact that it is often ahead of the member states as far as information is concerned. Its skills are needed by the negotiators of the member states, especially those from the smaller powers who often lack the apparatus to match their opponents. As an alternative they may use the facilities of the Secretariat which, in turn, creates a powerbase for the Council. Trust also plays an important role. The legitimacy of the Secretariat puts it in a central role as a neutral broker that can be trusted and will therefore be used by the players. The Commission, however, has not had the trust of the other actors as it is a player itself. As the Commission has compensated for this lack of trust by taking extremist positions, the effect has been a further loss of legitimacy and therefore of influence on the negotiation processes in the intergovernmental conferences. A general observation would be that the more complex the bargaining processes are, the more the institutions are needed to guide negotiators through the "forest."

Consequently member states are becoming more dependent on the institutions they have created, and they will therefore invest them with more possibilities for influencing the EU negotiation processes. By creating a power base for the common institutions, albeit an informal power base, the common good of the EU may be furthered but the individual bargaining positions will still suffer. As we have seen before, EU member states already have a diminishing range of options at their disposal because of the growth in the number of participating countries and the decrease in consensus decision making in favor of the increasing use of qualified-majority voting to decide the outcomes of EU negotiation processes. This not only applies to the regular bargaining processes but also to those outside the normal patterns of EU decision making such as the IGCs. This does not mean, however, that interstate negotiations are on the way out. On the contrary, as the multilateral process becomes more complex and more difficult to manage, bilateralism is on the rise. Countries will compensate for their lack of grip on the formal processes by being more active in the informal circuits such as lobbying. While this will facilitate the negotiation process in the European Union, it could also increase ambiguity and it will water down transparency. This, in its turn, will create more difficulties for individual actors to establish effective strategies; they will have to turn to allies and institutions to compensate for their own negotiating weakness.

What kind of negotiation does consensus decision making involve? This is an important topic as decision-making procedures have an enormous impact on the negotiation processes and their outcomes. The impact of qualified-majority voting has already been discussed, but the question remains: To what extent does QMV itself affect the negotiations, or can negotiators use it as a threat when, in practice, consensus remains the rule? A problem with the procedures in the EU is that they are often different from one issue area to the other. This limits transparency and enhances complexity. It should be noted that consensus decision making is also the rule in areas where QMV is allowed. One reason for this is the Luxembourg Compromise of 1966, a package deal whereby countries try to avoid using their veto while at the same time trying not to invoke actual voting. Thus, negotiating until general satisfaction is reached has become the reality in EU bargaining.

A major difference between EU and non-EU negotiations is the common understanding of EU negotiators that EU decision making is a non-zero-sum process: that the Commission is the agenda setter—with the European Council as an upcoming player in this realm—and will therefore enhance the possibility of coordinated solutions; and that the existence of the European Court of Justice guarantees implementation of the decisions agreed to by the member states. An additional factor is the long-standing influence of these factors on the negotiation process and, as a consequence, on the development of an EU negotiation culture with characteristics that cannot be found elsewhere. This evolution of cooperation creates an integrative bargaining process in which noncooperation and tit-for-tat tactics are rare. As negotiators meet each other on a day-to-day basis, EU negotiations are more personalized than other international negotiations. This, in turn, creates a chemistry that furthers integrative bargaining, just as the collective gathering of information shapes a common referential frame.

The enormous number of issues in the EU negotiation processes provides negotiators, in principle, with numerous possibilities for package deals, thereby facilitating integrative outcomes. As we have seen, however, there are several obstacles on the package-dealing horizon that obscure the view of the negotiators. Package deals sometimes work within one and the same dossier area if the deadline is approaching. Package dealing between dossiers is not really feasible, with the exception of trade-offs at the highest political level. Consensus is a more effective mechanism for constructing an efficient bargaining market than qualified-majority voting, as it creates more opportunities for new bargains in the Union. The necessity of meeting the demands of counterparts puts pressure on negotiators to be creative and to "enlarge the pie" of possible negotiation outcomes. This kind of voting makes it less important for the negotation process to steer in the direction of outcomes, as voting then takes the place of bargaining.

Negotiation and mediation in the EU Council of Ministers are important processes in view of the key role the institutions have to play as concession-making machinery. The highly institutionalized character of bargaining in the Council is of importance here. Agenda setting and initiating, the impact of procedures—among them voting rules—on negotiation behavior and coalition building, different mediator roles, and the effect of the institutional context on the negotiation process are vital ingredients in understanding the EU menu. We find consensus-seeking behavior and problem-solving approaches in EU bargaining because there is a perception on the part of member states that the EU will provide them with mutual efficiency gains on the basis of common values. As far as negotiation is concerned, it is easier to accept a proposal by majority vote than to amend it; the Council adopts a Commission proposal—the de facto single negotiation text for the Council of Ministers—by qualified majority but can amend it only by unanimity. For the Commission, therefore, agenda setting is a power resource, as is the prerogative to withdraw its proposals; but this counts only in first-pillar cases, for example, the common market. Quite often, however, the Commission resigns its power of initiative to the Presidency, while actual negotiation is a permanent process between the two.

In those EU areas where QMV is possible, constructive negotiations are imperative. Negotiations are first of all problem-solving exercises rather than the construction of minimal winning coalitions. Countries that are sure to be outvoted will normally go with the flow. Furthermore there is a long-standing Council norm to avoid (out)voting as much as possible. In practice consensus is the rule and voting is a last resort, thus negotiation gains in importance. Package dealing, facilitated by existing crosscutting cleavages and different coalitions depending on the dossier at hand, is the major tactical device used to obtain agreements. As far as coalition building is concerned, the emphasis is more on process coalitions than on voting ones. More QMV, however, is likely now that the European Union has been enlarged. Furthermore, the Commission plays a role both as a facilitative and as a preventive mediator, removing as many obstacles from the negotiation process as possible, while the Presidency is more of an ad hoc mediator. These mediators are not completely neutral; they have their own particular agendas. Some impartiality is needed, however, and this is one of the reasons why the chair of the Council and the leader of the delegation of the presiding country are always different individuals.

Negotiating European policy in the European Council—the multilateral negotiation between the political leaders of the EU countries is EU negotiation at its highest level. And this, the most important negotiation platform of the entire EU, is in crisis. The crisis in the negotiation process has been created by the malfunctioning of the Council of Ministers and by the working methods and proceedings of the European Council itself. One side of the problem is that too many issues are not finalized by the ministers and end up on the table of the heads of state and governments. Too many "low-political" topics have to be dealt with at too high a political level. This mismatch has to do with the risk-avoiding attitude of the lower political and diplomatic strata. As well as the problem of the leaders being swamped, there is the question of languages. As the Union grows, so too will the number of languages in use.

More perhaps than on other negotiation levels, the personal qualities of the leaders have an impact on the negotiation process. After all, they are vested with a great deal of power and therefore are highly "relevant" people. Character always counts, and some research (Meerts, 1997, 472) seems to indicate that, within the EU, character differences among negotiators have a greater impact on negotiation relationships and processes than culture. But for those who represent the states at the highest levels, personal characteristics may even be more relevant than for other representatives. We have seen the impact of people liking or disliking each other on the relationships between the leaders and therefore between the member states. This had nothing to do with political color. There have been German *bundeskanzler* who were able to work very well with French presidents of a different political color while having no chemistry with presidents of the French republic who were politically close to them. Other elements influencing mutual relationships are the power of the countries involved (size, population, economic performance) as well as the constitutional position and the seniority of the leader. Apart from these exogenous factors, changes of a procedural nature are needed to enhance the effectiveness of negotiations in the European Council.

Is there a **cookbook for the Presidency of the European Union** that will enlighten the actor on the role to be played in the EU negotiation processes? Here, factors such as the origin of the Presidency function play a role, as do the spoils a member state might win from holding this most-high function of the Union; also important are the duties and strategies required of the Presidency and finally the techniques for managing the process of negotiation and the national interests involved. One important duty of the Presidency is to guarantee the continuity of, and progress in, the negotiations on the various agenda issues. The country performing the role of the Presidency of the Union has a moral and political obligation to be successful during its six months in office. A failing Presidency shames the country that has the responsibility of guiding the Union through its official term. Its national honor and therefore the political position of the leader(s) are at stake. This is a strong incentive to invest plenty of energy into the presidential period. It is important to be successful and to avoid crisis situations as much as possible as they can lead to failure. The consequence is that presidencies often adopt a risk-avoiding style, as risk-taking presidencies have—until now—not been very successful. Hobbyhorses can be a serious obstacle to effective leadership in the negotiations presided over by the chair of the Union.

The Presidency has a decisive role to play, especially when the other actors fail. To be effective, planning is essential. Most countries prepare seriously for their term, and broad layers of the bureaucracy are trained to understand the issues at hand and to deal with them in an effective way. Pathfinders are sent out to gather information in EU capitals to obtain a thorough insight into the perceptions of the other member states concerning the issues that will be dealt with during the next half year. During its term in office the Presidency must keep in mind that technical chairing is just not enough. Maintaining order will not—by itself—lead to progress in the negotiation process. Corridor work, informal talks, mediation initiatives between opponents, performing well with the other institutions of the European Union as well as pleasing public opinion in member states, are the levels of activity that can help the chair to be seen as effective. But, with the conclusions drawn by the Convention on the Future of Europe regarding the rotation of the Presidency among all member states, new phenomena could enter the arena. The more participants and the more issues, the more important the chair will be, but at the same time, the more complicated its tasks.

Negotiating the enlargement is a very special element in EU negotiation processes. The negotiation processes of the Union with applicant states—and the internal negotiations that go with it—are of lasting importance, even after the recent extension of the EU by ten new member states, for this will not be the last group of countries to join. Other states, like Turkey and some Balkan countries, are bound to follow. It is thus of interest to look at the negotiation experiences involving the new countries to obtain a better insight into the processes we can expect for the coming five to fifteen years. The accession process provides a good example of the complexity of EU bargaining.

Five Directorates-General were involved in the enlargement process, plus the member states, the Council of Ministers, the European Council and, last but not least, the Commission. The Commission is the spider in the web of internal negotiations. It initiates, coordinates, and implements. In doing so it has its own strategies, for it tries to use the enlargement opportunity to create a more powerful position for itself. Fragmentation and complexity are, however, the most salient features of the Commission; thus it had some problems in negotiating the accession effectively. It tries to solve problems by tactics such as package dealing and side payments but it is not always successful at this as the inner fragmentation of its own subinstitutions makes effective bargaining a difficult task to perform. Furthermore, the Commission spends most of its time on negotiations with its own member states and only 10 percent on negotiations with applicant countries.

In other words enlargement negotiations are first and foremost internal EU bargaining processes. The result of this is a loss of flexibility in the external process, the internal process being so complicated that EU positions cannot easily be changed. In reality this means that the EU sets the terms and that they are not negotiable, leaving aside some exceptional high-level issues. Transitional arrangements and the way of implementing these terms, however, are negotiable. This inflexibility is also shown in the decision that all ten applicants of the most recent enlargement should join at the same time. A staggered admission, though originally advocated by the Commission, proved to be unworkable. After the accession of the ten new states the Union will have an even more complicated internal negotiation process than before. As a consequence room for real negotiations with the remaining applicants such as Bulgaria, Romania, and Turkey will even be more restricted than it was in the past.

Mutatis mutandis, this may mean that with the growth in the number of EU member states any external negotiations will be more difficult to deal with in terms of alternatives to the positions already taken by the Union. These positions will become more rigid than they are today, especially if external negotiations are about issues that will have a profound impact on the EU. The higher the stakes and the larger the Union, the less flexible the position it will take in negotiations with outside actors. This could seriously complicate its dealings with, for example, its transatlantic partners, and the inflexibilities could add to the present rift that has arisen as a result of different political aims and strategies. We can already see this process when we observe the difficulties the Council of Ministers has in compromising on its negotiation outcomes to reach consensus with the European Parliament. After internal negotiations, no space is left for further give-and-take. The bottom line has been reached.

Consequences

In 1998 the *International Negotiation Journal* devoted an issue to negotiating in the European Union, one of the earliest analyses of EU negotiation processes as such. According to the journal, "The European Union (EU) is a unique entity—neither a classic intergovernmental international organization nor an ongoing diplomatic negotiation" (Lodge and Pfetsch 1998, 289). All contributors to the book, *Negotiating European Union*, share this view of the uniqueness of EU negotiation processes. The enigma of the EU process hinges on eight main characteristics that distinguish it from other international negotiation processes.

1. The intertwining of national and international negotiation processes. More than any other international negotiation process, EU give-and-take has characteristics of national (e.g., quite controlled, often assured outcomes) and international

(e.g., more anarchistic, often nonassured outcomes) bargaining processes, often at the same time. This is a unique new blend that can be seen as a forerunner of other kinds of mixtures in other interstate negotiation processes as globalization makes national frontiers less important and as international interactions between national civil servants become more frequent. The negotiations within the EU, at least those outside the arena of the common foreign and security policy, are much less interstate than in other international processes. They are more at the interorganizational level, either the one above the national level (extrastate) or the one under the national level (intrastate). This new blend may provide lessons for classic international, interstate negotiation processes. The international negotiation processes at the global level may become less interstate and more interorganizational if enhanced European cooperation proves to be successful; and the latter may serve as a model for international cooperation. Diplomats may lose their (already) less-dominant position in international negotiation processes as the national experts of ministries rise to prominence.

2. Furthermore, most of the issues in the EU negotiation processes are questions of an internal rather than external nature (in the sense of outside the EU). Thus, it is all about internal EU issues. Even in negotiations with the outside world, as in the case of enlargement, the main focus is on the internal EU process. More than other international negotiation processes, this one is inward looking. This intertwining is further enhanced by the growing practice of using the EU as machinery for national change in situations where the national government is not able to implement the necessary new policies. Member states use, as it were, a contextual strategy. The population will then blame the EU acting as a *deus ex machina*. More than in other processes, the energy of the negotiating actors will have to be put into internal negotiation. There will be less time to look outside; external actors may feel ignored, and rightly so. Though there is no "fortress Europe," as the continent is still much too divided for that, the effects of the fortress mentality may already be there. Interest in international issues (questions outside the EU) may dwindle as is the case with the sometimes inward-looking nature of the United States. Europe's outward-looking nature could change and the continent could become a little "autistic." It is important then to study the consequences of focusing on the basket of member states' national interests and the effect this has on the priority given to international (i.e., outside the EU) questions. The importance of the international (i.e., global) negotiation processes could diminish as a consequence of the growing importance of intra-EU bargaining. The internal issues of the power blocs in the world could become more important than the external questions that may hamper international negotiation, and thereby cooperation, on a global scale.

3. The complexity of the internal EU negotiation process absorbs the attention of the partner states, and this results in an island mentality. Growing cleavages with

both the developing world and the major powers outside the Union—for example, the People's Republic of China, the Russian Federation, and the United States—will be difficult to avoid. The EU is much too entangled in managing its own mechanisms and may therefore become less of a global player. This is a strange paradox as one might partly explain the drive for integration as the wish to become a major global player. Internal considerations may, however, lead the EU to become less active at the global level. International negotiation processes on a world scale may become less intensive and less effective because of the nature of the internal international processes of the European Union. The study of the EU bargaining process and its effect on the global processes may therefore supply information about the future of state interaction at the global level. The European Union will either master its own complex nature or it will not be the EU that people envisaged, be they federalists or intergovernmentalists. It seems likely that the European Union will be able to deal with its internal workings only if it centralizes the EU negotiation processes to a much greater extent than it has done to date. By creating stronger intergovernmental actors (for example, a Presidency for a fixed number of years that can be held only by one of the dominant powers within the Union) as well as more powerful supranational bodies (a stronger Commission, for example) the Union will facilitate the more effective EU negotiation processes necessary to maintain its internal cohesion and its external position; though again, this could have an adverse effect on the global international negotiation process.

4. The characteristic of the EU process, that it leads to assured outcomes, will have an effect on negotiations both within member states and with the outside world. As the impact of the outcomes of internal EU negotiation processes becomes more and more substantial, the autonomy of national negotiation processes will be affected. In due course the outcomes at the EU level may determine on an ever-larger scale the outcomes at national levels within the Union. In other words the internal EU negotiation processes will become more important than the internal member-state processes. The predominance of international negotiation processes over national ones—on a permanent basis at least—would be a novelty. We do not know what the effect of this will be, but as control at the EU level will, at least for the time being, be less than at the national level, the consequences of this trend may be an internationalization of the national negotiation processes. In other words, the negotiation processes inside member states may become less effective and less assured because of the impact of the EU process even though, for a long time, it will lack the assured characteristics of the national negotiation process. At the same time, the nature of the processes at the EU level (i.e., processes that provide more assured outcomes than regular classic international negotiations) may influence the global negotiation scene again in the sense that it will be less open than before. The more independent actors there are at the global level, the more chances for

integrative bargaining and the fewer powers there will be, and the more distributive the process may become. An internal EU process that is strong because of the presence of EU institutions may provide for a problem-solving attitude inside the EU. Outside the EU the effect could be adverse. An effective assured-outcome-directed EU negotiation process could lead to less-assured outcomes at the global level as the chances for integrative bargaining diminish.

5. Another characteristic of the EU negotiation process, which it shares with other strong international organizations, is its continuity. The advantage of this, as we have seen, is that trust building will be facilitated, at least within the EU and also outside. Moreover, the group of countries that we call the Union may become more predictable than individual member states because of the need to compromise. Extremist positions cannot survive in an EU of twenty-five or more members. The EU will take a position that has been moderated by its internal negotiation processes and the necessity of give-and-take. Internally the bargaining process will become easier because of awareness of the long-term existence of the constellation of states. This will favor progress in the negotiation process within the Union. Outside powers will, in turn, be able to deal in a more strategic way with a Union that will be, to a certain extent, predictable.

6. The multitude of actors and issues in the EU is growing and provides us with a multitude of smoke screens. The characteristic of nontransparency will be a stumbling block for outside powers in understanding the Union's future steps. All international negotiation processes suffer from a lack of transparency, but the EU process with so many actors and so many issues suffers from it on a unique scale. As long as the internal negotiations are going on, it will often be unclear to outside partners what the assured outcome will be. This is a very difficult thing to predict, even where the partners have a good knowledge of the positions and interests of the member states and of the EU institutions. While the predictability of the EU as such may be enhanced, the predictability of the processes leading up to the final decisions could diminish.

7. Another important characteristic of the Union is, of course, that this coalition of states is more homogeneous than most of the other international negotiation groups. This creates that same integrated-negotiation network discussed previously. Its effect on the outside world will be to make intervention in questions concerning individual EU member states more difficult, as these member states will be shielded from the outside world. However, as long as the Union lacks homogeneity in certain policy areas such as common foreign and security policy, powerful outside actors like the United States will be able to play "divide and rule" and be successful at it. The effect of that strategy goes beyond the so-called second-pillar issues. It has, as we have seen in the Iraq crisis, a divisive effect on the Union as a whole. In other words, as long as there are important less-homogeneous spots in the EU negotiation

process, outside powers will be able to throw the EU into an extremely annoying disarray that will have a negative effect on the smoothness of the EU negotiation processes.

8. The negotiation process of the Union is based on more than a community of interests; it is based on a community of values as well. In that sense the EU process is quite unique, though we can also find similar aspects in other international organizations, for example, in the North Atlantic Treaty Organization. The Union's value-based nature strengthens its international bargaining position, the value patterns creating more stability as a supportive matrix for day-to-day, needs-based negotiations. On the other hand, it raises the danger of contradictions in values, of clashes over underlying perceptions and assumptions. In other words, it introduces an emotional dimension into EU negotiation processes, both internally and externally: an emotional dimension strengthened by cultural cleavages that undoubtedly exist in the Union and that will have an effect. Even if they are not seen as very important in the day-to-day dealings within the Union, values and culture are matters that can destroy the effectiveness of any negotiation processes, and it is very difficult, if not impossible, to control them once they get out of hand. Conflicts over values can be used very effectively by outside powers to weaken the internal cohesion they normally support and facilitate.

Taken together, the eight elements mentioned above distinguish the negotiation processes in the European Union from the negotiation processes in other international settings, though the overall tactical advice for multilateral negotiators applies to EU negotiators as well (Lang 1994, 210–11). The EU process is unique in the sense of its intensity. Elements of the process can and will be found in other international negotiation arenas, but not to the same extent. A single factor that, in general, plays a more prominent role in EU processes than in non-EU negotiations, is the notion of assured outcomes.

As we have seen, assured outcomes are a normal phenomenon in EU negotiation processes, partly because of mechanisms such as supranationality and the continuous nature of the process. Compared to, for example, environmental negotiations (Sjöstedt and Spector 1993, 303) the level of "unavoidability" is incomparably higher. The nature of the outcomes is overwhelmingly positive sum, while this is by no means evidently so in other negotiation processes where international economic relations are predominant (Zartman 2000, 327). Finally, the implementation of these outcomes, the strength of the EU institutions in enforcing compliance, is much greater than in, say, negotiations on the environment (Sjöstedt *et al.* 1994, 233).

Furthermore these outcomes are produced at a much faster pace and within a much larger time frame than in other international negotiation processes. The ability of the EU negotiation process to work as a continuous upside-down cascade (Zartman 2003, 180), where one level facilitates progress on a higher level of negotiations, sets it apart from the regular patterns of international negotiation processes. The necessity to come to an agreement in order to facilitate further steps at a later stage is the main explanation of the assured-outcomes character of EU negotiations processes—as is also the case in mandate-setting national negotiation processes.

Future

As has been observed, the European Union is one enormous negotiation process. What about this process in the EU today and in the years to come after further deepening and widening have taken place?

The EU started off as a confidence-building measure between the French and the German (Federal) Republic. Both countries wanted, through an economic arrangement (the European Coal and Steel Community), to prevent another war in Europe by creating a stable and secure situation with economic benefits as a spin-off. But Germany and France needed neutral partners to help them forge a durable balance; thus Italy and the Benelux countries stepped into the process. Ever since, this multilateral framework for international negotiation has been expanding: in the economic realm (first pillar), into the common foreign and security dimension (second pillar) and in the arena of justice and home affairs (third pillar). But as well as widening the number of new issue areas, the Union also enlarged its membership. The Union is broadening in two ways: by multiplying both its policy areas and the number of partners to be integrated. In several waves new countries have entered the ring: Denmark, Ireland, and the United Kingdom (1973), Greece (1981), Portugal and Spain (1986), and Austria, Finland, and Sweden (1995). The 15 then decided to accept 10 new members in 2004: Cyprus, the Czech Republic, Estonia, Hungary, Latvia, Lithuania, Malta, Poland, Slovakia, and Slovenia. In 2007 Bulgaria and Romania may enter; before that Croatia will probably be slotted in. Turkey will have to wait, let us speculate, until 2015. At that date countries like Albania, Bosnia, Macedonia, and Serbia will also be serious candidates, as will Norway and Switzerland. The EU may end up with some thirty-five states in the first quarter of the twenty-first century, some of which will have common borders with the nonmember states of the Organization of the Islamic Conference and the Commonwealth of Independent States—and with Israel of course, though some commentators also see that country as a future member of the Union.

The EU is not only broadening its horizons; it is also deepening its cooperation in two ways: by covering more and more aspects of the categories it sees as its domain and by strengthening the EU institutions. The supranational elements such as the European Commission, the European Parliament, and the European Court of Justice are being beefed up, as are the intergovernmental bodies such as the European Council of heads of states and government, the Council of Ministers and the whole range of working groups and committees served by negotiators from the public and—to a far lesser extent—the private sector.

Member states organize themselves in coalitions. Stable coalitions can be seen around the North-South cleavage (rich–poor, but primarily Germanic versus Latin cultures); there is a supranationalist–intergovernmentalist axis; an Atlanticist coalition verses a continentalist coalition; there are free traders versus protectionists; big versus small countries. All these cleavages are crosscutting: one country is always part of more than one "structural" alliance, and there are countless numbers of different coalitions on different dossiers. The effect of these coalition patterns is twofold: they both slow down and stabilize the EU negotiation processes. They constitute a negotiation arena that, while securing both European and national interests, does not enhance the strength of the Union as a global actor. The Union is (still) no match for the United States, which is capable of breaking EU consensus on vital world phenomena such as the war against terrorism, the criminal court at The Hague, and the intervention in Iraq. The European Union is, as a negotiated framework, both powerful and vulnerable, united and disunited. A fortress as well as a "fancy fair."

The present negotiation process can be characterized as an international multilateral process based on intranational multilateral negotiations. The international multilateral process, however, has been affected by two other dimensions, first of all the drive for supranationalism. From the very beginning member states realized that a workable EU would be impossible without the transfer of (at least partial) sovereignty to supranational bodies—in the first place, the Commission. The effect of this is that the EU negotiation processes cannot be seen as purely international. If we define an international negotiation process as an animal that cannot really be controlled because the world lacks a strong third party that can decide if international negotiations fail (with apologies to the UN institutions, especially the Security Council and the International Court of Justice) then—at least parts of—the EU negotiation processes cannot be branded as international. Where the Commission has a strong role to play and states can decide by qualified-majority voting (mainly in the first pillar and partly in the third)—though they will always try to reach consensus first—a distinct negotiation process has come into being, which has been labeled supranational negotiation. The difference between international and supranational negotiation, then, is a difference in control. While national negotiations are very much controlled by the national government, international negotiations have a more free-for-all character, and supranational negotiations are an in-between hybrid. In terms of the negotiation process it has been observed that supranational negotiations are more intense (because of the threat of being outvoted) than their international counterpart.

This drive toward supranationalism, in other words, the creation of a strong negotiation framework to enhance the effectiveness of international negotiations, is not a new development. After the fall of the Roman empire, whose former borders are still at the root of the cultural rift between the northern and southern countries of the EU, a rift that expresses itself, inter alia, in the use of French and English in EU plenary sessions, Europeans tried to replace the Roman order with a hierarchical framework of sovereign states. This structure decayed during the Middle Ages and came to an end in the middle of the seventeenth century at the peace conference at Westphalia (1648). Countries then tried to maintain the balance in a system of sovereign states that were formally equal although some, of course, were far more equal than others. Stability was constantly threatened by the use of force with international negotiation being used as a tool in warfare. States thought to reverse this by using warfare only as an ultimate tool in conflict management if negotiation did not work. To enhance the stability of the international negotiation processes among the European states more and more multilateral conferences such as the one at Westphalia were organized. One should note, however, that these conferences were multilateral only in the sense that more than two or three countries participated. The negotiations remained parallel bilateral. It was only at the Congress of Vienna at the beginning of the nineteenth century that real multilateral negotiations could be observed and only at the beginning of the twentieth century that this multilateralism led to institutionalism: the League of Nations, later the United Nations, and so forth. In terms of genuine peaceful cooperation and integration, however, this proved to be inadequate. Consequently, supranationalism was introduced as the highest stage of stable negotiation processes between states.

Does this mean that supranational negotiation will be the dominant negotiation mode in the EU at the end of the twenty-first century? There are no signs of this. Intergovernmentalism is on the rise again and thus international negotiation in its multilateral as well as its bilateral format. Why is this so? In some respects it has to do with the cyclical character of EU processes. Times of further integration are balanced by times of national reaction, followed by more internationalization and supranationalization. It also has to do with the character of negotiation processes themselves. The more actors, the more issues, the more complex the multilateral process. Supranational negotiations are only a partial solution to rising complexity, the other partial solutions being intergovernmental bilateral and trilateral negotiations, including lobbying. The negotiation process cannot be managed inside the multilateral mode as much as it could in the past (though many of the most important decisions in the EU have certainly been "precooked" in small caucuses). The result is a process within a process, making things more manageable perhaps but enhancing the lack of overall transparency and frustrating concerted cooperation. The growth of centered negotiation processes in the Union provokes a growth of centrifugal negotiation processes that tend to run in parallel instead of in an integrated way. Is this something of a regression to the seventeenth century? Whether it is or not, for the time being we will probably experience a mix of supranational and international negotiation processes at the European level, with a growing circus of bilateral and trilateral bargaining.

What then about national negotiations or, better yet, intrastate negotiation processes? As the Union grows in substance and area, national coordination becomes increasingly important and increasingly difficult—more important, too, because decisions taken in Brussels have an ever-growing impact on national policy making. Therefore ministries will have to set clear priorities and cooperate as effectively as possible. Where bigger member states can still relax a little here, smaller states have no time and power to lose and are obliged to be as effective as possible in their multilateral intrastate negotiations. This is especially a shock for the new member states of Central Europe which have only ten years of experience in coordinative negotiations between equal ministries, with the Soviet Union and the Communist party taking the decisions before that. The old member states are also confronted by multiplying coordination problems. The ministries of foreign affairs (MFAs) can scarcely cope with the growth of negotiation processes among the specialized ministries at a time when coordination is needed more than ever. Some policy makers have already started to think aloud about the option of decentralizing the tasks of the foreign ministries to specialized ministries, adding a foreign affairs coordination unit to their prime minister's office, doing away with the MFA; one additional argument is that as the bulk of the negotiation processes in the Union deal with national affairs, only second-pillar subject matter should remain in the foreign affairs domain, as should the world outside the EU, of course. But as more and more foreign-policy making is integrated into the Union, the room for independent external policies outside the Union is diminishing. What will the role of the diplomatic negotiator be?

We would like to postulate that, because of the process of deepening, the role of the diplomatic negotiator will be taken over—has already been taken over in many areas—by civil servant negotiators, both on the national as well as on the supranational and international levels. It has been noticed that specialized civil servants are not equipped to run the negotiation processes smoothly. Generalist civil servants will have to oversee the job—civil servants in diplomats' clothing, one might argue. Several problems arise here. The linkage between the different issue areas could be endangered as this new brand of negotiators direct their efforts into their own sectors and fail to take into account the packages between the areas. This might then secure a role, albeit no longer a dominant role as in the twentieth century, for the old-fashioned—but probably newly styled—EU diplomat. He/she will also be needed in the external negotiations of the Union as far as second-pillar subject matter is concerned but will lose out on first- and third-pillar external relations. While diplomats are trained to overcome cultural and other emotional rifts, civil servants may not be so good at this. The consequence could be a less-rational negotiation process in the European Union—a dangerous development on a continent that has been devastated by religious and ideological wars. More attention is needed to the emotional factor in EU negotiation processes. As it happens, negotiators from countries in the North have more difficulty in dealing with this than their counterparts from the South, whose bread and butter is networking.

We would also like to postulate that not only the deepening but also the broadening of the EU will complicate and change the Union's negotiation processes—first of all because of the rising number of actors. EU member countries are contemplating more institutionalization and even took some decisions on this in Nice under the French Presidency. This, however, will lead to a further loss of sovereignty or at least of political maneuverability; and European countries are not at all keen on this. Thus, the process will be slow, and even if it is successful there will be doubts about how much more effective institutionalized and formal negotiations will be than ad hoc and informal ones. But then culture comes into play again: systemic, political and bureaucratic, and societal. Systemic, because the variety of political cultures will increase, making matters less comparable and less transparent. The EU already faces such differences as those between centralized countries (France, Sweden) and decentralized ones (Belgium, Germany). These system incomparabilities already lead to confusion, behavioral differences between negotiators, and blockades to effective decision making. Political, because the existing behavioral differences between the network culture of the South and the process culture of the North will be further complicated by the hierarchical cultures in most of the new member states. Their political culture has been shaped by centralized democracy based on a much older layer of autocratic rule under the Austrian emperors, the Ottoman sultans, and the Russian tsars. As "take" seems to be more common sense than "give-and-take," the Union may be in for a surprise as far as negotiation processes are concerned. These differences in outlook are strengthened by bureaucratic and societal habits and will profoundly change the negotiations within and outside Brussels. Trust may be faltering, and it will take time to redress this. Furthermore, there is the multiplication of issue areas. New issues will be integrated into the process, more coordination will be needed, the negotiation process will be complicated further. There is a bright side to this, however. The more issues and the more options, the more likely are integrative rather than distributive negotiation processes.

To summarize we see an EU negotiation process that will be so complex that it may, in itself, be an obstacle to further integration. At the same time the opportunities for integrated solutions will be on the rise. The result could be a new balance where the EU will continue to grow as a system and process that will be larger than the sum of its parts. At the same time there will be important issue areas where a convergence of interests will not be possible. This disparity could develop in terms of an internal and an external position of the Union. Internally more power and opportunities will be generated. Externally the Union may remain what it is today, or may even regress slightly: a coalition that cannot get its act together. For EU negotiation this would mean growing interdependency of national, international, and supranational negotiation processes within the Union. Politicians and civil servants will dominate the scene, diplomats will lose their hegemony, while in the relations between the EU and the outside world the distribution of roles will be more balanced. Politicians, civil servants, and diplomats will be just as important as negotiators. They will have to find a balanced interplay. Power will be less centralized than inside the EU, and while external forces will have little impact on the internal EU negotiation process, they will be better able to distort the external negotiating processes. While internally a common negotiation market could be expected, a partial free-for-all will probably remain in the external sphere, especially as far as common foreign and security policy are concerned.

To conclude let us state that EU negotiation processes will be a sufficient tool for managing the common and diverging interests of the EU countries in the first quarter of the twenty-first century. After that they may hamper further integration as long as they remain rooted in intrastate negotiations as we know them today. A new format will have to be found then and, behold, the political system of the United States could be the answer here—as long as Europe can guard and enhance its own inherent cultural values. By its inherent nature, the EU negotiation process has and will have an enormous impact not only on the workings of the national negotiations within its own member states but also on international negotiations at the global level. The classic international negotiation processes as we have known them since the mid-seventeenth century will change dramatically because of globalization and of regionalization, as typified by the European Union.

Is there any policy advice to be given in view of the importance of the negotiation process as a factor in creating more unity in Europe? This is risky for an academic, even one working for decades at a policy-oriented institute, training diplomats and civil servants from the old and new countries in EU negotiation. But let us give it a try.

First it has been noted that the individual EU negotiator will become an even more important asset as the process becomes ever more complex and nontransparent. In that case, the inevitable conclusion is that the European Union and its member states will have to invest more in the human dimension, for example, by transforming the present-day, very modest, European diplomatic program into a fully fledged training curriculum or even establishing a European negotiation academy for diplomats and other civil servants. Such an academy would at least have the advantage of being able to enhance the level of the negotiations, familiarize the new breed of EU diplomats and civil servants with EU-specific negotiation, create a network within the group; and most importantly it might help to create a European diplomatic professional culture. And, as we know, professional cultures have a serious effect on negotiation processes (Sjöstedt 2003, 245). Another aspect of the human dimension has to do with the growing number of languages in the EU. It is not unlikely that this problem will be settled in favor of English as a lingua franca as French is already losing more and more ground in Brussels, undermining the claims of others (German for example) to also be seen as working languages.

Second, there is a need to harmonize policy-producing organizations, most of them ministries. Negotiation will be smoother if the institutions involved are more-or-less comparable in structure. This may also encompass the creation of uniform EU-coordination agencies in all member states, either as part of ministries of foreign affairs, or as separate ministries of European integration. It should be added, however, that separate ministries could create more bureaucracy, and experiments with this in some of the aspiring member states have not shown very positive results to date.

Third, it seems unavoidable that the larger member states will have to take special responsibility for the efficiency of the negotiation process through enhanced cooperation between them. They already work much more closely together than their sometimes hefty disagreements on issues such as common foreign and security policy might suggest. Three have a tacit agreement not to support any coalition that may affect the vital interests of each of them concerning issues where qualified-majority voting casts its shadow on the negotiation processes. More guidance for the EU by the major EU powers will, of course, demand a better cooperative process between the three (France, Germany, UK) or the six (plus Italy, Poland, Spain) major players in concert with the Commission, the Parliament, and the smaller EU member states in the Council of Ministers.

Harmonious leadership may be established in the QMV arenas, but for CFSP it remains quite unlikely for the time being. In a way the EU does not "exist" in that area. It may well be that France and the UK should hand over their veto right in the United Nations Security Council to the European Union, but it is extremely unlikely that this will ever happen. However centralized the EU negotiation processes become, some basic issues may always remain out of reach, especially on international politics in the sense of external EU politics, or, as far as military matters are concerned, given the very useful EU-U.S. cooperation in the context of the North

Atlantic Treaty Organization. It is, however, in the interests of the European Union to become more integrated into the external negotiation processes for these can create major upheaval in internal processes, as we have seen quite recently. All this to say that effective negotiation processes in the European Union will be sustained by a more effective integration of the EU into international negotiation processes outside its realm. External disturbances can upset the internal balance.

Fourth and last, we come to the leadership by the Presidency. The present system will change, but a good piece of advice would be to stick to the mores for EU chairing developed in past decades: impartiality; legitimacy; being strict on rules and regulations without becoming inflexible and bureaucratic; sticking to the time limits; explaining how the chair wishes to guide the meetings; having fallback positions ready in the form of more than one draft final text; making effective use of the corridors as time for arguments in the plenary will be lacking after enlargement; giving the floor first to those who support the chair; and not forgetting that holding the Presidency does not entitle your member state to push for its own interests. The Presidency must represent the common good.

And finally, it may be true that the member states of the Union cannot escape further integration into the EU negotiation processes if they want to survive in the world outside Europe. But it could also be true that the EU as such cannot escape the globalization of the process of international negotiation and will have to adapt to this trend by taking more responsibility in the realm of conflict resolution through international negotiation. After all, the European Union negotiation process may be an enigma, but it is very much a part of the overall negotiation processes needed to run world affairs in a peaceful and effective way. In that sense negotiation is a central element in international relations, deserving attention by practitioners and theoreticians alike. It is hoped that this book contributes to the understanding of that process as far as European integration is concerned.

References

Allison, G., and P. Zelikow. 1999. *Essence of Decision: Explaining the Cuban Missile Crisis*. New York, N.Y.: Longman.

Anderson, C.J., and C. Guillory. 1997. Political Institutions and Satisfaction with Democracy: A Cross-National Analysis of Consensus and Majoritarian Systems. *American Political Science Review*, **91**(1):66–81.

Aspinwall, M.D., and G. Schneider. 2000. Same Menu, Separate Tables: The Institutionalist Turn in Political Science and the Study of European Integration. *European Journal of Political Research*, **38**:1–36.

Avery, G. 1995. *The Commission's Perspective on the EFTA Accession Negotiations*. Sussex European Institute Papers No. 12.

Avery, G., and F. Cameron. 1998. *The Enlargement of the European Union*. Sheffield, England: Sheffield Academic Press.

Axelrod, R. 1984. *The Evolution of Cooperation*. New York: Basic Books.

Bal, L.J. 1995. *Decision-Making and Negotiations in the European Union*. University of Leicester, Centre for the Study of Diplomacy, Discussion Paper No. 7.

Beach, D. 2004. *The Dynamics of European Integration—When and Why EU Institutions Matter*. Basingstoke, Hampshire: Palgrave Macmillan.

Bengtsson, R. 2002. Soft Security and the Presidency. *Cooperation and Conflict*, **37**(2):212–18.

Bjurulf, B., and O. Elgström. 2004. Negotiating Transparency: The Role of Institutions. *Journal of Common Market Studies*, **42**(1).

Bogaards, M., and M. Crepaz. 2002. Consociational Interpretations of the European Union. *European Union Politics*, **3**(3).

Bostock, D. 2002. Coreper Revisited. *Journal of Common Market Studies*, **2**(40):215–34.

Börzel, T. 2002. Member State Responses to Europeanisation. *Journal of Common Market Studies*, **2**(40):194.

———. 2003. *Shaping and Taking EU Policies: Member States' Responses to Europeanisation*. Belfast: Queen's Papers on Europeanisation No. 2.

Budden, P. 2002. Observations on the Single European Act and "Relaunch of Europe": A Less "Intergovernmental" Reading of the 1985 Intergovernmental Conference. *Journal of European Public Policy*, **9**(1):76–97.

Bull, H. 1977. *The Anarchical Society: A Study of Order in World Politics*. London: Macmillan.

Bulmer, S. 1983. Domestic Politics and EC Policy-Making. *Journal of Common Market Studies*, **21**(4).

———. 1994. The Governance of the European Union: A New Institutionalist Approach. *Journal of Public Policy*, **13**(4):351–80.

Carnevale, P.J., and S. Arad. 1996. Bias and Impartiality in International Mediation, in J. Bercovitch, ed., *Resolving International Conflicts—The Theory and Practice of Mediation*. London: Lynne Rienner Publishers, 39–53.

Charlemagne, V.O. 1994. L'équilibre entre les états membres, in *L'équilibre européen. Etudes rassemblées et publiées en hommage*. Brussels: B. Niels Ersbøll. Edition provisoire, 69–78.

Christiansen, T. 2001. The European Commission: Administration in Turbulent Times, in J. Richardson, ed., *European Policy-Making—Power and Policy-Making*. London: Routledge.

———. 2002. The Role of Supranational Actors in EU Treaty Reform. *Journal of European Public Policy*, **9**(1):33–53.

Christoffersen, P. S. 1992. *Traktaten om Den Europæiske Union—Baggrund, Forhandling, Resultat*. Kobenhavn: Jurist-og Okonomforbundets Forlag.

Corbett, R. 1987. The 1985 Intergovernmental Conference and the Single European Act, in R. Pryce, ed., *The Dynamics of European Union*. London: Croom Helm, 238–72.

Costa, O. 2000. La présidence française de l'Union: quelques éléments pour un bilan. *L'Année Sociale*: 386–96.

Council Guide: Presidency Handbook. 2001. Brussels: General Secretariat of the Council of the European Union.

Council of the European Union. 2002. *Measures to Prepare the Council for Enlargement*. Report by the Presidency to the European Council (drawn up jointly with the General Secretariat of the Council). Brussels, 13 June, 9939/02, POLGEN25.

Cowles, M. G., J.A. Caporaso, and T. Risse, eds. 2001. *Transforming Europe. Europeanization and Domestic Change*. Ithaca, N.Y.: Cornell University Press.

Crombez, C. 2000. Codecision: Towards a Bicameral European Union. *European Union Politics*, **1**(3):363–68.

Daemen, H., and M.C.P.M. van Schendelen. 1998. The Advisory Committee on Safety, Hygiene, and Health Protection at Work, in M.C.P.M. van Schendelen, ed., *EU Committees as Influencial Policymakers*. Aldershot, Hampshire; Brookfield, V.T.: Ashgate, 129–47.

de Ruyt, J. 1987. *L'acte unique Européen: commentaire*. Brussels: Editions de l'Université Libre de Bruxelles.

de Schoutheete, P. 1988. The Presidency and the Management of Political Cooperation, in A. Pijpers, E. Regelsberger and W. Wessels, eds., *European Political Cooperation in the 1980s*. Dordrecht: Martinus Nijhoff Publishers.

———. 2002. The European Council, in J. Peterson and M. Shackleton, eds., *The Institutions of the European Union*. Oxford: Oxford University Press.

de Winter, L., and H. Türsan. 2001. *The Belgian Presidency 2001*. Research and Policy Paper No. 13. Paris: Groupement d'Etudes et de Recherches. Text available at: <http://www.notre-europe.asso.fr/fichiers/Etud13-en.pdf>.

den Boer, M. 2002. A New Area of Freedom, Security and Justice, in F. Laursen, ed., *The Amsterdam Treaty: National Preference Formation, Interstate Bargaining, Outcome and Ratification*. Odense: Odense University Press, 509–35.

Dinan, D. 1994. *An Ever Closer Union? An Introduction to the European Union*, 1st edition. Basingstoke, Hampshire: Palgrave Macmillan.

———. 1997. The Commission and the Reform Process, in G. Edwards and A. Pijpers, eds., *The Politics of European Treaty Reform: The 1996 Intergovernmental Conference and Beyond*. London: Pinter.

———. 2000a. *An Ever Closer Union? An Introduction to the European Union*, 2nd edition. Basingstoke, Hampshire: Palgrave Macmillan.

———. 2000b. The Commission and the Intergovernmental Conferences, in N. Nugent, ed., *At the Heart of the Union: Studies of the European Commission*, 2nd edition. London: Macmillan, 250–69.

Dosenrode, S. 2002. *The Danes, the European Union and the Forthcoming Presidency*. Research and European Issues No.18. Paris: Groupement d'Etudes et de Recherches.

Dyson, K., and K. Featherstone. 1999. *The Road to Maastricht: Negotiating Economic and Monetary Union*. Oxford: Oxford University Press.

Edwards, G., and A. Pijpers. 1996. *The 1996 IGC and the EU Presidency*. Paper presented at the Netherlands' Presidency of the European Union, The Hague, 15–16 November.

Eising, R. 2002. Policy Learning in Embedded Negotiations: Explaining EU Electricity Liberalization. *International Organization*, **56**(1):85–120.

Elgström, O. 2001. *The Honest Broker? The Council Presidency as a Mediator*. Paper presented at the 4th Pan-European IR Conference in Canterbury, Kent, England.

Elgström, O., and C. Jönsson. 2000. Negotiation in the European Union: Bargaining or Problem-Solving? *Journal of European Public Policy*, **7**(5):684–704.

European Commission. 1996. *Reinforcing Political Union and Preparing for Enlargement*. Commission Opinion of 28 February. COM(96)90 final.

Evans, P., H.K. Jacobson, and R.D. Putnam. 1993. *Double-Edged Diplomacy*. Berkeley: University of California Press.

Fisher, R., and W. Ury 1978. *International Mediation: A Working Guide. Ideas for the Practitioner*, 4th edition. Harvard: Harvard Negotiation Project.

Fisher, R., W. Ury, and B. Patton. 1997. *Getting to Yes: Negotiating an Agreement Without Giving In*, 2nd edition. London: Arrow Business Books.

Forster, A. 1999. *Britain and the Maastricht Negotiations*. Basingstoke, Hampshire: Macmillan.

Frank, C., and T. de Wilde d'Estmael. 1994. L'Union européenne et la Présidence belge: juîllet-décembre 1993. *Courrier Hebdomadaire du Crisp*: 1432–33.

Friedrich, C.J. 1974. *Limited Government*. Englewood Cliffs, N.J.: Prentice Hall.

Friis, L. 1998. *The End of the Beginning of Eastern Enlargement—Luxembourg Summit and Agenda Setting*. See <http://eiop.or.at>.

Garrett, G. 1992. International Cooperation and Institutional Choice: The European Community's Internal Market. *International Organization*, **46**:533–60.

———. 1995. From the Luxembourg Compromise to Codecision: Decision Making in the European Union. *Electoral Studies*, **14**(3):289–308.

Garrett, G., and G. Tsebelis. 1996. An Institutional Critique of Intergovernmentalism. *International Organization*, **50**(2):269–99.

———. 2000. Legislative Politics in the European Union. *European Union Politics*, **1**(1):9–36.

———. 2001a. Understanding Better the EU Legislative Process. *European Union Politics*, **2**:3.

———. 2001b. The Institutional Foundations of Intergovernmentalism and Supranationalism in the European Union. *International Organization*, **55**(2):357–90.

General Report 2002 of the European Union. The text can be found in full at: <http://europa.eu.int/abc/doc/off/rg/en/2002/somm.000.htm>.

George, S., and M. Sowemimo. 1998. Europe Looks to London. *The World Today*, **541**:18–20.

Gower, J. 1999. EU Policy to Central and Eastern Europe, in K. Henderson, ed., *Back to Europe: Central and Eastern Europe and the European Union*. London: UCL Press.

Grant, C. 1994. *Delors: Inside the House that Jacques Built*. London: Nicholas Brealey Publishing.

Gray, M. 2002. Negotiating the Treaty of Amsterdam: The Role and Influence of the European Commission, in F. Laursen, ed., *The Amsterdam Treaty: National Preference Formation, Interstate Bargaining, Outcome and Ratification*. Odense: Odense University Press, 381–404.

Gray, M., and A. Stubb. 2001. The Treaty of Nice: Negotiating a Poisoned Chalice? *Journal of Common Market Studies* (Annual Review EU 2001), **39**:5–23.

Greenwood, J. 1997. *Representing Interests in the EU*. London: The Macmillan Press.

Gruber, L. 2000. *Ruling the World: Power Politics and the Rise of Supranational Institutions*. Princeton, N.J.: Princeton University Press.

Hall, P.A., and R. Taylor. 1996. Political Science and the Three New Institutionalisms. *Political Studies*, **XLIV**:936–57.

Hanf, K., and B. Soetendorp. 1996. *Adapting to European Integration. Small States and the European Union*. Harlow: Longman.

Harrems, N. 1998. The Leghold Trap Regulation and Potential Pitfalls during the Dutch Presidency of the EU. *Environmental Law Review*, **71**:7–12.

Hayes-Renshaw, F., and H. Wallace. 1997. *The Council of Ministers*. London: Macmillan.

Helsinki European Council 1999. *Presidency Conclusions*. See full text at: <http://europa. eu.int/council/off/conclu/dec99/dec99_en.htm>.

Henderson, D. 1998. *The British Presidency of the EU and British European Policy*. Discussion Paper, Center for European Integration Studies, Universität Bonn.

———. 1999. The British Presidency: An Insider's View. *Common Market Studies*, **364**:563–72.

Héritier, A. 1996. The Accommodation of Diversity in European Policy-Making and Its Outcomes: Regulatory Policy as a Patchwork. *Journal of European Public Policy*, **3**(2):149–67.

Hirschman, A.O. 1970. *Exit, Voice, and Loyalty*. Cambridge, Mass.: Harvard University Press.

Hix, S. 1999. *The Political System of the European Union*. Basingstoke, Hapshire: The Macmillan Press.

Hoffman, S. 1966. Obstinate or Obsolete? The Fate of the Nation-State and the Case of Western Europe. *Daedalus*, **95**(3).

Hooghe, L., and G. Marks. 2001. *Multilevel Governance and European Integration*. Oxford: Rowman & Littlefield Publishers.

Hopmann, T.P. 1996. *The Negotiation Process and the Resolution of International Conflicts*. Columbia, S.C.: University of South Carolina Press.

Hosli, M. 1993. The Admission of the European Free Trade Association to the European Community: Effects on Voting Power in the European Community Council of Ministers. *International Organization*, **47**(4):629–43.

———. 1995. The Balance between Small and Large: Effects of a Double-Majority System on Voting Power in the European Union. *International Studies Quarterly*, **39**(3):351–70.

Hull, R. 1993. Lobbying Brussels: A View from Within, in S. Mazey and J. Richardson, eds., *Lobbying in the European Community*. Oxford: Oxford University Press.

Humphreys, P.C. 1997. *The Fifth Irish Presidency of the European Union: Some Management Lessons*. Dublin: Committee for Public Management Research.

Iklé , F.C. 1967. *How Nations Negotiate*. New York: Praeger.

Jönsson, C., B. Bjurulf, O. Elgström, A. Sannerstedt, and M. Strömvik. 1998. Negotiations in Networks in the European Union. *International Negotiation*, **3**:319–44.

Johnston, A.I. 2001, Treating International Institutions as Social Environments. *International Studies Quarterly*, **45**(4):487–515.

Kassim, H., B.G. Peters, and V. Wright. 2000. *The National Coordination of EU Policy: The Domestic Level*. Oxford: Oxford University Press.

Kassim, H., and B.G. Peters. 2001. Conclusion: Co-ordinating National Action in Brussels—A Comparative Perspective, in H. Kassim, A. Menon, B.G. Peters, and V. Wright, eds., *The National Coordination of EU Policy: The European Level*. Oxford: Oxford University Press.

Keohane, R.O. 1983. The Demand for International Regimes, in S. D. Krasner, ed., *International Regimes*. London: Cornell University Press, 141–72.

Keohane, R.O., and J. Nye. 1989. *Power and Interdependence*, 2nd edition. Glenview, Ill.: Scott, Foresman.

Kirchner, E. 1992. *Decision-making in the European Community: The Council Presidency and European Integration*. Manchester: Manchester University Press.

Kirchner, E., and A. Tsagkari, eds. 1993. *The EC Council Presidency. The Dutch and Luxembourg Presidencies*. London: UACES.

Kitzinger, U. 1973. *Diplomacy and Persuasion. How Britain Joined the Common Market*. London: Thames and Hudson.

Kleiboer, M.A. 1997. *International Mediation: The Multiple Realities of Third-Party Intervention*. University of Leiden Dissertation.

Knill, C. 1998. European Policies: The Impact of National Administrative Tradition. *Journal of Public Policy*, **18**:1–28.

Kohler-Koch, B. 1996. Catching Up with Change: The Transformation of Governance in the European Union. *Journal of European Public Policy*, **3**(3):359–80.

———. 1998. Organised Interests in the EU and the EP, in P. Claeys, C. Gobin, I. Smets, and P. Winand, eds., *Lobbying, Pluralism and European Integration*. Brussels: EIP, 126–58.

Kremenyuk, V.A. ed. 2002. *International Negotiations—Analysis, Approaches, Issues*. San Francisco: Jossey-Bass Publishers.

Kwast-van Duursen, M. 1996. *The 1996 IGC: The Netherlands Debate. A Shifting Policy on Europe*. Paper presented at the Netherlands' Presidency of the European Union, The Hague.

Laffan, B. 2001. The European Union Polity: A Union of Regulative, Normative and Cognitive Pillars. *Journal of European Public Policy*, **85**:709–27.

Lang, W. 1994. Lessons Drawn from Practice, Open Covenants, Openly Arrived At, in I.W. Zartman, ed., *International Multilateral Negotiation*. San Francisco: Jossey-Bass Publishers.

Lax, D.A., and J.K. Sebenius. 1996. *The Manager as Negotiator*. New York: The Free Press.

Lewicki, R.J. 2003. *Negotiation*, 4th edition. Boston: McGraw-Hill/Irwin.

Lijphart, A. 1999. *Patterns of Democracy: Government Forms and Performance in Thirty-Six Countries*. New Haven: Yale University Press.

Lipsius, J. 1995. The 1996 Intergovernmental Conference. *European Law Review*, **20**(3):235–67.

Lodge, J.E., and F.R. Pfetsch 1998. Negotiating the European Union: Introduction. *International Negotiation*, **3**(3).

Ludlow, P. 1993. The UK Presidency: A View From Brussels. *Journal of Common Market Studies*, **31**(2):246–68.

———. 1998. *The 1998 UK Presidency: A View from Brussels*. Center for European Policy Studies.

Luther, K.R. 1998. From West European Periphery to the Centre of Europe? in K.R. Luther and I. Ogilvie, eds., *Austria and the European Union Presidency: Background and Perspectives*. Keele, England: Keele European Research Centre, Keele University.

March, J.G., and J.P. Olsen. 1998. The Institutional Dynamics of International Political Orders. *International Organization*, **52**(4):943–69.

Matlary, J. 1993. Now You See It, Now You Don't. Exposé and Critique of Approaches to the Study of European Integration, in T. Tiilikainen and I. Damgaard Petersen, eds., *The Nordic Countries and the EEC*. Copenhagen: Copenhagen Political Studies Press, 107–35.

Mattila, M., and J.-E. Lane. 2001. Why Unanimity in the Council? A Roll Call Analysis of Council Voting. *European Union Politics*, **2**(1):31–52.

Maurer, A., J. Mittag, and W. Wessels. 2001. *National Parliaments on Their Way to Europe: Losers or Latecomers?* Baden Baden: Nomos.

Mayhew, A. 1998. The European Union's Policy toward Central Europe: Design or Drift? in C. Rhodes, ed., *The European Community in the World Community*. Boulder: Lynne Rienner Publishers, 105–25.

McDonagh, B. 1998. *Original Sin in a Brave New World: An Account of the Negotiation of the Treaty of Amsterdam*. Dublin: Institute of European Affairs.

Meerts, P.W. 1997. Negotiating in the European Union: Comparing Perceptions of EU Negotiators in Small Member States. *Group Decision and Negotiation*, **6**.

Mény, Y., P. Muller, and J.-L. Quermonne, eds. 1996. *Adjusting to Europe. The Impact of the European Union on National Institutions and Policies*. London and New York: Routledge.

Metcalfe, L. 1987. *Comparing National Policy Coordination; Do Differences Matter?* Paper presented at the Ehrenstein Colloquium, EIPA, Maastricht.

———. 1994. International Policy Coordination and Public Management Reform. *International Review of Administrative Sciences*, **60**:271–90.

———. 1998. Leadership in European Union Negotiations: The Presidency of the Council. *International Negotiation*, **3**:413–34.

Michalksi, A. ed. 2003. *An Assessment of the European Convention: The Political Dynamics of Constitutional Reform—Seminar Report*. The Clingendael Institute, 5 June. See <www.clingendael.nl>.

Middlemas, K. 1995. *Orchestrating Europe*. London: Fontana Press.

Miles, L. 1996. The Nordic Countries and the Fourth EU Enlargement, in L. Miles, ed., *The European Union and the Nordic Countries*. London: Routledge, 63–78.

———. 2002. Enlargement: From the Perspective of "Fusion." *Cooperation and Conflict*, **372**:190–98.

Moravcsik, A. 1991. Negotiating the Single European Act: National Interests and Conventional Statecraft in the European Community. *International Organization*, **45**(1):19–56.

———. 1993. Preferences and Power in the European Community: A Liberal Intergovernmentalist Approach. *Journal of Common Market Studies*, **11**:471–524.

————. 1998. *The Choice for Europe: Social Purpose and State Power from Messina to Maastricht*. Ithaca: Cornell University Press.

Nicoll, W. 1998. *The Evolution of the Office of the Presidency*. Paper presented at the Conference on the Presidency of the European Union, Belfast, 15–16 October.

Nielsen, T. 1971. Aspects of the EEC: Influence of the European Groups in the Decision-Making Process. *Government and Opposition*, **6**:539–60.

Norgaard, A. 1996. Rediscovering Reasonable Rationality in Institutional Analysis. *European Journal of Political Research*, **29**:31–57.

Nugent, N. 1999. *The Government and Politics of the European Union*, 4th edition. London: The Macmillan Press.

————. 2001. *The European Commission*. New York: Palgrave.

O'Nuallain, C., and J.-M. Hoscheit, eds. 1985. *The Presidency of the European Council of Ministers: Impacts and Implications for National Governments*. London; Dover, N.H.: Croom Helm.

Paemen, H., and A. Bensch. 1995. *From the GATT to the WTO: The European Community and the Uruguay Round*. Leuven, Belgium: Leuven University Press.

Peters, B.G., and V. Wright. 2001. The National Coordination of European Policy-Making: Negotiating the Quagmire, in J. Richardson, ed., *European Union, Power and Policy-Making*, 2nd edition. London: Routledge, 148–69.

Peters, B.G. 1994. Agenda Setting in the EU. *Journal of European Public Policy*, **1**:9–26.

Peterson, J., and E. Bomberg. 1999. *Decision-Making in the European Union*. London and New York: Macmillan and St. Martin's Press.

Pfetsch, F.R. 1998. Negotiating the European Union: A Negotiation-Network Approach. *International Negotiation*, **3**(3).

Phinnemore, D. 1999. The Challenge of EU Enlargement: EU and CEE Perspectives, in K. Henderson, ed., *Back to Europe: Central and Eastern Europe and the European Union*. London: UCL Press, 71–88.

Piris, J.-C. 1999. Does the European Union have a Constitution? Does it Need One? *European Law Revue*, **24**(6):557–85.

Pollack, M.A. 1997. Delegation, Agency, and Agenda Setting in the European Community, *International Organization*, **51**(1):99–134.

————. 2003. *The Engines of Integration. Delegation, Agency and Agenda Setting in the European Union*. Oxford: Oxford University Press.

Preston, C. 1995. Obstacle to EU Enlargement: The Classical Community Method and the Prospects for a Wider Europe. *Journal of Common Market Studies*, **33**(3):451–63.

Putnam, R. 1988. Diplomacy and Domestic Politics: The Logic of Two-Level Games. *International Organization*, **42**(3):427–60.

Raunio, T., and M. Wiberg. 1998. Winners and Losers in the Council: Voting Power Consequences of EU Enlargements. *Journal of Common Market Studies*, **36**(4).

Rittberger, B. 2001. Which Institutions for Post-War Europe? Explaining the Institutional Design of Europe's First Community. *Journal of European Public Policy*, **85**:673–708.

Rometsch, D., and W. Wessels, eds. 1996. *European Union and the Member States: Towards Institutional Fusion*. Manchester, England and New York: Manchester University Press.

———. 1997. The Commission and the Council of the Union, in G. Edwards and D. Spence eds., *The European Commission*, 2nd edition. London: Cartermill Publishing, 213–38.

Rood, J. Q. T. 1997. De angst van het Nederlandse voorzitterschap. *Internationale Spectator*, **513**:128–31.

Rood, J.Q.T., and M. van Keulen. 2001. De Gordiaanse Knoop van de Nederlandse EU coördinatie. *Internationale Spectator*, **55**(3):287–92.

Ross, G. 1995. *Jacques Delors and European Integration*. Cambridge: Polity Press.

Ruiz Tartas, C. 1995. La Présidence du Conseil de l'Union européenne et la deuxième Présidence espagnole. *Eipascope*, **3**:2–10.

Sandholz, W. 1992. ESPRIT and the Politics of International Collective Action. *Journal of Common Market Studies*, **30**:1–22.

Scharpf, F.W. 1998. The Joint-Decision Trap: Lessons from German Federalism and European Integration. *Public Administration*, **66**:239–78.

Schmidt, S.K. 2000. Only an Agenda-Setter? The European Commission's Power over the Council of Ministers. *European Union Politics*, **1**(1):37–61.

———. 2001. A Constrained Commission: Informal Practices of Agenda-Setting in the Council, in G. Schneider and M.D. Aspinwall, eds., *The Rules of Integration. Institutional Approaches to the Study of Europe*. Manchester, England: Manchester University Press, 125–46.

Schneider, G., and M.D. Aspinwall. 2001. *The Rules of Integration. Institutional Approaches to the Study of Europe*. Manchester, England: Manchester University Press.

Schneider, V., G. Dang Nguyen, and R. Werle. 1994. Corporate Actor Networks in European Policy-Making: Harmonizing Telecommunications Policy. *Journal of Common Market Studies*, **32**(4):105–30.

Schout, A. 1997. *The Domestic Management of European Affairs: Draining the Quagmire*. Paper, EIPA, Maastricht.

———. 1998. The Presidency as a Juggler. Managing Conflict Expectations. *EIPASCOPE*, **2**:1–19.

Schout, A., and S. Vanhoonacker. 2002. *Preparing the Presidency: A Guidebook for National Administrations*. Maastricht: EIPA.

Schreurs, R. 2002. *Europees procesmanagement: Nederlandse belangenbehartiging in de EU*. Paper, The Hague: Clingendael.

Scully, R. 1997. The European Parliament and the Co-Decision Procedure: A Re-Assessment. *Journal of Legislative Studies*, **3**:58–73.

———. 2001. The European Parliament as a Non-Legislative Actor. *Journal of European Public Policy*, **8**:162–69.

Sergeev, V. 2002. Metaphors for Understanding International Negotiation, in V.A. Kremenyuk, ed., *International Negotiation: Analysis, Approaches, Issues*, 2nd edition. San Francisco: Jossey-Bass Publishers.

Shepsle, K.A. 1989. Studying Institutions. Some Lessons from the Rational Choice Approach. *Journal of Theoretical Politics*, **1**(2):131–47.

Sherrington, P. 2000. *The Council of Ministers. Political Authority in the European Union*. London and New York: Pinter.

Sjöstedt, G. 2003. Lessons for Research and Practice, in G. Sjöstedt, ed., *Professional Cultures in International Negotiation: Bridge or Rift?* Lanham, Boulder,

Sjöstedt, G., and B.I. Spector. 1993. Conclusion, in G. Sjöstedt, ed., *International Environmental Negotiation. Insights for Practice*. Newbury Park, London, New Delhi: Sage Publications.

Sjöstedt, G., B.I. Spector, and I.W. Zartman 1994. Looking Ahead, in B.I. Spector, G. Sjöstedt, and I.W. Zartman, eds., *Negotiating International Regimes: Lessons Learned from the United Nations Conference on Environment and Development*. London, Dordrecht, Boston: Graham and Trotman/Martinus Nijhoff. New York, Oxford: Lexington Books.

Soetendorp, B., and M. Hosli. 2000. *The Hidden Dynamics of EU Council Decision-Making*. Paper presented at the 41st Annual Convention of the International Studies Association (ISA), Los Angeles.

Spence, D. 1995. Negotiations, Coalitions, and the Resolution of Inter-State Conflicts, in M. Westlake, ed., *The Council of the European Union*. London: Cartermill, 373–89.

Steinberg, R.H. 2002. In the Shadow of Law or Power? Consensus-Based Bargaining and Outcomes in the GATT/WTO. *International Organization*, **56**(2):339–74.

Stenelo, L.-G. 1972. *Mediation in International Negotiations*. Lund: Studentlitteratur.

Steunenberg, B. 2000. Seeing What You Want to See: The Limits of Current Modelling on the European Union. *European Union Politics*, **1**(3):368–73.

Stone Sweet, A., and W. Sandholtz, eds. 1998. *Supranational Governance: The Institutionalization of the European Union*. Oxford: Oxford University Press.

Stubb, A. 2002. *Negotiating Flexibility in the European Union*. Basingstoke, Hampshire: Palgrave Macmillan.

Susskind, L., S. McKearnan, and J. Thomas-Larner, eds. 1999. *The Consensus Building Handbook*. London: Sage.

Svensson, A.-C. 2000. *In the Service of the European Union: The Role of the Presidency in Negotiating the Amsterdam Treaty 1995–1997*. Uppsala: Acta Universitatis Upsaliensis- Skrifter utgivna av statsvetenskapliga föreningen i Uppsala.

Tallberg, J. 2001. *Responsabilité sans pouvoir*. Paper presented at the 4th Pan-European IR Conference in Canterbury, Kent.

Torreblanca, J. 1998. Overlapping Games and Cross-Cutting Coalitions in the European Union. *West European Politics*, **21**(2):134–53.

———. 2001. *The Reuniting of Europe, Promises, Negotiations and Compromises*. Aldershot, Hampshire: Ashgate Publishing.

Tsebelis, G., and G. Garrett. 2000. Legislative Politics in the European Union. *European Union Politics*, **1**(1):9–36.

van den Bos, J.J.M. 1991. *Dutch EC Policy Making: A Model-Guided Approach to Coordination and Negotiation*. University of Utrecht: Dissertation.

van Grinsven, P. 2002. *The Evolution of the European Council: From a Serial Summit to a Permanent Arena for Leadership Negotiations*. Paper presented at the Summitry Conference, Department of International Relations, Boston University, Boston, Mass., 19–20 March.

van Grinsven, P., and J. Melissen. 2002. Europese Raad tussen marginale aanpassing en radicale hervorming. *Internationale Spectator*, 56(9).

van Kippersluis, R. 1998. The Waste Management Committee, in M.C.P.M. van Schendelen, ed., *EU Committees as Influencial Policymakers*. Aldershot, Hampshire; Brookfield, V.T.: Ashgate, 47–67.

van Schendelen, M.C.P.M. 1993. *National Public and Private EC Lobbying*. Aldershot: Dartmouth.

———. 1996. "The Council Decides": Does the Council Decide? *Journal of Common Market Studies*, **34**:4.

———. ed. 1998. *EU Committees as Influential Policymakers*. Aldershot, Hampshire; Brookfield, V.T.: Ashgate.

———. 2002. *Machiavelli in Brussels: The Art of Lobbying the EU*. Amsterdam: Amsterdam University Press.

———. 2003. The In-Sourced Experts, in M.C.P.M. van Schendelen and R. Scully, eds., *The Unseen Hand: Unelected EU Legislators*. London: Frank Cass.

Verdun, A. 1999. The Role of the Delors Committee in the Creation of EMU: An Epistemic Community. *Journal of European Public Policy*, **6**(2):308–28.

Walch, J. 2001. *Le bilan de la Présidence suédoise*. Défense national, **57**(10):144–52.

Wallace, H. 1985. The Presidency of the Council of Ministers of the European Community: Tasks and Evolution, in C.O'Nuallain and J.M. Hoscheit, eds., *The Presidency of the European Council of Ministers: Impacts and Implications for Natial Governments*. London; Dover, N.H.: Croom Helm.

———. 1989. The Best is the Enemy of the "Could." Bargaining in the European Community, in S. Tarditi, K. Thompson, P. Pierani, and E. Croci-Angelilni, eds., *Agricultural Trade Liberalization and the European Community*. Oxford: Clarendon Press, 193–206.

Wallace, H., and G. Edwards. 1976. European Community: The Evolving Role of the Presidency of the Council. *Internationale Spectator*: 535–50.

Wallace, H., and W. Wallace, eds. 2000. *Policy-Making in the European Union*, 4th edition. Oxford and New York: Oxford University Press.

Walton, R. E., and R. B. McKersie. 1991. *A Behavioral Theory of Labor Negotiations*. Ithaca, N.Y.: ILR Press. (1st edition, 1965).

Wehr, P., and J.P. Lederach. 1996. Mediating Conflict in Central America, in J. Bercovitch, ed., *Resolving International Conflicts. The Theory and Practice of Mediation*.

Boulder and London: Lynne Rienner Publishers, 55–74. (First published in the 1991 *Journal of Peace Research*, **28**[1].)

Wendt, A. 1999. *Social Theory of International Politics*. New York: Cambridge University Press.

Werts, J. 1992. *The European Council*. Elsevier Science Publishers, 98.

Westlake, M. 1995. *The Council of the European Union*. London: Cartermill.

———. 1999. *The Council of the European Union*, revised edition. London: John Harper Publishing.

Woolcock, S. 2000. European Trade Policy, in H. Wallace and W. Wallace, eds., *Policy-Making in the European Union*, 4th edition. Oxford and New York: Oxford University Press, 372–400.

Wurzel, R. 2000. Flying into Unexpected Turbulence: The German EU Presidency in the Environmental Field. *German Politics*, **93**:23–42.

———. 2002. Environmental Policy. *Cooperation and Conflict*, **37**(2):206–11.

Young, O.R. 1967. *The Intermediaries. Third Parties in International Crises*. Princeton, N.J.: Princeton University Press.

———. 1991. Political Leadership and Regime Formation: On the Development of Institutions in International Society. *International Organization*, **45**(3):281–308.

———. 1999. Commentary on *A New Statecraft? Supranational Entrepreneurs and International Cooperation* by Andrew Moravcsik. *International Organization*, **53**(4):805–809.

Zartman, W.I. 2000. Negotiation Analysis Perspective in International Economic Negotiation, in V.A. Kremenyuk and G. Sjöstedt, eds., *International Economic Negotiation: Models versus Reality*. Cheltenham, Northampton, England: Edward Elgar.

———. 2002. The Structure of Negotiation, in V. Kremenyuk, ed., *International Negotiations—Analysis, Approaches, Issues*. San Francisco: Jossey-Bass Publishers, 65–78.

———. 2003. Conclusion: Managing Complexity. *International Negotiation*, **8**(1).

Zeff, E.E., and E.B. Pirro. 2001. *The EU and the Member States*. Boulder, C.O.: Lynne Rienner Publishers.